John Buchan's 1914:
The World at War

John Buchan's 1914: The World at War

The Naval Conflict & Global Campaigns of the Opening Year of the First World War

John Buchan

LEONAUR

John Buchan's 1914: The World at War
The Naval Conflict & Global Campaigns of the Opening Year of the First World War
by John Buchan

FIRST EDITION

Leonaur is an imprint of Oakpast Ltd

Copyright in this form © 2014 Oakpast Ltd

ISBN: 978-1-78282-305-6 (hardcover)
ISBN: 978-1-78282-306-3 (softcover)

http://www.leonaur.com

Publisher's Notes

Contents

Publisher's Note

The story of the First World War by renowned author, John Buchan, began in John Buchan's 1914: The war in the West. That book examines the events that led to the outbreak of the war before describing the German invasion of Belgium and France and the campaigns that followed on the western front to the end of the year. This book excludes that background material moving immediately to the war at sea and the global conflicts which erupted in the sideshow theatres during the early months of the war.

The Beginning of the War at Sea

The landing of the British Expeditionary Force in France in 1914 and the utilisation of the resources of the Empire depended upon the Allies retaining a sufficient control of the sea-routes of the world. The security of British territory and the provision of food for its people were in the keeping of our navy. Further, since the chief antagonist was the second greatest of the Sea Powers, the war must be conducted by water as well as by land. "It is upon the navy," it is set forth in the Articles of War, "that, under the good Providence of God, the wealth, prosperity, and peace or these islands and of the Empire do mainly depend." We must briefly consider the naval position of the different combatants at the beginning of August.

The British navy at that date had reached a point of efficiency both in quality and quantity which was unprecedented in its history, it is true that, the growth of German sea-power had relatively reduced its pre-eminence, hut the existence of a bold claimant for 'he Empire of the Ocean had stimulated the spirit of our fleet, and perfected its organization for war. This is not the place to enter into the interminable discussions which since 1906 had raged around the subject. The attempts at reduction, happily frustrated, may well be relegated to oblivion. Ever since Lord Selborne's period at the Admiralty a steady advance may be noted in training and equipment. The establishment of the Royal Fleet Reserve and the Volunteer Naval Reserve, the provision of North Sea bases, the admirable work done by the Committee of Imperial Defence, the development of armament and of battleship designing, the immense improvement in gunnery practice, the revision of the rates of pay, the opening up of careers for the lower deck, and the provision of a naval air service, are landmarks in the advance. Much was due to Lord Fisher and the other Sea Lords; something was due, also, to the civilian First Lords, Mr. M'Kenna and Mr. Winston Churchill. The latter especially flung himself into the work of his department with a zeal and intelligence which were of incalculable value to the country in the hour of need. In the Navy Estimates of March 1914, Parliament sanctioned over fifty-one millions For naval defence—the largest sum ever granted for the purpose.

The Home Fleet, available for the war in the North Sea, was arranged in three units. The First: was divided into four battle squadrons, together with the flagship of the commander-in-chief. The first squadron was made up of eight battleships—Dreadnoughts and super-Dreadnoughts seven of which carried ten 12-inch guns, while one. the *Marlborough*, had ten 13.5-inch guns, besides secondary armaments. The second squadron contained eight super-Dreadnoughts, each armed with ten 13.5-inch guns. The third squadron was composed of eight pre-Dreadnoughts of the *King Edward VII.* class, carrying four 12-inch, four 9.2 inch, and ten 6-inch guns. The fourth squadron consisted of three Dreadnoughts, each carrying ten 12-inch, guns, and one pre-Dreadnought, carrying four 12-inch and ten 9.2-inch guns.

Attached to the First Fleet was a battle-cruiser squadron of four ships, three of which carried eight 13.5-inch guns, and the fourth eight 12-inch guns; the second cruiser squadron of four armoured cruisers; the third cruiser squadron of four cruisers of the *Devonshire* class; the fourth cruiser squadron of four ships of the *Monmouth* class, and one light cruiser, the *Bristol*; the first light cruiser squadron; a squadron of six gunboats for mine-sweeping; and four flotillas of destroyers, each with a flotilla cruiser attached.

This, the first line of defence of our shores, had behind it the Second Fleet, which had two battle squadrons, the first consisting of eight pre-Dreadnoughts and the second of six. It contained also the fifth and sixth cruiser squadrons; a mine-layer squadron of seven, vessels; four patrol flotillas consisting of destroyers and torpedo-boats; and seven flotillas of submarines. Behind the Second Fleet came the Third, containing two battle-squadrons, mainly composed of comparatively old ships, and six cruiser squadrons.

Our strength outside home waters may be very roughly summarised. In the Mediterranean fleet we had three battle cruisers, four armoured cruisers, four ordinary cruisers, and a flotilla of seventeen destroyers, besides submarines and torpedo boats. In Eastern waters we had a battleship, two cruisers, and four sloops in the East India squadron; a battleship, two armoured cruisers, two cruisers, a number

H.M.S. "Marlborough"

of gunboats, eight destroyers, besides submarines and torpedo boats, in the China squadron; and four cruisers in the New Zealand division. The Australian fleet showed a battle cruiser, three cruisers, three destroyers, and two submarines. Various cruisers and gunboats were stationed at the Cape, the west coast of Africa, and the east and west coasts of America, while four armoured cruisers and one ordinary cruiser patrolled the Western Atlantic.

To arrive at our total naval strength we must add the two destroyers purchased from Chile, and the two Turkish battleships, building in England, which were commandeered by the British Government at the outbreak of war. This would give us the following figures for the principal classes:—

BATTLESHIPS AND BATTLE CRUISERS.

Super-Dreadnought type	14
Dreadnought type	18
Pre-Dreadnought types (1895-1908)	38
Super-Dreadnoughts completing	3
Total	73
Armoured Cruisers (1901-1908)	34
Cruisers (1890-1914)	87
Destroyers (1893-1914)	227
Torpedo-boats (1885-1908)	109
Submarines (1904-1913)	75

The German Navy, the second in the world, was a creation of the past fifteen years, deliberately undertaken for the purpose of challenging British supremacy. The chief begetter was an obscure naval officer called Tirpitz, who in 1897 succeeded Admiral von Hollmann as Naval Minister. With the support of the emperor, he began to wring money for the navy out of a reluctant Treasury, and in the face of a jealous army; and, by dint of a skilful press campaign, succeeded in arousing in the German people a new enthusiasm for maritime power. At the outbreak of war he had held office for fifteen years, and had built up a navy which in *matériel* and personnel was second only to one—a marvellous performance for so short a period. The High Sea Fleet consisted of twenty-one battleships, thirteen of them of the Dreadnought type, four battle cruisers, eight light cruisers, and eighty torpedo boats. The total naval strength was—

"King Edward VII." class battleships on manoeuvres.

Dreadnought type	13
" (completing)	3
Pre-Dreadnought (1891-1908)	22
Old types (1889-1893)	8
Total	46
Armoured cruisers (1892-1913)	40
Cruisers (1893-1910	12
Destroyers (1889 1913)	152
Torpedo-boats (1887-1898)	45
Submarines	40

The German Navy was originally regarded as a branch of the army; naval strategy was conceived of only as an auxiliary to land strategy, and ships were units for coast defence. It had been the task of the modern German sea-lords to emancipate the fleet from the military tradition. The result was that the navy had become a far more democratic profession than the sister service, and had drawn to it many able men of middleclass birth who were repelled by the junkerdom of the army. It was manned chiefly by conscription; but about a quarter consisted of volunteers, chiefly dwellers on the coast and on the Frisian and Baltic islands, and men who had deliberately made it their career. The term of service for conscripts was three years, and the training, concentrated in so short a space, was strenuous and highly specialized. The officers were almost to a man professional enthusiasts; and our own sailors, who had fraternised with them in foreign ports, had borne witness to their efficiency and seamanlike spirit.

The navy of Austria-Hungary had expanded in recent years like that of her ally. Under the inspiration of Admiral Montecuccoli naval expenditure was trebled in the last ten years, and an elaborate shipbuilding programme undertaken. On the outbreak of war the fleet comprised fifteen battleships, three of them being Dreadnoughts, two armoured and nine light cruisers, fifteen destroyers, fifty-eight torpedo boats, and six submarines. The Dual Monarchy possessed three main naval stations in the Adriatic—Pola, the fleet's headquarters, Trieste, and the Hungarian port of Fiume—while an additional station had been established at Sebenico in Dalmatia.

The French Navy had in the matter of invention given the lead to the world, but till recently its size had not kept pace with the quality

H.M.S. "DEVONSHIRE"

of its officers, and it had dropped from second to fifth place among the navies of the world. When Admiral Boué de Lapeyrère became Minister of Marine a great upward movement began, and this was continued under M. Delcassé, who insisted that France must possess a fleet to give her indubitable supremacy in the Mediterranean. When Admiral Boué de Lapeyrère became commander-in-chief of the navy he gathered about him a brilliant *coterie* of young flag-officers, and sea-training and gunnery made rapid strides. At the beginning of the war France had twenty-four battleships, including ten Dreadnoughts, armed with 12-inch guns, twenty-four cruisers, eight light cruisers, eighty destroyers, 140 torpedo boats, and some fifty submarines, the two last classes representing the very latest types. Her principal base was Toulon on the Mediterranean, and she had also Rochefort on the Bay of Biscay, Brest and Lorient on the Atlantic. Cherbourg on the Channel, as well as Ajaccio and Bonifacio in Corsica, Algiers and Gran in Algeria, and Bizerta in Tunis,

Russia, after the war with Japan, was faced with the problem of constructing her navy anew, and by August 1914 the reconstruction was far from complete. The Navy Bill of 1912 had provided for the expenditure of £50,000,000 on a building programme to be completed in 1917, and she had aimed at creating a powerful Baltic battle fleet, which should be scarcely inferior to any power Germany could place in these waters. But this policy was not given time to mature. On the outbreak of war she had in the Baltic only four Dreadnoughts, ten armoured cruisers, two light cruisers, eighty destroyers, and twenty-four submarines, and a fleet of about half the strength in the Black Sea. Its bases were Kronstadt, an ice-bound port in winter, the minor ice-free base of Libau, and Sveaborg for torpedo craft. The projected ice-free base of Reval was not yet completed.

The mere enumeration of ships does not give any real clue to the effective naval strength of a Power at any one moment, since much depends upon where the fleets are chiefly concentrated. To take the Mediterranean first, the union of France and Britain made the Allies easily superior there; for, if Italy remained neutral, the Austrian Navy could be shut up securely in the Adriatic. This superiority was needed, if France were to transport her African troops in safety and British commerce were to be free to continue the Suez Canal route to India and the East.

But the vital theatre of the naval war was the North Sea and the Baltic, where Germany had all her fleet, except one battle cruiser (the famous *Goeben*), two armoured cruisers, and a few light cruisers.

The German seaboard is divided by the peninsula of Denmark into two completely separate areas—the North Sea and the Baltic coasts. The entrance to the Baltic was virtually closed to an enemy from the west, as the Sound and the Great Belt had been mined by Denmark, a neutral, and an enemy's fleet was forbidden to seek neutral pilotage. At the same time, passage between the two seas was possible for Germany by means of the Kiel Canal, widened in 1914 so as to admit the largest battleships, and running from Kiel Bay on the Baltic to the estuary of the Elbe. A certain portion of the German fleet must remain in the Baltic to watch the Russian fleet and protect the north coast of Prussia; but this portion need not be fixed, but could be added to or subtracted from at pleasure.

The strength of Russia lay chiefly in torpedo craft, and the German Baltic fleet was, therefore, likely to be composed of fast cruisers and destroyers. At the outbreak of war it seems to have consisted of nine of the older battleships, several armoured, and one or two smaller cruisers, and a number of destroyers, from which it would appear that Germany contemplated using the Baltic as an exercise ground, since the high seas were forbidden her.

The German High Sea Fleet was inferior to the British Home Fleet, so far as capital ships were concerned, by more than 40 *per cent.*, and this inferiority was much greater in the class of cruisers and destroyers. It was, therefore, the aim of Admiral von Ingenohl to avoid a battle, until he had reduced our lead by the slow attrition which submarines, mines, and the casualties of the sea might be expected to produce. The policy of a sudden raid—that "day" which German naval officers had regularly toasted, under the inspiration of Admiral Livonius's heroics—was made almost impossible by the manner in which war broke out and the complete preparedness of the British at sea. The Fabian line of strategy had many advantages from the German point of view. It gave ample scope for the ingenuity and boldness of mine-layers and submarines, two branches of her sea-service to which Germany had paid special attention.

It kept Germany's fleet intact against the time when, her arms victorious on land, she could sally forth to fight a dispirited enemy. Further, a period of forced inaction must have a wearing effect upon the nerves of the British navy. For a fleet which believes itself invincible and longs for combat, it is a hard trial to wait day after day without descrying an enemy's pennon on the horizon. The modern battleship

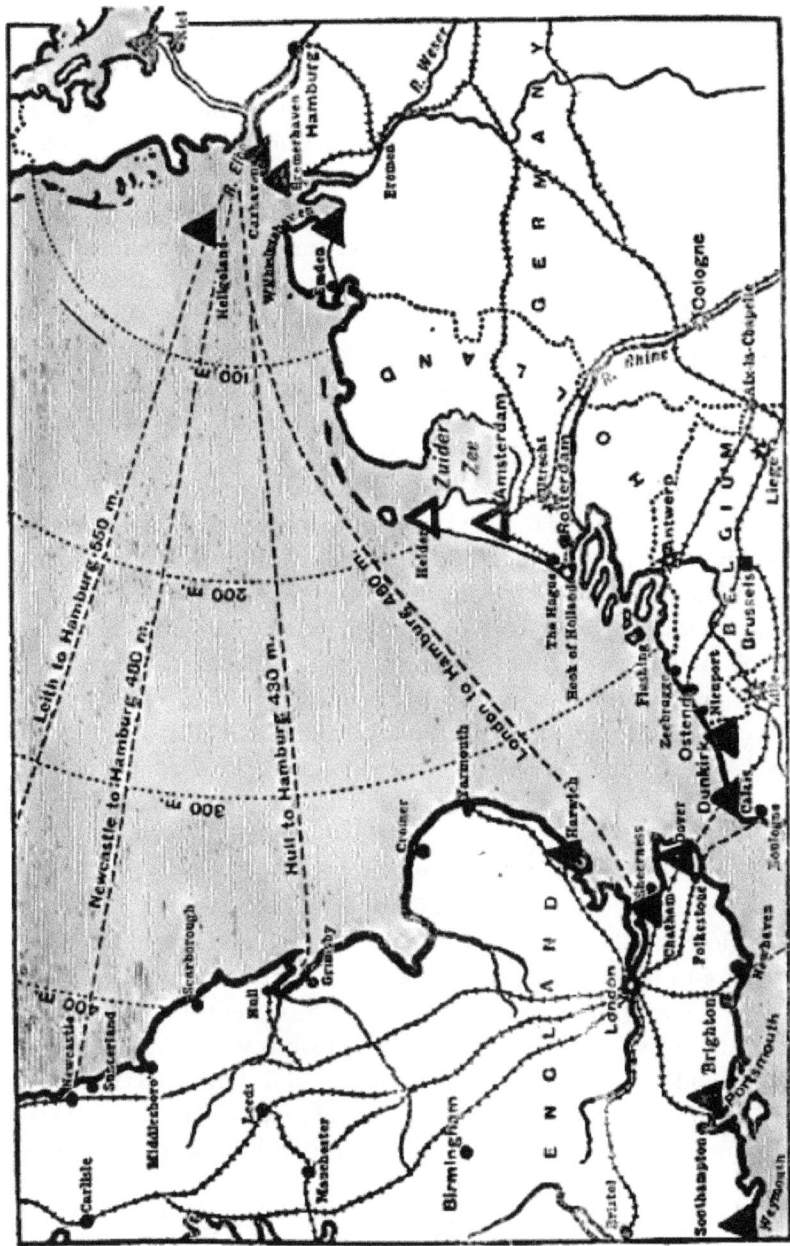

Map of Naval Bases in the North Sea.

▲ Bases of Belligerents. △ Dutch Bases.

has not the constant small duties which existed in the ships of Nelson's time, and it was hoped that the men and officers might grow stale and apathetic. Or, in the alternative, they might risk an attack upon the German fleet in its home waters, an attack which, in the German view, would result in the crushing defeat of the invader.

The German plan, perfectly sound strategy in the circumstances, was made possible by the peculiar configuration of the German coast, and the magnificent shelter it provided. The few hundred miles between Emden and the Danish frontier are deeply cut by bays and river mouths, and the western part is screened by the chain of Frisian islands from Borkum to Wangeroog. In the centre of the bight lies Heligoland, a strong fortress with a wireless station. Close to the Dutch frontier is the estuary of the Ems, with the town of Emden. Then comes a low, sandy stretch of coast, indented with tidal creeks, till the estuary of the Jade is reached at Wilhelmshaven, which is the fortified base of the North Sea Fleet. Next comes the estuary of the Weser, with the important dockyard of Bremerhaven. Last comes the estuary of the Elbe, with Cuxhaven at its mouth, opposite the debouchment of the Kiel Canal, and at its head the great city and dockyard of Hamburg.

Each estuary is a network of mazy channels among the sands, requiring skilful piloting, and in themselves a strong defence against a raid. There is, further, the screen of the islands, behind which operations could take place unnoticed, and there is the Kiel Canal to furnish a back-door to the Baltic. The coast is followed by a double line of railway from Hamburg to Emden, which taps no populous district and carries no traffic, but is meant solely for strategic purposes. This Frisian corner was the key to German naval defence. Visitors had always been shepherded away from vital points, and the notion of espionage there had given the German people sleepless nights. Captain Bertrand Stewart, an English Territorial officer—the first to give his life in this war—was condemned to three years' imprisonment in a fortress on the charge of visiting various towns and islands where he had never set foot; and so feverish was public and official feeling in Germany on the subject that the evidence of a single and much discredited spy was sufficient to secure this officer's conviction without a word of German protest.

At the great review of the British fleet in July two hundred and sixteen ships of war passed before the king—only half the total number, but in itself the most powerful fleet ever mustered in British waters in a state of instant readiness for battle. Though diplomacy had not yet broken down, the conduct of Germany had given the chiefs of the navy much to think about. It had been reported on good authority that the German fleet was being placed on a war footing, that certain German liners which could be used as transports or auxiliary cruisers had altered or cancelled their sailings, and that German naval officers in foreign countries had been recalled. No sooner was the review over than our work of preparation began. The squadrons went to the stations appointed to them, took in war stores, and sent ashore whatever might impede them in battle.

On Monday, 3rd August, at the memorable Cabinet meeting which decided British policy, Mr. Churchill was able to inform his colleagues that that morning the last steps had been taken, and that the whole sea power of Britain was in readiness for war.

From that moment the fleet disappeared. Dwellers on our southern and eastern coasts in the bright weather of early August could see an occasional cruiser or destroyer speeding on some errand, or an escorted mine-sweeper busy at its perilous task. But the great battleships had gone. Somewhere out on the blue waters, or hidden in some nook of our northern or western shores, lay the vigilant admirals of England.

The British fleet had not fought a great battle at sea since Trafalgar. Since those days, only a century removed in time, we had changed the conditions of naval warfare more than they had changed between Themistocles and Nelson. The old wooden walls, the unrifled guns, the boarders with their cutlasses, belonged to an earlier world. We had no longer to scour the ocean for the enemy's fleet. Wireless telegraphy, aerial reconnaissance, and swift destroyers brought us early news of a foe. The gun power of a modern battleship would have wrecked the Spanish Armada with one broadside, and the enemy could now be engaged at a distance of many miles. Sea lighting was no more the clean and straightforward business of the old days. Destruction dwelt in every element when there was no sign of a hostile pennon. Aircraft dropped bombs from the clouds; unseen submarines, like sword-fish, pierced the hull from the depths; and anywhere might lurk those mines which destroyed, like some convulsion of nature, with no human enemy near.

We had to fight under new conditions, with new strategy and new weapons, with far greater demands on the intellect and a far more deadly strain on the nerves. Most things had changed, but two things

21

remained unaltered—the cool daring of our sailors and the conviction that the seas were the unquestionable heritage of our race.

To the command of the fleet there had been appointed Admiral Sir John Jellicoe, with Rear-Admiral Charles Madden as his Chief of Staff. Those who shared R. L. Stevenson's view as to the racy nomenclature of British seamen must have found something reassuring in the name of the new commander-in-chief. Admiral Jellicoe had served as a lieutenant in the Egyptian War of 1882. Specialising in gunnery, he had become a commander in 1891, and was one of the few survivors of the ill-fated *Victoria*, which went down off the Syrian coast. He became a captain in 1897, and served on the China station, commanding the Naval Brigade and acting as chief staff officer at the Peking expedition of 1900, where he was severely wounded.

Thereafter he became successively Naval Assistant to the Controller of the Navy, Director of Naval Ordnance and Torpedoes, Rear-Admiral in the Atlantic Fleet, a Lord Commissioner of the Admiralty, and Controller of the Navy, Vice-Admiral commanding the Atlantic Fleet, Vice-Admiral commanding the Second Division of the Home Fleet, and second Sea Lord of the Admiralty. He brilliantly distinguished himself by the command of the "Red" Fleet at the naval manoeuvres of 1913. Rear-Admiral Madden, his Chief of Staff, who was also his brother-in-law, had already served with him at the Admiralty. Sir John Jellicoe was one of the officers chiefly responsible for the modern navy of Britain, and enjoyed not only the admiration and complete confidence of his colleagues, but a peculiar popularity among all grades of British seamen. His nerve and self-possession were not less conspicuous than his professional skill, and in the wearing months ahead of him he had need of all resources of mind and character.

Those who expected a speedy and decisive Trafalgar in the south end of the North Sea were doomed to disappointment. Admiral von Ingenohl was too wise a commander to indulge in quixotic adventures. But the day after the declaration of war the first shots were fired. German minelayers, there is reason to believe, had been busy in various pacific guises for the past week, dropping mines over a wide area extending from opposite Harwich to far up in the Scottish waters. On Wednesday, 5th August, the mine-layer *Koenigen Luise* was overtaken by the destroyer *Lance* and sunk in six minutes. On Thursday morning the British light cruiser *Amphion*, Captain Cecil Fox, struck one of the mines laid by the *Koenigen Luise*, and foundered, with serious loss of life, though the captain, the principal officers, and the larger half of the crew were saved.

On Sunday, the 9th, German submarines attacked a cruiser squadron of the main British fleet, without doing any damage, and one submarine was sunk by the protected cruiser *Birmingham*, which steamed straight for it, and ran it down.

Meantime during the week rumours came from the Baltic of a German success off the Aland Isles and the sinking of a Russian battleship, rumours which proved later to be unfounded. On 2nd August, however, the German cruiser *Augsburg* had made an attack on the port of Libau, but the bombardment was weak, and the damage done was insignificant. The aim of such a movement was to force Russia to keep a considerable number of men on the Baltic coast. There was always the danger that Germany might make an attempt on Petrograd by way of Finland.

It was in the Mediterranean that during that week the naval interest was keenest. At the outbreak of war two German warships, the *Goeben* and the *Breslau*, were off the Algerian coast. This can scarcely have come about by accident, and it is not improbable that when these ships received their first sailing orders Germany calculated either upon the assistance of Italy or the neutrality of Britain, and intended her finest battle cruiser to assist in the one case Italy and Austria against France and Britain, or in the other Austria against France. The *Goeben* was the fastest armoured vessel in the German fleet, displacing 22,640 tons, attaining a speed of 28 knots, and carrying as armament ten 11-inch, twelve 5.9-inch, and twelve 21-pounder guns.

The *Breslau* was a fast light cruiser, with about the same rate of speed, and a displacement of 4,478 tons. She was the vessel sent, by Germany to Albanian waters to join the international squadron which kept the unfortunate *Mpret* in countenance. Both of these ships had specially great coal capacity, and the *Breslau* could cover 6,000 knots without taking in fresh fuel. They were, therefore, admirably suited for commerce destroyers, and had they continued at large might have done much to embarrass the sea-borne trade of the Allies.

They began by firing a few shots into the unprotected Algerian coast towns of Bona and Philippeville, but did little harm. They then turned northwest, with the object, apparently, of running for the Strait of Gibraltar, but were headed off by the British fleet. They seem to have shown their pursuers a very clean pair of heels, and early on Wednesday morning, 5th August, appeared at Messina. There they went through a somewhat theatrical performance. The captains and officers made their wills, and deposited their valuables, including signed portraits of the Kaiser, with the German consul; the decks were cleared for action, and with the bands playing "*Heil dir im Siegerkranz*," sailed out—so said the German papers—under a blood-red sunset. But the blood was only in the sunset, for they sought not battle but safety.

Escaping by some mischance our fleet, and going at full speed eastward, they encountered, off Cape Matapan, a British cruiser, the *Gloucester*, a ship slightly larger than the *Breslau*, which, with great gallantry, attempted to engage, and damaged the plates of the *Goeben* and the smoke stack of the *Breslau*. But the superior speed of the Germans brought them through. They were next heard of in the Dardanelles at the end of the week. Presently they had reached Constantinople, where they passed into the power of the Turkish Government, and thereby began that disquieting of the diplomatic relations of the Porte which was to end in war. It was not a brilliant achievement for Germany's chief battle cruiser, and for the moment it gravely lowered the prestige of the untried German Navy.

But more important than any isolated incident was the swift and methodical sweeping in of the German mercantile marine, which began on 4th August. The blockade, which the more sober of German naval writers had always feared, had come to pass. In every quarter of the globe our cruisers spread their net. German merchantmen in the ports of the Empire were detained, and hundreds of ships were made prizes of in the high and the narrow seas. Some escaped to the shelter of neutral ports, especially those of the United States, but none got back to Germany. In a week German sea-borne commerce had virtually ceased to exist. Without striking a blow, by the sheer menace of our omnipresent navy, we had annihilated the trade of the enemy and protected our own.

A few German cruisers and armed merchantmen were still at large, but their number was too small and their life too precarious to affect our commerce. The government very properly began by guaranteeing part of the risks of maritime insurance; but soon the rates fell of their own accord to a natural level, as it became clear how ample was our security. It was calculated at the outbreak of war that British losses in the first six months might rise to 10 *per cent.* of vessels engaged in foreign trade. A return issued in the beginning of October showed that of our mercantile marine we had lost up to that date only 1.25 *per cent.*, while Germany and Austria had lost each 10 *per cent*, of their total shipping.

It is true that no Power has complete command of the sea so long as a hostile fleet remains undestroyed. But if the hostile fleet chooses to shut itself up in port, then, for all practical purposes, and until it comes forth, the command lies with the fleet that keeps the open water. The German fleet behind Heligoland, and the Austrian in Pola, might as well not have existed for all the influence they had on the oceans of the world. Every sea except the Baltic was a *mare clausum* to our enemies, and presently in the Pacific appeared a new ally.

On 15th August Japan delivered an ultimatum to Germany, in order, as she put it, to safeguard general interests as contemplated in the Agreement of Alliance between herself and Great Britain. She asked for (1) an immediate withdrawal from Japanese and Chinese waters of all German armed vessels, and (2) the delivery at a date not later than 15th September of the leased territory of Kiao-chau, in order that it might be restored to China. The wheel had come full circle with a vengeance. After the war with China, Germany had interposed to rob Japan of the fruits of her victory, and, on the plea of murdered missionaries, had forced from China the Kiao-chau lease. Now the tables were turned on the aggressor. Japan required an answer by noon on 23rd August, and, not receiving it, promptly declared war, and proceeded to the investment of the Tsingtau peninsula.

THE SURE SHIELD OF BRITAIN—A SCENE AT THE NAVAL REVIEW

The Battle of the Bight of Heligoland

The work of the British navy during the first two months of war was so completely successful in its main purpose that the ordinary man scarcely recognised it. He expected a theatrical *coup*, a full-dress battle, or a swift series of engagements with enemy warships. When he found that nothing happened, he began to think that something was amiss. But the proof of our success was that nothing happened— nothing startling, that is to say, for every day had its full record of quiet achievement. Three-fourths of the game was already ours without striking a blow. The British people depended for their very livelihood on their sea-borne commerce; that went on as if there were no war. The rates of marine insurance fell, and freights did not increase beyond the limits dictated by the law of supply and demand. We moved our armed forces about the world as we desired, not as our enemies permitted. Germany's foreign trade, on which she depended in the long run for munitions of war and the maintenance of most of her industries, ceased with dramatic suddenness. Our naval predominance was instantly proved by the impotence of our opponents.

The German policy was what the wiser among our people had always desired. No doubt if Admiral von Ingenohl had sailed forth with his Grand Fleet in the early days of August and been summarily sent to the bottom, it would have been even more convenient. But, short of such a wholesale destruction, things could not have fallen out more opportunely than they did. Assume that they had gone otherwise, and that the German admiral, instead of sheltering in the Elbe, had sent out some of his best cruisers and battle cruisers to scour the high seas. The performances of the *Emden*, which we shall later consider, would have been many times multiplied. We should have lost scores of mer-

Saving the crew of "Audacious" a "King George V"-class battleship of the Royal Navy. Sunk by a German naval mine off the northern coast of Donegal, Ireland in 1914, without seeing any combat in the First World War

chantmen, and a number of our smaller fighting units. Marine insurance rates and freights would have mounted high, prices would have risen, and there would have been heard at home the first mutterings of commercial panic.

The transport of troops from South Africa, Australia, and Canada would have been difficult, and we should have had to weaken dangerously our Grand Fleet to supply escorts. Indeed, with a dozen big German cruisers at large, it might have seemed for a week or two that the offensive had passed to the enemy, and that Britain, not Germany, was on her defence. Of course, we should have ended by destroying the raiders; the cruisers would have had a short life or a long life, but they would not have returned home. Nevertheless this weakening of the enemy's naval strength would have been dearly paid for by the congestion of our ordinary life at that most critical time, the first weeks of war, and by the inevitable interference with our military plans. Had Germany been bolder at sea there might have been no British force to hold the Allied left in the difficult days from the Sambre to the Marne.

One of the chief objects of a navy in war is to protect the commerce of its country. This purpose we achieved with ease, and it would have been mere folly to throw away capital ships in an assault on the retreat of an enemy which had virtually allowed our mastery of the sea to go unchallenged. On land an army fights its way yard by yard to a position from which it can deal a crushing blow. But a fleet needs none of these preliminaries. As soon as the enemy chooses to appear the battle can be joined. Hence von Ingenohl was right in saving his fleet for what he considered a better chance, and we were right in not forcing him unduly. Naval power should be used, not squandered, and the mightiest fleet on earth may be flung away on a fool's errand. It should not be forgotten that the strength of a fleet is a more brittle and less replaceable thing than the strength of an army. New levies can be called for on land, and tolerable infantry trained in a few months. But in the navy it takes six years to make a junior officer, it takes two years to build a cruiser, and three years to replace a battleship. A serious loss in fighting units is, for any ordinary naval war, an absolute, not a temporary, calamity.

It was the business, then, of the British fleet to perform its principal duty, the protection of British trade; it was not its business to break its head against the defences of Wilhelmshaven or Kiel. At the same time, it had to watch incessantly for the emergence of German ships, and, if possible, entice them out of their sanctuary. Cautious and well-reasoned boldness was the quality demanded, and on 28th August, the day when Sir John French's retreat from Mons had reached the Oise, it earned its reward in the first important naval action of the war.

The Battle of the Bight of Heligoland was in its way such a little masterpiece of naval strategy and tactics that it deserves to be examined with some attention. First, we must realize the various forces engaged, which may be set down in the order of their appearance in the action.

1. Eighth Submarine Flotilla (Commodore Roger Keyes).—
   Parent ships: Destroyers *Lurcher* and *Firedrake*.
   Submarines: D2, D8, E4, E5, E6, 7, 8, 9.

2. Destroyer Flotillas (Commodore R. Y. Tyrwhitt).—Flagship:
   Light cruiser *Arethusa*.

   First Destroyer Flotilla: Light cruiser *Fearless* (Captain
   Blunt).—Destroyers: *Acheron, Archer, Ariel, Attack,
   Badger, Beaver, Defender, Ferret, Forester, Goshawk, Hind,
   Jackal, Lapwing, Lizard, Phoenix, Sandfly*.

   Third Destroyer Flotilla: *Laertes, Laforey, Lance, Landrail,
   Lark, Laurel, Lawford, Legion, Leonidas, Lennox, Liberty,
   Linnet, Llewelyn, Louis, Lucifer, Lydiard, Lysander*.

3. First Light-Cruiser Squadron (Commodore W. R.
   Goodenough).—*Southampton, Falmouth, Birmingham,
   Lowestoft, Nottingham*.

4. First Battle-Cruiser Squadron (Vice-Admiral Sir
   David Beatty).—*Lion, Princess Royal, Queen Mary,
   New Zealand*. Joined at sea by *Invincible* (Rear-Admiral
   Moore) and by destroyers: *Hornet, Hydra, Tigress,* and
   Loyal.

5. Seventh Cruiser Squadron (Rear-Admiral A. H.
   Christian).—Armoured cruisers: *Euryalus, Cressy, Hogue,
   Aboukir, Sutlej, Bacchante*, and light cruiser *Amethyst*.

The battle cruisers were the largest and newest of their class, displacing some 27,000 tons, with a speed of 29 knots, and an armament each of eight 13.5 and sixteen 4-inch guns. The First Light-Cruiser Squadron contained ships of the "town" class—5,500 tons, 25 to 26 knots, and eight or nine 6-inch guns. The Seventh Cruiser Squadron were older ships from the Third Fleet—12,000 tons and 21 knots. The

THE BRITISH FLEET AT SEA

First Destroyer Flotilla contained destroyers each of about 800 tons, 30 knots, and two 4-inch and two 12-pounder guns. The Third Flotilla was composed only of the largest and latest type—965 tons, 32 knots, and three 4-inch guns. Of the accompanying cruisers the *Arethusa*—the latest of an apostolical succession of vessels of that name—was the first ship of a new class; her tonnage was 3,750, her speed 30 knots, and her armament two 6-inch and six 4-inch guns. Her companion, the *Fearless*, had 3,440 tons, 26 knots, and ten 4 -inch guns. The two small destroyers which accompanied the submarines, the *Lurcher* and the *Firedrake*, had 765 tons, 35 knots, and two 4-inch and two 12-pounder guns.

Ever since the 9th of August the seas around Heligoland had been assiduously scouted by the submarines E6 and E8. German cruisers—apparently the *Strassburg* and the *Stralsund*—had shown a certain activity, and had succeeded in sinking a number of British trawlers; but the several "drives" which we organized had sent them back to their territorial waters. The *Fearless* had also been on patrol work, and on 21st August had come under the enemy's shell fire. By the 26th our intelligence was complete, and at midnight the submarine flotilla, under Commodore Keyes, sailed from Harwich for the Bight of Heligoland. All the next day, the 27th, the *Lurcher* and the *Firedrake* scouted for the submarines. At five o'clock on the evening of the 27th the First and Third Destroyer Flotillas, under Commodore Tyrwhitt, left Harwich, and some time during that day the Battle-Cruiser Squadron, the First Light-Cruiser Squadron, and the Seventh Cruiser Squadron also put to sea. The rendezvous appointed was reached early on the morning of the 28th, the waters having been searched for hostile submarines before dawn by the *Lurcher* and the *Firedrake*.

The chronicle must now concern itself with hours and minutes. The first phase of the action began just before 7 a.m. on the 28th. The morning had broken windless and calm, with a haze which limited the range of vision to under three miles. The water was like a millpond, and out of the morning mist rose the gaunt rock of Heligoland, with its forts and painted lodging-houses and crumbling sea-cliffs. It was the worst conceivable weather for the submarines, since in a calm sea their periscopes were easily visible.

The position at seven o'clock was as follows. Close to Heligoland, and well within German territorial waters, were Commodore Keyes' eight submarines, with his two small destroyers in attendance.

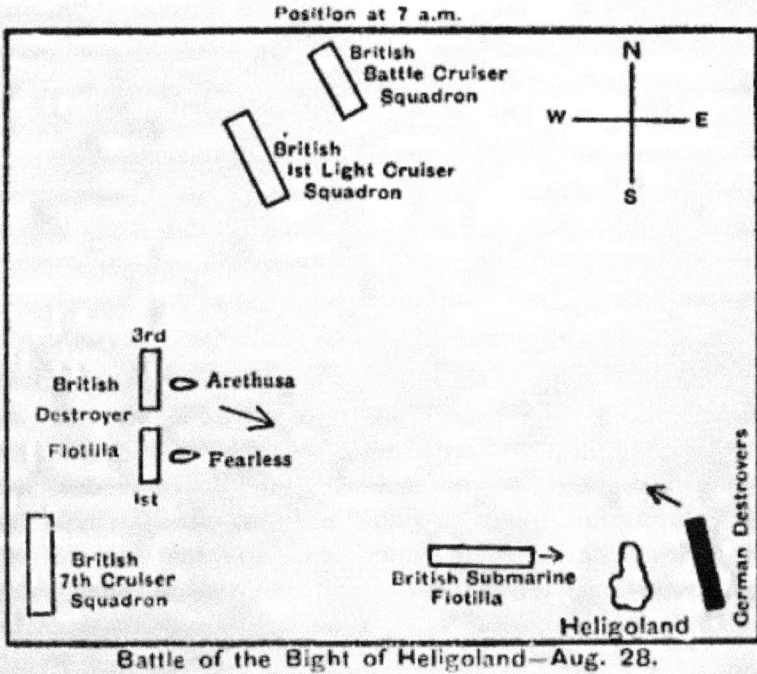

Position at 7 a.m.

British Battle Cruiser Squadron

British Ist Light Cruiser Squadron

N
W —|— E
S

3rd

British
Destroyer
Flotilla

Arethusa

Fearless

Ist

British
7th Cruiser
Squadron

British Submarine
Flotilla

German Destroyers

Heligoland

Battle of the Bight of Heligoland—Aug. 28.

Approaching rapidly from the north-west were Commodore Tyr-whitt's two destroyer flotillas, while behind them, at some distance and a little to the east, was Commodore Goodenough's First Light-Cruiser Squadron. Behind it lay Sir David Beatty's battle cruisers, with the four destroyers in attendance. A good deal to the south, and about due west of Heligoland, lay Admiral Christian's Seventh Cruiser Squadron, to stop all exit towards the west.

The submarines, foremost among them E6, E7, and E8, performed admirably the work of a decoy. They were apparently first observed by a German seaplane, and presently from behind Heligoland came a number of German destroyers. These were presently followed by two cruisers, and the submarines and their attendant destroyers fled westwards, while the British destroyer flotillas came swiftly down from the northwest. At the sight of the latter the German destroyers turned to make for home; but the British flotillas, led by the Third, along with the *Arethusa*, altered their course to port in order to head them off. the official report says:

The principle of the movement was to cut the German light

craft from home and engage them at leisure in the open sea.

The destroyers gave little trouble, and our own ships of that class were quite competent to deal with them. But between our two attendant cruisers and the two German cruisers a fierce battle was waged. About eight o'clock the *Arethusa*—*praeclarum et venerabile nomen*—was engaged with the German *Ariadne*, while the *Fearless* was busy with a four-funnelled vessel which some of our men thought was the *Yorck*, but which was probably the *Strassburg*. The *Arethusa*, till the *Fearless* drew the *Strassburg's* fire, was exposed to the broadsides of the two vessels, and was considerably damaged. About 8.25, however, one of her shots shattered the fore-bridge of the *Ariadne* and killed the captain, and the shattered vessel drew off towards Heligoland, whither the *Strassburg* soon followed.

Meantime the destroyers had not been idle. They had sunk the leading boat of the German flotilla, V187, and had damaged a dozen more. With great heroism they attempted to save the German sailors now struggling in the water, and lowered boats for the purpose. These boats, as we shall see, came into deadly peril during the next phase of the action.

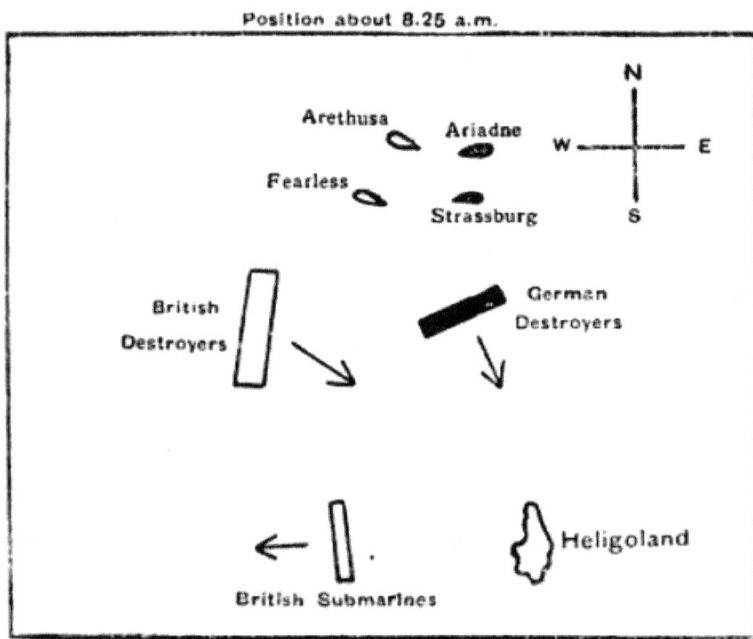

Battle of the Bight of Heligoland—Aug. 28.

On the retreat of the *Ariadne* and the *Strassburg* the destroyer flotillas were ordered to turn westward. The gallant *Arethusa* was in need of attention, for a water-tank had been hit, and all her guns save one were temporarily out of action. She was soon repaired, and only two of her 4-inch guns were left still out of order. Between nine and ten o'clock, therefore, there was a lull in the fight, which we may take as marking the break between the first and second phases of the battle. The submarines, with their attendants, *Lurcher* and *Firedrake*, were still in the immediate vicinity of Heligoland, as well as some of the destroyers which had boats out to save life.

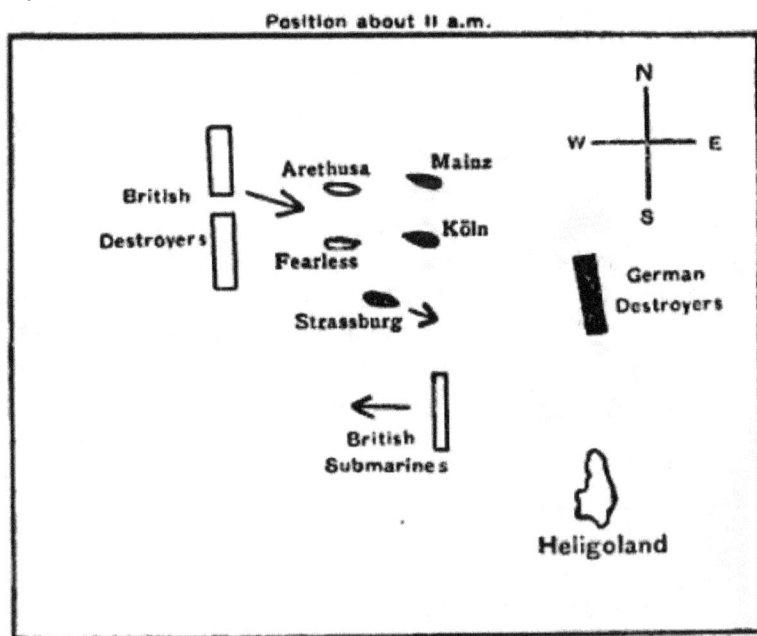

Position about 11 a.m.

Battle of the Bight of Heligoland—Aug. 28.

About ten o'clock the second phase began. The Germans believed that the only hostile vessels in the neighbourhood were the submarines, destroyers, the *Arethusa* and the *Fearless*, and they resolved to take this excellent chance of annihilating them. About ten Commodore Tyrwhitt received a wireless message from Commodore Keyes that the *Lurcher* and *Firedrake* were being chased by three German cruisers. These were the *Mainz*, the *Köln*, and a heavier vessel, which may have been the *Yorck* or the *Strassburg*. The German cruisers came on the boats of the First Flotilla busy saving life, and thinking apparently that the British had adopted the insane notion of boarding, opened a heavy fire on them. The small destroyers were driven away, and two boats, belonging to the *Goshawk* and the *Defender*, were cut off under the guns of Heligoland. At this moment submarine E4 (Lieutenant-Commander E. W. Leir) appeared alongside. By the threat of a torpedo attack he drove off the German cruiser for a moment, and took on board the British seamen.

The *Arethusa*, the *Fearless*, and the destroyers boldly engaged the three enemy cruisers, and for a little were in a position of great peril. They had already suffered considerably, and their speed and handiness must have been reduced. The first incident was an artillery duel between the *Arethusa* and the vessel which we may call the *Strassburg*, which resulted in the retirement of the latter. Then came the *Mainz*, which was so severely handled that her boilers blew up, and she became little better than a wreck. There remained the *Köln*, which began a long-range duel with the *Arethusa*. So far the destroyer flotillas had covered themselves with glory, but their position was far from comfortable.

They were in German home waters, not far from the guns of Heligoland (which the fog seems to have made useless at that range); they were a good deal crippled, though still able to fight; and they did not know but that at any moment the blunt noses of Admiral von Ingenohl's great battleships might come out of the mist. The battle had now lasted for five hours ample time for the ships in the Elbe to come up. Commodore Tyrwhitt about eleven had sent a wireless signal to Sir David Beatty asking for help, and by twelve o'clock that help was sorely needed.

It was on its way. Admiral Beatty, on receipt of the signal, at once sent the First Light-Cruiser Squadron south-eastwards. The first vessels, the *Falmouth* and the *Nottingham*, arrived on the scene of action about twelve o'clock, and proceeded to deal with the damaged *Mainz*. By this time the First Destroyer Flotilla had retired westward, but the Third Flotilla and the *Arethusa* were still busy with the *Köln*. Admiral Beatty had to take a momentous decision. There was every likelihood that some of the enemy's great armoured and battle cruisers were close at hand, and he wisely judged that "to be of any value the support must be overwhelming." It was a risky business to take his vessels through a mine-strewn and submarine-haunted sea; but in naval warfare the highest risks must be run.

Hawke pursued Conflans in a stormy dusk into Quiberon Bay, and Nelson before Aboukir risked in the darkness the shoals and reefs of an uncharted sea. So Admiral Beatty gave orders at 11.30 for the battle cruisers to steam E.S.E. at full speed. They were several times attacked by submarines, but their pace saved them, and when later the *Queen Mary* was in danger she avoided it by a skilful use of the helm. By 12.15 the smoke-blackened eyes of the *Arethusa's* men saw the huge shapes of our battle cruisers emerging from the northern mists.

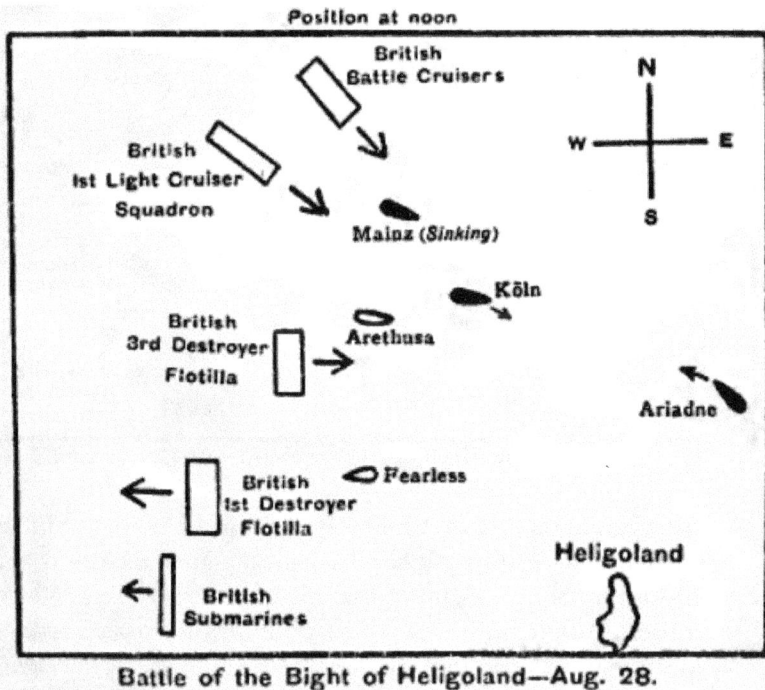

Battle of the Bight of Heligoland—Aug. 28.

Their advent decided the battle. They found the *Mainz* on fire and sinking by the head, and steered north-eastward to where the *Arethusa* and the *Köln* were hard at work. The *Lion* came first, and she alone among the battle cruisers seems to have used her guns. Her immense fire power and admirable gunnery beat down all opposition. The *Köln* fled before her, but the *Lion's* guns at extreme range hit her and set her on fire. Presently the luckless *Ariadne* hove in sight from the south—the forerunner, perhaps, of a new squadron. Two salvos from the terrible 13.5-inch guns sufficed for her, and, burning furiously, she disappeared into the haze. Then the battle cruisers circled north again, and in ten minutes finished off the *Köln*. She sank like a plummet with every soul on board.

N

W ——— E

S

British
1st Light Cruiser
Squadron

Köln (Sunk)

British
Battle
Cruisers

Mainz
(Sunk)

Ariadne
(Sunk)

British
Destroyers

Arethusa

Fearless

German
Destroyers

Heligoland

Strassburg
(Damaged)

British
Submarines

Battle of the Bight of Heligoland—Aug. 28.

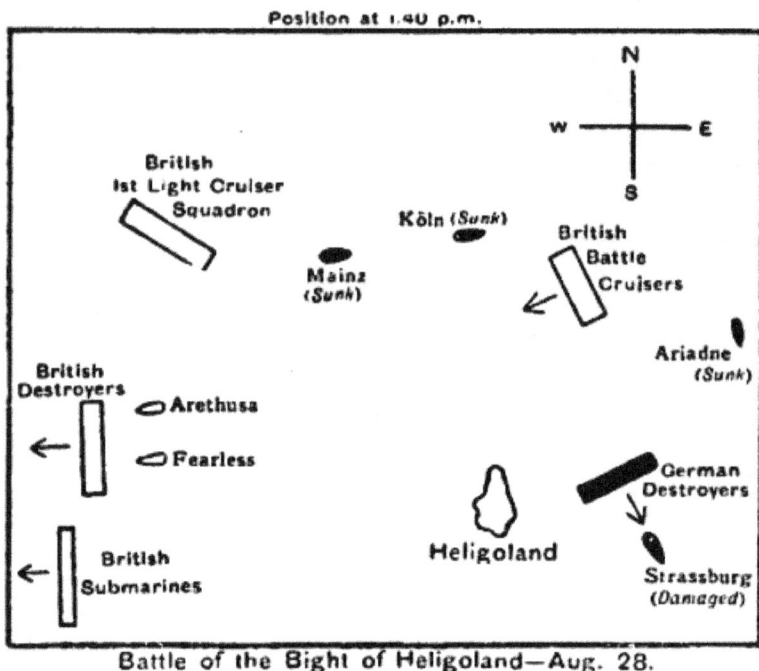

At twenty minutes to two Admiral Beatty turned homeward. The submarines and the destroyer flotillas had already gone westward, and the Light-Cruiser Squadron, in a fan-shaped formation, preceded the battle cruisers. Admiral Christian's squadron was left to escort the damaged ships and defend the rear. By that evening the whole British force was in our own waters without the loss of a single unit. The *Arethusa* had been badly damaged, wounded, among the former being two brilliant officers, Lieutenant-Commander Nigel Barttelot of the destroyer *Liberty*, and Lieutenant Eric Westmacott of the *Arethusa*.

The Germans lost two new cruisers, the *Mainz* and the *Köln*, and one older cruiser, the *Ariadne*. A four-funnelled cruiser, the *Strassburg* or the *Yorck*,[1] was seriously damaged, as were at least seven destroyers. Only one destroyer, the V187, was actually sunk, though our Admiralty mentioned two. The broken destroyers which put into Kiel some days later did not suffer, as we at first believed, from the Heligoland fight, but from a misadventure in the Baltic. At least 700 of the German crews perished, and there were 300 prisoners.

---

1. The *Yorck* was destroyed by a mine on November 3. The *Strassburg* was one of the vessels engaged in the raid on Scarborough and Hartlepool in December.

HELOGOLAND–SINKING OF THE "MAINZ"

Of the Battle of the Bight it may fairly be said that it was creditable to both victors and vanquished. The Germans fought in the true naval spirit, and the officers stood by their ships till they went down. The gallantry of our own men was conspicuous, as was their readiness to run risks in saving life, a readiness which the enemy handsomely acknowledged. The submarine flotilla fought under great disadvantages, but the crews never wavered, and their attendant destroyers, the *Lurcher* and the *Firedrake*, were constantly engaged with heavier vessels. The two destroyer flotillas were not less prominent, and, having taken the measure of the German destroyers, did not hesitate to engage the enemy's cruisers. But the chief glory belongs to the *Arethusa* and the *Fearless*, who for a critical hour bore the chief brunt of the battle.

For a time they were matched against three German cruisers, which between them had a considerably greater force of fire. Nowadays much of naval fighting is a mathematical certainty, for, given the guns and the speed, you can calculate the result. But it was the good fortune of the *Arethusa* to show her mettle in a conflict which more resembled the audacious struggles of Nelson's day. It is a curious fact that though we had some sixty vessels in the action from first to last, only four or five were hit. The light-cruiser squadron and the battle cruisers decided the battle, and while their blows were deadly, the enemy never got a chance of retaliation. From twelve o'clock onward it was scientific modern destruction; before that it was any one's fight.

The strategy which devised the action was admirable in conception and execution, and not less admirable was the tactical skill which provided for the co-operation of different classes of vessels, proceeding from different bases, within a narrow area and at the right moment. Had the German battleships emerged it may be presumed that we were prepared for that eventuality. Undoubtedly the action justified to the full three classes of our recent naval constructions—the big battle cruisers, the new light cruisers of the *Arethusa* type, and the large destroyers that belonged to the Third Flotilla. It proved, too, that the largest ships might safely operate among the enemy's submarines if only their speed was high—a lesson of immense importance for future naval warfare.

The immediate consequence of the Battle of the Bight was a change in German naval policy. Von Ingenohl was confirmed in his resolution to keep his battleships in harbour, and not even a daring sweeping movement of the British early in September, when our vessels came within hearing of the church bells on the German coast, could goad him into action. But he retaliated by an increased activity in mine-laying and the use of submarines. In the land warfare of the Middle Ages there came a time when knights and horses were so heavily armoured that they lost mobility, and what had been regarded as the main type of action ended in stalemate. Wherefore, since men must find some way of conquering each other, came the chance for the hitherto despised lighter troops, and the archers and spearmen began to win battles like Courtrai and Bannockburn. A similar stalemate was now reached as between the capital ships of the rival navies. The British battleships were vast and numerous; the German fleet, less powerful at sea, was strong in its fenced harbour. No decision could be reached by the heavily armed units, so the war passed into the hands of the lesser craft. For a space of more than two months the Germans fought almost wholly with mines and submarines.

One truth should be remembered, which at this period was somewhat forgotten by the British people. Command of the sea, unless the enemy's navy is totally destroyed, does not mean complete protection. This has been well stated in a famous passage by Admiral Mahan[2]:—

> The control of the sea, however real, does not imply that an enemy's single ships or small squadrons cannot steal out of ports, and cross more or less frequented tracts of ocean, make harassing descents upon unprotected points of a long coast-line, enter blockaded harbours. On the contrary, history has shown that such evasions are always possible, to some extent, to the weaker party, however great the inequality of naval strength.

This has been true in all ages, and is especially true now that the mine and submarine have come to the assistance of the weaker combatant. Our policy was to blockade Germany, so that she should suffer and our own life go on unhindered. But the blockade could only be a watching blockade; it could not seal up every unit of the enemy's naval strength. To achieve the latter we should have had to run the risk of missing the very goal at which we aimed. It was our business to see that Germany did nothing without our knowledge, and to encourage her ships to come out that we might fall upon them. Her business was to make our patrolling as difficult as possible. To complain of British losses in such a task was to do precisely what Germany wished us to do, in order that caution might take the place of a bold and aggressive vigilance.

---

2. *Influence of Sea Power upon History.*

THE BATTLE OF HELIGOLAND BIGHT: H.M.S. "ARETHUSA" LEADING THE DESTROYERS INTO ACTION.—AFTER A R.N. OFFICER'S SKETCH.

The idea of the attack in Heligoland Bight was for a force of destroyers, backed by the light armoured-cruiser "Arethusa," to stand in and cut off the German light squadron from their port, and then attack them on the open sea. The "Arethusa," a ship of a new type, only commissioned a few days ago, under Commodore Tyrwhitt, commanding the destroyer flotillas of the First Fleet, led the destroyers and opened the attack, engaging two German cruisers. While the destroyers were rounding up the nearest German destroyers and "punish'ng" them severely, the "Arethusa" was sharply engaged for 10 irty-five minutes at a range of about 3000 yards until the two cruisers fled.—[Drawn by Norman Wilkinson from a Sketch by an Officer who took part in the action.—*The Illustrated London News*.]

Germany had laid in the first days of the war a large mine-field off our eastern coasts, and early in September, by means of trawlers disguised as neutrals, she succeeded in dropping mines off the north coast of Ireland, which endangered our Atlantic commerce and the operations of our Grand Fleet. The right precaution—the closing of the North Sea to neutral shipping, unless specially accompanied—was not taken till too late in the day, and even then was too perfunctorily organised. A section of the Royal Naval Reserve was detached for the task of mine-sweeping, and trawlers, manned by East Coast fishermen, were busy at all hours off our shores. It was a hard and perilous employment, how perilous the many casualties revealed; and the work of these crews, inconspicuous and unadvertised as it was, deserves to be ranked along with more sounding deeds among the heroisms of the war. The mine-field, for all its terrors, was not productive of much actual loss to our fighting strength. During the first two months of war, apart from the *Amphion*, the only casualty was the old gunboat *Speedy*, which struck a mine and foundered in the North Sea on 3rd September.

The submarine was a graver menace. On 5th September the *Pathfinder*, a light cruiser of 2,940 tons, with a crew of 268, was torpedoed off the Lothian coast and sunk, with great loss of life. Eight days later the German light cruiser *Hela*, a vessel slightly smaller than the *Pathfinder*, was sunk by the British submarine E9 (Lieutenant Max Horton) in wild weather between Heligoland and the Frisian coast—an exploit of exceptional boldness and difficulty. During that fortnight a great storm raged, and our patrols found it hard to keep the seas, many of the smaller destroyers being driven to port. This storm led indirectly to the first serious British loss of the war. Three cruisers of an old pattern, the *Cressy*, *Hogue*, and *Aboukir*, which had been part of Admiral Christian's Seventh Cruiser Squadron in the Battle of the Bight of Heligoland, had for three weeks been engaged in patrolling off the Dutch coast. It does not appear why three large ships carrying heavy crews were employed on a duty which could have been performed better and more safely by lighter vessels. No screen of destroyers was with them at the moment, owing to the storm.

On the 22nd of September the sky had cleared and the seas fallen, and about half-past six in the morning, as the cruisers proceeded to their posts, the *Aboukir* was torpedoed, and began to settle down. Her sister ships believed she had struck a mine, and closed in on her to save life. Suddenly the *Hogue* was struck by two torpedoes, and began to sink. Two of her boats had already been got away to the rescue of the *Aboukir's* men, and as she went down she righted herself for a moment, with the result that her steam pinnace and steam picket-boat floated off. The *Cressy* now came up to the rescue, but she also was struck by two torpedoes, and sank rapidly. Three trawlers in the neighbourhood at the time picked up the survivors in the water and in the boats, but of the total crews of 1,459 officers and men only 779 were saved. In that bright, chilly morning, when all was over within a quarter of an hour, the British sailor showed his unsurpassed discipline and courage. Men swimming in the frosty sea or clinging naked to boats or wreckage cheered each other with songs and jokes. An eye-witness wrote:

> The men on the *Hogue* stood quietly by waiting for the order
> to jump, and passing the time in slipping off their clothes.

The survivors were positive that they saw at least three submarines, but the German official account mentions only one—the U9, under Captain-Lieutenant Otto Weddigen.

The fate of the three cruisers was not only a disaster; it was a mistake, of the kind which is inevitable at the beginning of a naval war, before novel conditions are adequately realised. Faulty staff work somewhere at headquarters was to blame. There was no reason why three such vessels should have been employed at all on patrol duty; and if they were to be employed they should never have been sent out without a screen of destroyers. Again, they had been kept promenading on the same beat for some time, which was simply an invitation to submarines to come out and attack them. Lastly, no instructions had been given them as to what to do in the case of one of their number being torpedoed, with the result that the *Hogue* went to assist the *Aboukir*, and the *Cressy* to assist the *Hogue*, and all three perished. The Admiralty realized this grave omission too late, and a few days after the disaster issued a statement, from which we quote:—

> The sinking of the *Aboukir* was, of course, an ordinary hazard
> of patrolling duty. The *Hogue* and *Cressy*, however, were sunk
> because they proceeded to the assistance of their consort, and
> remained with engines stopped endeavouring to save life, thus
> presenting an easy and certain target to further submarine at-
> tacks. The natural promptings of humanity have in this case led
> to heavy losses which would have been avoided by a strict ad-
> hesion to military considerations. Modern naval war is present-
> ing us with so many new and strange situations that an error

THE BATTLE OF HELOGOLAND BLIGHT, THE FIRST NAVAL ENGAGEMENT OF THE WAR

of judgment of this character is pardonable. But it has become necessary to point out for the future guidance of His Majesty's ships, that the conditions which prevail when one vessel of a squadron is injured in a mine-field, or is exposed to submarine attack, are analogous to those which occur in an action, and that the rule of leaving ships to their own resources is applicable so far at any rate as large vessels are concerned.

The Admiralty correctly attributed the catastrophe to an error of judgment, but the error was not that of the captains of the lost vessels.

The third method of weakening British sea power was by the attack upon merchantmen by light cruisers. Apparently Germany sent forth no new vessels of this type after the outbreak of war, and her activities were confined to those which were already outside the Narrow Seas, especially those under Admiral von Spee's command at Kiao-chau. So far as September is concerned, we need mention only the *Emden* and the *Koenigsberg*. The former was to provide the world with a genuine tale of romantic adventure, always welcome among the grave realities of war, and in her short life to emulate the achievements and the fame of the *Alabama*. She appeared in the Bay of Bengal on 10th September, and within a week had captured seven large merchantmen, six of which she sank.

Next week she arrived at Rangoon, where her presence cut off all sea communication between India and Burma. On 22nd September she was at Madras, and fired a shell or two into the environs of the city, setting an oil tank on fire. On the 29th she was off Pondicherry, and the last day of the month found her running up the Malabar coast. There for the present we leave her, for the tale of her subsequent adventures belongs to another chapter. The *Koenigsberg* had her beat off the East Coast of Africa. Her chief exploit was a dash into Zanzibar harbour, where, on 20th September, she caught the British cruiser *Pegasus* while in the act of repairing her boilers. The *Pegasus* was a seventeen-year-old ship of 2,135 tons, and had no chance against her assailant. She was destroyed by the *Koenigsberg's* long-range fire.

The exploits of the two German commerce-raiders were magnified because they were the exceptions, while the British capture of German merchantmen was the rule. We did not destroy our captures, because we had many ports to take them to, and they were duly brought before our prize courts. In addition, we had made havoc of Germany's converted liners. The *Kaiser Wilhelm der Grosse*, which had escaped from Bremerhaven at the beginning of the war, and which had preyed for a fortnight on our South Atlantic commerce, was caught and sunk by the *Highflyer* near the Cape Verde Islands. On 12th September the *Berwick* captured in the North Atlantic the *Spreewald*, of the Hamburg-Amerika line. On 14th September the *Carmania*, Captain Noel Grant, a British converted liner, fell in with a similar German vessel, the *Cap Trafalgar*, off the coast of Brazil. The action began at 9,000 yards, and lasted for an hour and three-quarters. The *Carmania* was skilfully handled, and her excellent gunnery decided the issue. Though the British vessel had to depart prematurely owing to the approach of a German cruiser, she left her antagonist sinking in flames.

Other instances might be quoted, but these will suffice to show how active British vessels were in all the seas. The loss of a few light cruisers and a baker's dozen of merchantmen was a small price to pay for an unimpaired foreign trade and the practical impotence of the enemy. Modern inventions give the weaker power a better chance for raiding than in the old days; but in spite of that our sufferings were small compared with any other of our great wars. It is instructive to contrast our fortunes during the struggle with Napoleon. Then, even after Trafalgar had been fought, French privateers made almost daily captures of English ships in our home waters.

Our coasts were frequently attacked, and the inhabitants of the seaboard went for years in constant expectation of invasion. In the twenty-one years of war we lost 10,248 British ships. Further back in our history our inviolability was even more precarious. In the year after Agincourt the French landed in Portland. Seven years after the defeat of the Armada the Spanish burned Penzance and ravaged the Cornish coasts. In 1667 the Dutch were in the Medway and the Thames. In 1690 the French burned Teignmouth, and landed in Sussex; in 1760 they seized Carrickfergus; in 1797 they landed at Fishguard. In 1775 Paul Jones captured Whitehaven, and was the terror of our home waters. The most prosperous war has its casualties in unexpected places.

As for the alleged slowness in bringing the enemy's fleet to book, it should be remembered that in the Revolution Wars England had to wait a year for the first naval battle, Howe's victory of the 1st of June; while Nelson lay for two years before Toulon, and Cornwallis for longer before Brest. To quote Admiral Mahan:—

They were dull, weary, eventless months, those months of waiting and watching of the big ships before the French arsenals. Purposeless they surely seemed to many, but they saved England. The world has never seen a more impressive demonstration of the influence of sea power upon its history. Those far-distant, storm-beaten ships, upon which the Grand Army never looked, stood between it and the dominion of the world.

In Nelson's day we had one advantage which is now lost to us. We were not hampered by a code of maritime law framed in the interests of unmaritime nations. The Declaration of Paris of 1856, among other provisions, enacted that a neutral flag covered enemy's merchandise except contraband of war, and that neutral merchandise was not capturable even under the enemy's flag. This Declaration, which was not accepted by the United States, has never received legislative ratification from the British Parliament; but we regarded ourselves as bound by it, though various efforts had been made to get it rescinded in times of peace by those who realized how greatly it weakened the belligerent force of a sea power. The Declaration of London of 1909 made a further effort to codify maritime law.[2] It was signed by the British plenipotentiaries, though Parliament refused to pass the statutes necessary to give effect to certain of its provisions. In some respects it was more favourable to Britain than the Declaration of Paris, but in others it was less favourable, and it was consistently opposed by many good authorities on the subject. Generally speaking, it was more acceptable to a nation like Germany than to a people situated like ourselves. (See note at end of chapter).

When war broke out the British Government announced that it accepted the Declaration of London as the basis of our maritime practice. The result was a position of some confusion, for the consequences of the new law had never been fully realised. Under it, for example, the captain of the *Emden* could justify his sinking of British ships instead of taking them to a port for adjudication. One provision, which seems to have been deduced from it, was so patently ridiculous that it was soon dropped that belligerents (that is, enemy reservists) in neutral ships were not liable to arrest. Presently successive Orders in Council, instigated by sheer necessity, altered the Declaration of London beyond recognition. The truth was, that we were engaged in a war to which few a priori rules could be made to apply. Germany had become a law unto herself, and the wisest course for the Allies was to

---

2. Parliamentary Paper, Cd. 4554 of 1909.

frame their own code, which should comply not only with the half-dozen great principles of international equity, but with the mandates of common sense.

Note:—The following are a few examples of the way in which it impaired our naval power: It was made easy to break a blockade, for the right of a blockading Power to capture a blockade-runner did not cover the whole period of her voyage and was confined to ships of the blockading force (Articles 14, 16, 17, 19, 20); stereotyped lists of contraband and non-contraband were drawn up, instead of the old custom of leaving the question to the discretion of the Prize Court (Articles 22, 23, 24, 25, 28); a ship carrying contraband could only be condemned if the contraband formed more than half its cargo; a belligerent warship could destroy a neutral vessel without taking it to a port for judgment; the transfer of an enemy vessel to a neutral flag was presumed to be valid if effected more than thirty days before the outbreak of war (Article 55); the question of the test of enemy property was left in high confusion (Article 58); a neutral vessel, if accompanied by any sort of warship of her own flag, was exempt from search; belligerents in neutral vessels on the high seas were exempt from capture (based on Article 45). With the Declaration of London would go most of the naval findings of the Hague Conference of 1907. The British delegates who assented to the Declaration of London proceeded on the assumption that in any war of the future Britain would be neutral, and so endeavoured to reduce the privileges of maritime belligerents.

The War in Africa

By the end of August the war had spread beyond Europe to every quarter of the globe where Germany possessed a square mile of territory. British Australasian and African dominions were engaged in defending or enlarging their borders, and, though the fighting was on a small scale compared with the gigantic European struggle, it had important strategical bearings, and for Britain was scarcely less vital than the battlefields of France. The war in the Pacific, in which Japan was our partner, must be left to another chapter. Here we propose to consider only the campaigns conducted in the different parts of Africa, where Germany owned four colonies, contiguous to those of France and Britain. This was fighting of a familiar type, such as almost every year had shown on some portion of the Empire's frontiers. We fought with and against armies largely composed of native troops, and the country was that bush and desert which had been for a century the common theatre of our armed adventures.

Germany's colonial ambitions awoke with her great development after the victory over France. She desired to emulate Britain in finding an outlet under her flag for her surplus population, which had hitherto emigrated to North and South America; she wished to have producing grounds of her own from which she could draw raw material for new factories; she sought to share in the glory of conquest and colonization, which had done so much for France and Britain; and, as a coming maritime power, she was anxious to have something for her navy to defend. Her thinkers as well as her statesmen fostered the new interest. List and Friedel and Treitschke pointed out that trade followed the flag, and that the flag might also follow trade; while Bismarck discerned in the movement a chance of getting fresh assets to bargain with in that European game which he played with such consummate skill.

Especially Germany's eyes turned towards Africa, and not without justification. Her travellers had been among the greatest pioneers of that mysterious continent. In the history of South African exploration honourable place must be given to the names of Kolbe and Lichtenstein, Mohr and Mauch. In West and Northern Africa the roll of honour contained such great adventurers as Hornemann and Barth, Ziegler and Schweinfurth, Rohlfs and Nachtigal. It was a German, Karl von der Decken, who first surveyed Kilimanjaro, and the story of African enterprise contains few more heroic figures than that of von Wissmann. Germany was resolved to share in what is called the scramble for Africa, and she had admirable pathfinders in her missionaries and explorers.

This is not the place to describe in detail the tortuous events from 1880 onwards which led to the foundation of the four German African colonies. It is a fascinating tale, for Germany made adroit use of the suspicions and supineness of the Powers in possession. So far as the British Governments of the day were concerned, she might have had all she wanted for the asking; and it was only by the efforts of clear-sighted private citizens that her bolder schemes were checkmated. Her first attempts were directed towards the Portuguese colony of Delagoa Bay, which would bring her in touch with what she believed to be the bitterly anti-British people of the Transvaal. In Pondoland and at St. Lucia Bay, on the Zululand coast, she endeavoured to get grants of land from the native chiefs, and was only stopped by a tardy British intervention, forced upon the mother-country by the people of Cape Colony. Few at home realised the significance of the attempts, and Mr. Gladstone in the House of Commons publicly thanked God for them, and looked forward to her alliance, "in the execution of the great purposes of Providence for the advantage of mankind." In 1884 the work was fairly begun. Sir Bartle Frere from Cape Town had warned Lord Carnarvon as early as 1878 that Britain must be mistress up to the Portuguese frontier on both the east and west coasts. He wrote:—

> There is no escaping from the responsibility which has been already incurred ever since the English flag was planted on the castle here. All our difficulties have arisen, and still arise, from attempting to evade or shift this responsibility.

But presently Herr Luderitz had founded his settlement at Luderitz Bay, and on April 25, 1884, the German flag was hoisted in Damaraland, and the colony of German South-West Africa was constituted. Two months later Nachtigal landed from a gunboat at Lome, the port of Togoland, and by arrangement with the local chiefs declared the country a German Protectorate. A month after he did the same thing in the Cameroons, and the British consul, sent to frustrate him, arrived five days too late.

Bismarck, desiring to regularise his acquisitions, summoned the famous Berlin Conference, which met on 15th November of the same year. Many of its phrases are still in common use—"Occupation to be valid must be effective," "Spheres of influence," and such like. Meanwhile German agents, including the notorious Karl Peters, were busy in Zanzibar, intriguing with the *sultan*, and sending expeditions into the interior to secure concessions. Some day the history will be written of the part played in that contest by men like Sir Frederick Lugard, who, while they could not prevent the creation of German East Africa, saved Uganda and the East African Protectorate for Britain. In 1890 came the Caprivi Agreement, as a consequence of which Heligoland was ceded to Germany. It settled the boundaries of German East Africa, but it did more, for it gave to German South-West Africa a strip of land running north-east to the Zambesi, which formed a wedge separating the Bechuanaland Protectorate from Angola and North-West Rhodesia.

There could be no objection in international law or ethics to Germany's African activity, though there might be much to her methods of conducting it. She had a right to get as much territory as she could, and to profit by the blindness of her rivals. But by 1890 a new and more watchful spirit was appearing in British Africa, and to some extent in the mother-country. Cecil Rhodes was beginning his great struggle with Paul Kruger for the road to the north, and the dream of a Cape to Cairo route seized upon the popular imagination. Imperialists sighed for a Monroe doctrine for Africa, but the day for that had long gone by. A solid German fence had been built across that northern avenue which might have joined up Nyassaland and North-East Rhodesia with Uganda and the Sudan. Meanwhile Germany, having got her colonies, did not handle them with great discretion. She was much out of pocket over them, for she lavished money on the construction of roads and railways, and especially on that cast-iron type of administration which was the Prussian ideal.

Her first blunder was her treatment of her settlers, who found themselves terribly swathed in red tape, and were apt to trek over the

FORT DACHANG, CAMEROONS 1915

border to more liberal British climes. Her second was her attitude towards the native population. Unaccustomed to allow ancient modes of life to continue side by side with the new—which is the British plan—she attempted to make of the Bantu peoples decorous citizens on the Prussian model; and, when they objected, gave them a taste of Prussian rigour. One of the ablest of German students of colonial policy, Dr. Moritz Bonn of Munich, has noted the result so far as concerns South-West Africa:—

> We solved the native problem by smashing tribal life and by creating a scarcity of labour.

Beginning from the west, the first colony, Togoland, is about the size of Ireland, and is bounded on one side by French Dahomey, and on the other by the British Gold Coast, It is shaped like a pyramid, with its narrow end on the sea, for its coast line is only thirty-two miles. About a million natives inhabit it, chiefly Hausas, and the whites number about four hundred. It was a thriving little colony, with a docile and industrious population, and a large trade in palm oil, cocoa, rubber, and cotton, while the natives were considerable owners of cattle, sheep, and goats. One railway ran inland from Lome, and there was a network of admirable roads, which were a credit to any tropical country. Farther south the German Cameroons lay between British Nigeria and French Congo, and extended from Lake Chad in the north to the Ubangi and Congo Rivers. Its area was about one-third larger than the German Empire in Europe, and its population of 3,500,000 contained 2,000 whites, and the rest Bantu and Sudanese tribes.

In the south lay the Spanish enclave of Rio Muni, or Spanish Guinea, which was an enclave owing to the arrangements which followed the trouble with France over Morocco in 1911, when Germany obtained a long, narrow strip of French Congo to the south and east of the Cameroons. This Naboth's vineyard was one of the pieces of territory which Bernhardi had marked down for speedy German acquisition. The Cameroons was a colony of great possibilities, for it contains a range of high mountains, which might form a health station for white residents, while the soil is rich and water abundant. Its products were much the same as Togoland, but its forests provided also valuable timber, and there was a certain mineral development. Some roads had been made, and 150 miles of railway, but trouble with the native tribes had done much to handicap progress.

Following the western coast-line past the Congo mouth and the Portuguese territory of Angola, we reach a more important colony in German South-West Africa. Its area is some 320,000 square miles, considerably larger than the Cameroons, and it stretches from the Angola border to its march with Cape Colony on the Orange River. Its native population used to be 300,000, but at the beginning of the war, owing to the Herero campaign, it was little over 100,000—chiefly Bushmen, Hottentots, and Ovambo; while the whites numbered 15,000 and included many agricultural settlers. German South-West Africa was the only German colony where the small farmer, as opposed to the planter, seemed to flourish. In spite of the dryness of the climate the land makes excellent pasturage, and there is considerable mineral wealth in the shape of copper and diamonds. The latter were discovered in 1906 near Luderitz Bay, and promised at one time to become a serious competitor to the mines of Kimberley and the Transvaal.

The colony has two chief ports—Swakopmund, half-way down the coast-line, and just north of the little British enclave of Walfish Bay, and Luderitz Bay, or Angra Pequena, nearer the southern border. The capital, Windhoek, is 200 miles from the coast, in a direct line east from Swakopmund. Some note must be taken of the railways, which were built with a strategical as well as a commercial purpose. A railway quadrilateral had been formed, of which the northern side was Swakopmund to Windhoek, the eastern Windhoek to Keetmanshoop, and the southern Keetmanshoop to Luderitz Bay. From Swakopmund an unfinished line runs for several hundred miles northeast towards the Caprivi strip which abuts on the Zambesi. But the most important strategical extension is in the south, where a branch runs from Reitfontein to Warmbad, which is within easy distance of the Orange River and the frontier of the Cape Province.

The last and greatest of the German colonies is German East Africa, which is about twice the size of European Germany. It has a population of 8,000,000, which includes in normal times about 5,000 white men. The wide variations of climate and landscape which it contains give it endless possibilities. Its northern frontier runs from the coast south of Mombasa, just north of the great snow mass of Kilimanjaro, to the Victoria Nyanza, of which two-thirds are in German territory. Going westward, it includes the eastern shores of Lakes Kivu and Tanganyika, as well as the north-eastern shore of Lake Nyassa. It has Britain for its neighbour on the north and part of the west borders, while the remainder of the west marches with the Belgian Congo and the whole of the south with Portuguese Mozambique. The islands of Pemba and Zanzibar, under British protection, dominate the northern part of its coast-line of 620 miles. It will be seen that the vast lake region of the west provides admirable means of transit, and is eminently suitable for tropical agriculture. Elsewhere water is a difficulty, for the only river of any size is the Rufiji, and the snows of Kilimanjaro largely drain towards British territory.

Nevertheless it is a land of great potential agricultural and pastoral wealth; its forest riches are enormous; gold is known to exist in large quantities, as well as base metals and soda deposits. On this colony Germany especially expended money and care. It was resolved to make it a planter's country, and huge agricultural estates were the rule. Four excellent ports, Lindi, Kilwa, Tanga, and the capital, Dar-es-Salam, made commerce easy, and the colony was well served by the great German steamship lines. Two railways ran into the interior, and competed with the Uganda railway to Port Florence.

One, running from Tanga to Moschi, served the rich foothills of Kilimanjaro, and was destined to be continued to Victoria Nyanza. A second, which was only completed this year, ran from Dar-es-Salam to Tabora, an important junction of caravan routes, and was continued thence to Ujiji, on Tanganyika. All such railways were intended under happier circumstances to be connected at their railheads by the great Cape to Cairo route. It will be seen that, if in West Africa Germany had acquired no more than ordinary tropical colonies, and in South-West Africa something of a white elephant, in East Africa she had won a territory which might some day be among the richest of African possessions.

The first blow in the war was struck in Togoland. That small colony was in an impossible strategic position, with French and British territory enveloping it on three sides, and a coast-line open to the attack of British warships. Its military forces were at the outside 250 whites and 3,000 natives. In the early days of August a British cruiser summoned Lome, and the town surrendered without a blow. The German forces fell back one hundred miles inland to Atakpame, where was situated Kamina, one of the chief German overseas wireless stations. Meantime Captain Bryant of the Royal Artillery had led part of the Gold Coast Regiment across the western frontier in motor cars, while the French in Dahomey had entered on the east. By Monday, the 10th of August, the whole of southern Togoland was in the hands

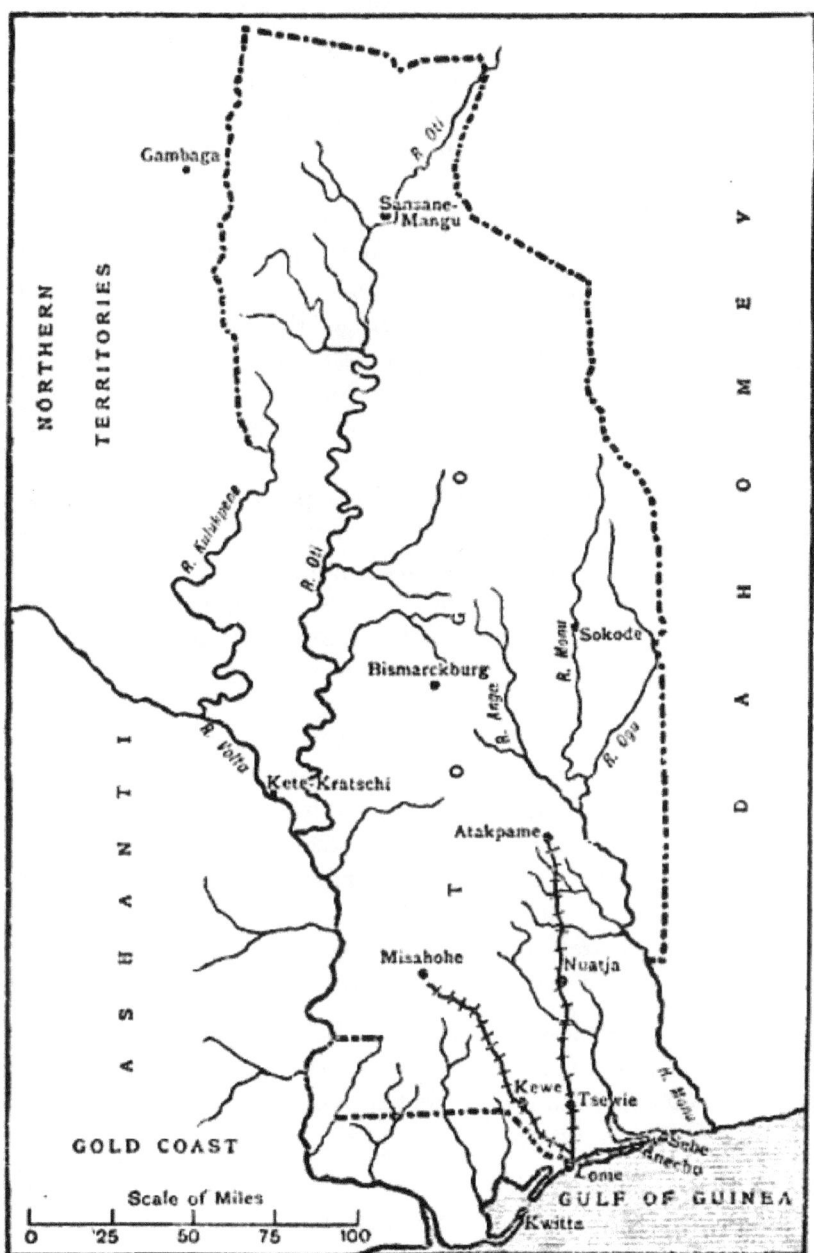

Togoland.

of the Allies, and Captain Bryant, with a small French contingent, advanced against the Government station of Atakpame. On 25th August he crossed the River Monu, and by 27th August, with very few casualties, he occupied Atakpame, destroyed the wireless station, and secured the unconditional surrender of the German troops. Togoland had become a colony of the Allies, normal trade was resumed, and in two months' time there was nothing to distinguish it from Dahomey and the Gold Coast.

A far more difficult problem was presented by the Cameroons. Strategically this colony also was hemmed in by the Allies, but the great distances and the difficulty of communication made a concerted scheme not easy to execute. It was arranged that two French columns should move from French Congo, while the British columns should enter at several points on the Nigerian frontier. There is reason to believe that both on the French and British side the advance was made without adequate preparation. It was the rainy season in West Africa, and any campaign in a tangled and ill-mapped country was liable to awkward surprises. A mounted infantry detachment of the West African Frontier Force left Kano on 8th August, under the command of Lieutenant-Colonel Maclear, and seems to have crossed the frontier on 25th August after a heavy march, and occupied the German post of Tepe, on the Benue River.

Next day it advanced along the Benue as far as Saratse, and on the 29th attacked the river station of Garua. One fort was captured, but next day the Germans counter-attacked in force, and drove back the British troops to Nigerian soil. In this fighting Lieutenant-Colonel Maclear and four other British officers were killed, several were wounded or missing, and forty *per cent*, of the native force was lost. Apparently we suffered chiefly from Maxim fire, for the Germans, having once located our trenches, had the exact range, and simply mowed down our troops. In the words of one of the survivors:—

> It was a terrible loss, and there was absolutely no glory in the whole fighting, taking place as it did in a little out-of-the-way spot 5,000 miles from England, that not one person in a thousand has ever heard of.

No better luck attended the other two expeditions which about the same time entered from Nigeria at more westerly points on the frontier.

One entering from Ikom met with little resistance, and about the

30th occupied the German station of Nsanakong, five miles from the border. The other expedition, moving in from Calabar close to the coast, occupied Archibong on 29th August. A week later, at Nsanakong, as at Garua, the Germans counter-attacked in force. They arrived about two in the morning, and met with a stubborn resistance until the British ammunition was exhausted, when the garrison endeavoured to cut its way out with the bayonet. The bulk of them managed to retreat to Nigeria, but three British officers and one hundred natives were killed, and many were taken prisoners. Thereupon the Germans crossed the frontier, and occupied the Nigerian station of Okuri, north-east of Calabar, from which, however, they soon retired.

The land attack having failed, recourse was had to the sea. For some time the British warships *Cumberland* and *Dwarf* had been watching the mouth of the Cameroon River and the approaches to the German port, Duala. On 14th September a bold attempt was made to blow up the *Dwarf* by an infernal machine. Two days later, a German merchantman, the *Nachtigal* tried to ram the British gunboat, but was wrecked, with the loss of thirty-six men. A few days later two German launches made another attempt with spar-torpedoes, but once again the attack miscarried.

On 27th September the Anglo-French force appeared before Duala, and the bombardment resulted in its unconditional surrender. Bonaberi, the neighbouring coast town, fell to an Anglo-French force, under Brigadier-General Dobell, and the *Cumberland* captured eight merchantmen belonging to the Woermann and Hamburg-Amerika lines. All were in the Cameroon River, and were reported to be in good order, "most of them containing general and homeward cargoes, and considerable quantities of coal." At the same time a German gunboat, the *Soden*, probably constructed for river work, was seized, and put into commission in the British navy. Meanwhile the French, operating from Libreville in French Congo, and covered by the warship *Surprise*, attacked Ukoko on Corisco Bay, and sank two armed vessels, the *Khios* and the *Itolo*.

With the chief port in our hands, and the coast as a base, the Allies could now advance with better hopes of success. The Germans retreated by the valley of the River Wuri, and by the two interior railways. During October the half-circle of conquered territory was rapidly widened, while isolated entries were made from the northern and southern frontiers. Jabassi, on the Wuri, was taken, and Japoma, the

BRITISH WARSHIP "DWARF"

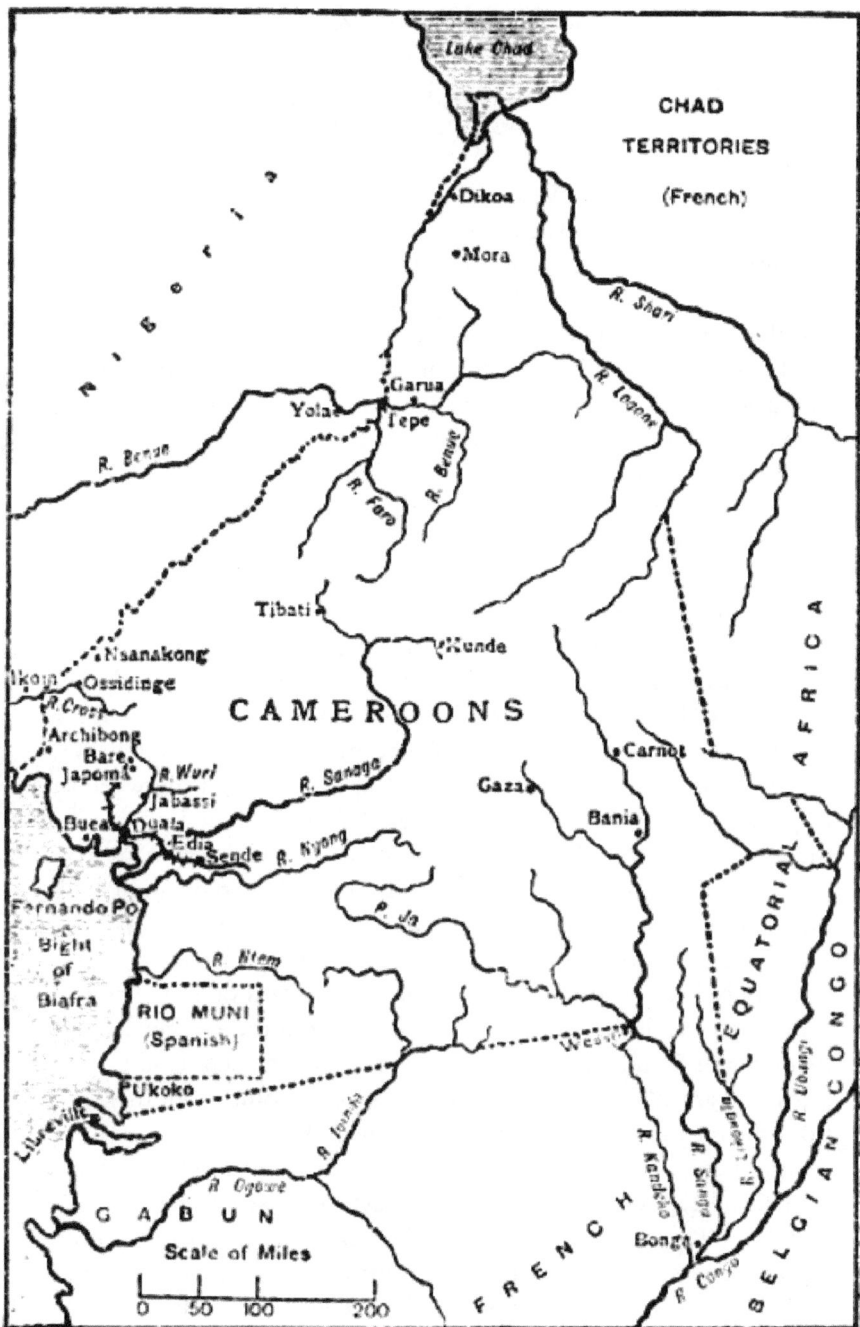

The Cameroons.

railway terminus. We had now the measure of the enemy, and could afford to advance at our leisure. By 1st October the Cameroons, so far as it was of any value to Germany in the struggle, was virtually captured. The wireless stations had been destroyed, the coast was ours, and the German troops were reduced to defensive warfare in a difficult hinterland.

In German South-West Africa the situation was different from that in the other German colonies of the East and West. Here over the frontier lay not a British Crown possession, but a self-governing dominion. Elsewhere a cable from the Colonial Office could mobilize the British defence, but in South Africa there was an independent Parliament and a hotchpotch of parties to be persuaded. Further, the ground had been carefully baited. Intrigues had been long afoot among the irreconcilable elements in the Dutch population, and the highest of German authorities had not thought it undignified to speak words in season, and to hold out hopes of a new and greater Afrikander republic. Elsewhere the German colonies had to fight their battles unaided, but here there was every expectation of powerful assistance from within the enemy's camp.

Till the situation developed the campaign on Germany's part must be defensive, and for this role German South-West Africa had many advantages. Her capital was far inland, and, since she could hope for no assistance by sea, it mattered little if her ports were seized. Her railways on the south ran down almost to the Cape frontier, but between the Cape railheads and her border stretched the desert of the Kalahari, and the dry and waterless plains of North-West Cape Colony. At least two hundred miles separated the branch railways at Carnarvon and Prieska from the nearest German territory, and the distance from Kimberley on the main northern line was little less than four hundred. At one point only had the British forces reasonable means of access by land. From Port Nolloth a line runs inland to serve the copper lands of Namaqualand, and from one station on it, Steinkopf, a sixty-mile track leads to Raman's Drift, on the Orange River, a point about fifty miles from the terminus of the German railway at Warmbad.

As to the German forces, it is not possible to speak with certainty. In their official returns before the war they claimed a military force of some 3,500 men, mainly whites; but by calling up reserves and enrolling volunteers from among the civil population of German blood they probably increased this to not less than 6,000. The figure may have been higher, for the Cape Town estimates put the German strength at not less than 10,000, as well as a camel corps 500 strong. The Germans were believed to be strong in artillery, and to have sixty-six batteries of Maxims, half of which were concentrated at Keetmanshoop, in the south of the colony.

On the declaration of war the German governor, Dr. Seitz, put at once into force the long-prepared scheme of defence. The Germans, about 10th August, abandoned their two principal stations on the coast, Swakopmund and Luderitz Bay, and retired with all military stores to their inland capital of Windhoek. Before leaving they destroyed the jetty, and dismantled and sank the tugs in the harbour of Swakopmund. By 20th August they had made small incursions into British territory, entrenching themselves in certain places among the kopjes, and skirmishing with the frontier farmers. When General Botha met the Union Parliament on 8th September he was able to inform it that Germany had begun hostilities.

In a later chapter we shall consider the political situation in the Union of South-West Africa which led to a dramatic and not unexpected rebellion. Here it is sufficient to say that General Botha, in a speech of great dignity and force, announced that after careful consideration he and his colleagues had decided to carry the war into German territory, "in the interests of South Africa as well as of the Empire." He had information about German machinations which was denied to the ordinary politician, and the great majority of the members of Parliament were ready to trust his judgment. The sole opposition came from General Hertzog, who succeeded in mustering only twelve votes in the House of Assembly and five in the Senate.

Yet it is clear that his views were largely held in the country, and that many *burghers* looked with alarm upon a policy of active operations. These men lived chiefly in the districts bordering upon German South-West Africa, in the Orange Free State, and in the Western Transvaal, and they argued that, as long as Germany left Union territory alone, no offensive measures should be taken against her. It did not require any great amount of political acumen to foresee that such an attitude was impossible. Sleeping dogs may be best left alone, but when ninety-nine of the pack are tearing in full cry across Europe it is folly to suppose that the hundredth will continue its slumbers.

The beginning of September saw scattered fighting in the southeastern angle of the frontier. Information was received that a considerable German force was advancing to Raman's Drift, on the Orange, with the intention of entrenching themselves and disputing the north-

GUN TEAM IN AFRICA

ward passage of British troops. Colonel Dawson, with the 4th South African Rifles, left the Port Nolloth railway at Steinkopf, marched the sixty miles to the river, and surprised a German garrison at the drift on 15th September.

After a fight in which only one man was killed, he captured the German blockhouse, and received the surrender of the garrison. He sent patrols up the Orange, and ousted the enemy from the *kopjes*, while with a larger force he compelled the Germans to evacuate an entrenched position farther north. To set against this success, the Germans on 17th September surprised a small British post at Nakob, a point near the Orange just outside the south-eastern angle of the frontier. The victors carried off some cattle and a number of prisoners, and retired, leaving a small garrison. The next day witnessed a British counter-stroke by sea. On 18th September a force sailing to Luderitz Bay occupied the town, and hoisted the Union Jack on the town hall. The Germans had destroyed the wireless station, but otherwise the place was undamaged.

While this frontier fighting was taking place there was a widespread martial enthusiasm throughout the Union. General Botha, who had agreed to take command of the army, called for 7,000 men—5,000 foot and 2,000 mounted infantry—and to his appeal there was an immediate and adequate response. Recruiting was stimulated by the news of three unimportant German raids, two across the Orange at Pella and Rietfontein, which they occupied, and one upon Walfish Bay, which failed disastrously. Meantime the Rhodesian Police had occupied the far north-western post of Schuckmansburg, in the Caprivi strip, and had forestalled any danger from that quarter. At this time the strategical idea seems to have been a British advance simultaneously from Rhodesia, down the Orange River and from the Port Nolloth railway, while a movement would also be made inland from the coast ports.

With the end of September there came heavier fighting. On the 27th, between Kolmanskop and Grassplatz, a German patrol was surprised by some Rand Light Infantry, and found its retreat barred by a body of Imperial Light Horse. In the skirmish three British and four Germans were killed. Our forces in this affair were operating from Luderitz Bay, and, using the same base, we surprised a German post at Anichab. Meantime, at the south-eastern angle a more serious encounter took place which ended in a British reverse. Between Warmbad and Raman's Drift lies a place called Sandfontein, important as

German South West Africa.

one of the few spots where water can be got in that arid desert. On 25th September a small force of South African Mounted Rifles and Transvaal Horse Artillery pushed forward to the water-hole, which lay in a cup-shaped hollow, commanded by *kopjes*, and with the only retreat through an awkward defile. Early on the 26th the Germans brought up guns to the heights, and till noon bombarded the water-hole, while a considerable force held the pass in the rear. The British troops, under Colonel Grant, made a gallant fight till their ammunition was exhausted, and then, having first rendered their guns useless, were forced to surrender. Our total strength seems to have been no more than 200, and out of it we lost 16 killed, 43 wounded, and a large number of prisoners and missing. The German commander, Lieutenant-Colonel von Heydebreck, behaved like a good soldier, complimented the survivors on their defence, and buried the British dead with the honours of war.

The affair at Sandfontein was in many ways mysterious. It looked as if we had had false information, or treacherous guides, to have been betrayed into so hopeless a battle. A fortnight later came news which explained much and revealed a very ugly state of things in the northwest of the Cape Province. The British forces there were under the command of a certain Lieutenant-Colonel S. G. Maritz, who had fought on the Dutch side in the South African War, and had assisted the Germans in their struggles with the Hereros. Maritz was the ordinary type of soldier of fortune, not uncommon in South Africa, florid, braggart, gallant after his fashion, and with little scientific knowledge of war. General Botha found reason to suspect his loyalty, and dispatched Colonel Conrad Brits to take over his command.

Maritz refused to come in, and challenged Colonel Brits to come himself and relieve him. The latter sent Major Ben Bouwer as his deputy, who was made prisoner by Maritz, but subsequently released, and sent back with an ultimatum to the Union Government. This ultimatum declared that, unless the government guaranteed that before a certain date Generals Hertzog, De Wet, Beyers, Kemp, and Muller should be allowed to come and meet him and give him their instructions, he would forthwith invade the Union.

Major Bouwer had other interesting matters to report. To quote the dispatch of the governor-general:—

Maritz was in possession of some guns belonging to the Germans, and held the rank of general commanding the German

67

troops. He had a force of Germans under him, in addition to his own rebel commando. He had arrested all those of his officers and men who were unwilling to join the Germans, and had then sent them forward as prisoners to German South-West Africa. Major Bouwer saw an agreement between Maritz and the Governor of German South-West Africa, guaranteeing the independence of the Union as a republic, ceding Walfish Bay and certain other portions of the Union to the Germans, and undertaking that the Germans would only invade the Union on the invitation of Maritz. Major Bouwer was shown numerous telegrams and helio messages dating back to the beginning of September. Maritz boasted that he had ample guns, rifles, ammunition, and money from the Germans, and that he would overrun the whole of South Africa.

The immediate result of this discovery was the proclamation of martial law throughout the Union and a general strengthening of the Union forces. The time had now come for every man in South Africa to reveal where lay his true sympathies, and the centre of action was soon to shift from the western borders to the very theatre where for three years the British army had striven against the present generalissimo of the Union forces. Meantime Maritz proved a broken reed to his new allies. His one asset was an intimate local knowledge of the waterless north-west. He had small notion of serious warfare, and was incompetent to control his ill-assorted forces. He fixed his base near Upington, on the Orange, and dispatched a portion of his command of 2,000 to march southward up the Great Fish River against Kenhart and Calvinia. Colonel Brits lost no time in harrying the Upington commando, and on 15th October captured a part of it at Ratedrai, many of the men voluntarily surrendering.

On the 22nd Maritz attacked Keimoes, a British station on the Orange, south-west of Upington. But its small garrison of 150, after holding on till reinforcements reached it, drove him back, and captured four of his officers. Maritz then moved west down the Orange to Kakamas, where Colonel Brits fell upon him so fiercely that he lost all his tents and stores, and was compelled to withdraw, wounded, over the German frontier. He made another sally on the 30th, but was conclusively beaten by Brits at Schuit Drift, and driven finally out of the colony. Meantime the commando which had marched up the Great Fish River had no better success. It travelled fast, and by

25th October had covered 200 miles, and was close to Calvinia. Here Colonel van der Venter beat it heavily, taking ninety prisoners and the two Maxim guns which Maritz had confiscated from the Union army. The commando was hopelessly broken, and "drives," organized by van der Venter and Sir Duncan Mackenzie, collected its remnants at their leisure. It was fortunate for the British cause, for a far more formidable rebellion under abler soldiers than Maritz was now threatening in the very heart of the Union.

The situation in East Africa in the first months of war was the gravest which a British colony had to face. The German province was rich, well-organised, and strategically well-situated, for our Uganda railway, which formed the sole communications between Uganda, the East African plateau, and the sea, ran parallel with the northern frontier at a distance of from fifty to one hundred miles, and offered a natural and easy object of attack. There is reason to believe that the German scheme of operations, while providing for invasions of Nyassaland, North-East Rhodesia, and the British shores of Victoria Nyanza, aimed especially at an advance by land against Mombasa and the railway, which should be assisted by the *Koenigsberg* from the sea. The size of the German forces is hard to estimate.

Lord Crewe, in the House of Lords, spoke of native infantry and police to the number of 2,000; but there is little doubt that the native levies were at least 5,000, and that there were some 3,000 whites, recruited partly from the residents and partly from German reservists in the East, who had come thither by sea at the outbreak of war. The Germans got their native forces largely from the Sudan, which was the chief recruiting ground of the King's African Rifles; but they also enlisted the local tribesmen, especially the Masai and the Manyumwezi. They were especially strong in machine-guns, of which they had four to each company.

The British forces at the start were almost non-existent. In British East Africa and Uganda they consisted of the 3rd and 4th battalions of the King's African Rifles, numbering under 1,000. These troops were mainly stationed on the northern frontier and in Jubaland, where a punitive expedition had just been dispatched against some of the Somali and Abyssinian tribes. All companies were at once recalled, and about 500 King's African Rifles were concentrated. Some 200 police were obtained for the defence of the railway line, by means of calling out the reserves and weakening police posts wherever possible. Two volunteer corps were raised among the white settlers—the East African Mounted Rifles and the East African Regiment. The latter was a failure, and never reached a higher figure than 50, but the former was nearly 400 strong. The existing Uganda Railway Volunteers—less than 100—were also called out, and employed in guarding bridges. As time went on further volunteer units were raised from Indian residents. A small body of Somali scouts was created, and a number of Arabs were recruited by Captain Wavell, one of the few Englishmen who have made the pilgrimage to Mecca. In Nyassaland and North-East Rhodesia there were small bodies of police, aided by white volunteers.

The total British defence force, therefore, in the first three weeks of war may be put at under 1,200, much of it of doubtful quality. The King's African Rifles were first-class fighting men, and the new Mounted Rifles, recruited from young British settlers of good blood and from the Boers of Uasin Gishu, were a force whose members reached a remarkable standard of shooting and *veldcraft*. But it is difficult to believe that so small an army could have made a serious stand if the Germans had pushed their northern invasion with vigour. For some obscure reason Germany did little in this direction during August, but contented herself with attacks on the south and west borders.

On 13th August the campaign began by an attack of a British cruiser on the German capital, Dar-es-Salam. The port was bombarded, and landing parties made their way into the harbour and completely destroyed the new wireless installation. They finished their work by dismantling the German ships, and by sinking the floating dock and the *Moewe*, a survey ship of 650 tons. On the same day, on Lake Nyassa, the British steamer *Gwendolen* surprised the German steamer *Von Wissmann* at Sphinxhaven on the eastern shore, took her crew and captain prisoners, and rendered her helpless. Three weeks later two vigorous attacks were made in the south-west.

At Karongwa, one of the chief British ports on Lake Nyassa, a small garrison of 50 was attacked by a force of 400, but held on long enough for supports to arrive. These supports decisively defeated the invaders, and drove them over the border with the loss of half their white officers. The second attack was made upon Abercorn in North-East Rhodesia, just south of Lake Tanganyika. A body of Rhodesian police drove it back, and captured a field-gun. Fighting continued intermittently all along this part of the frontier, but the balance leaned heavily in the British favour. Germany was keeping her best troops for her northern campaign.

German East Africa.

On 3rd September reinforcements arrived for the British. Brigadier-General J. M. Stewart reached Nairobi and assumed command of all the British troops. He brought with him the 29th Punjabis, a battalion of Imperial Service troops, one battery of Calcutta Volunteer Artillery, one battery of Maxim guns, and one mountain battery. He had come only just in time, for the Germans were beginning operations against the Uganda railway. About 20th August they had seized the small frontier post of Taveta under Kilimanjaro, which was in dangerous proximity to their chief northern military post of Moschi. They had also taken the frontier post of Vanga, on the coast, due south from Mombasa. Early in September they sent a detachment to blow up the Uganda railway at Maungu.

The history of this expedition is curious. They arrived comfortably within twenty miles of the line, guided by the excellent German maps. There, however, the maps stopped, and they were compelled to have recourse to English ones. The result was that they missed the water-holes, went eight miles out of their course, and were captured to a man. Thus may the deficiencies of a Survey Department prove an asset in war.

A more serious advance was made on 6th September, when a force of Germans, about 600 strong, marched down the Tsavo River. They were much delayed by Lieutenant Hardingham with a mounted infantry company of King's African Rifles, who harassed them day and night, and gave time for a half battalion of the 20th Punjabis and several companies of the King's African Rifles to come up. An engagement was fought about five miles from the Tsavo railway bridge, and the enemy were driven back in some confusion. This success enabled us to establish advance posts at Mzima and Campiya Marabu, which managed to maintain their position against repeated German assaults.

Three days later, on 10th September, the northern frontier was crossed at its extreme western end. The Germans occupied the frontier town of Kisi, near the Victoria Nyanza. On the 12th two companies of King's African Rifles, with two Maxims and some native police, surprised this force, who retired in disorder upon the lake port of Karungu. About the same time an action was fought on the lake itself. Two German *dhows* were sunk, and the British steamer *Winifred* sailed into Karungu Bay to relieve the town. At first it was driven off, but it returned with a colleague, the *Kavirondo*, and in the face of the British strength the Germans evacuated Karungu and fell back over the border.

ARMOURED CARS (ROLLS ROYCE) IN THE BUSH

During September there were other attacks on the northern frontier, making a total of seven in all, but much the most dangerous was the advance along the coast from Vanga towards Mombasa. The expedition was to be supported by the *Koenigsberg*, which was to shell the town and occupy the island, while the land forces were to destroy the bridge connecting Mombasa with the mainland. Something prevented the *Koenigsberg* from playing its part—perhaps the presence of British warships—but the land attack came very near succeeding. The Germans were 600 strong, with six machineguns, and they were met at Gazi by Captain Wavell's Arab company, strengthened by some King's African Rifles from Jubaland. This little force held up the invaders for several days, and on 2nd October were reinforced by some Indian troops. Gazi was a very fine performance, for practically all the European officers were wounded before help arrived, and the command of the King's African Rifles passed to a native colour-sergeant, who handled his men with great coolness and skill, and headed the charge which drove back the enemy.

Towards the end of October the German attacks slackened, and the position resolved itself into a stalemate. The British troops remained on the defensive, waiting until a big Indian contingent should arrive in the beginning of November. The Germans occupied British territory at Taveta and at Longido on the Romba River, and they had an advance post between the Romba and the Tsavo. The defence had had great luck, but had on the whole acquitted itself well. In such a campaign the attackers had to fight against the country as well as against human opponents. All along the northern border the waterless desert is covered with thorny scrub, which makes military operations desperately difficult. At a time when our soldiers elsewhere were shivering in the mud of the Aisne, the East African force had to contend with intolerable heat and thirst. Much of the country was wholly virgin; there were no maps or roads; and wild beasts made picketing and scouting a sensational task. Happily, most of the men engaged in the work were familiar with the conditions. Most of the officers had hunted big game over a similar country, and the African levies were bush-bred and expert *shikaris*.

One officer's letter ran:—

This is an awful country to fight in, and an ideal one for way-laying. It is one mass of bush and thorny scrub, in which you can walk right on to the enemy without being seen. Last night they put me out on picket duty on the hills. I got a grand view of Kilimanjaro in the moonlight—it looked awfully fine with its snowy peak; but really the job was a nervy one, considering that the place was teeming with rhino and lion, and we had to stand in the open without even a fire. The lions could be heard roaring quite close by, and besides that many other sounds of animal life could be heard. All this is very nice, but awe-inspiring.

The War in Eastern Waters

While the armies were ranging themselves in Europe and the British navy was sealing up the Narrow Seas, a vigorous campaign was being conducted both by land and water in the Far East, where the units of Germany's colonial empire were, one by one, taken by the Allies. Her dominions there were so widely scattered that they could get no aid from the Fatherland or from one another. Each had to fight its battle alone, with such resources as the outbreak of war found in its possession.

In the Pacific, Germany owned 100,000 square miles of territory, mainly in New Guinea. Her possessions there, officially known as Kaiser Wilhelm's Land, were in the northern part of the south-eastern section of the island A long straight line running south-east and north-west divided them from Papua or British New Guinea, while another straight line, running north and south, separated them from the Dutch colony in the west. Kaiser Wilhelm's Land had an area of 70,000 square miles, and a population of half a million, three hundred of whom were Germans. The country had been little developed, but exported from its chief ports, Friedrich Wilhelmshafen and Constantinhafen, a fair amount of copra, cocoa, and rubber.

The German protectorate of New Guinea included not only Kaiser Wilhelm's Land, but a large number of islands lying off its coast, and its official headquarters were at Rabaul, on the island of New Pomerania. Chief among these islands was the group known as the Bismarck Archipelago, which lay to the north-east of Kaiser Wilhelm's Land, and included New Pomerania, New Mecklenburg, New Lauenburg, New Hanover, Admiralty Island, and some two hundred little isles. Their population consisted of some 200,000 natives, and a few hundred Chinamen and Germans. The chief island was New Pomerania, with its two considerable ports of Herbertshohe and Simpsonhafen.

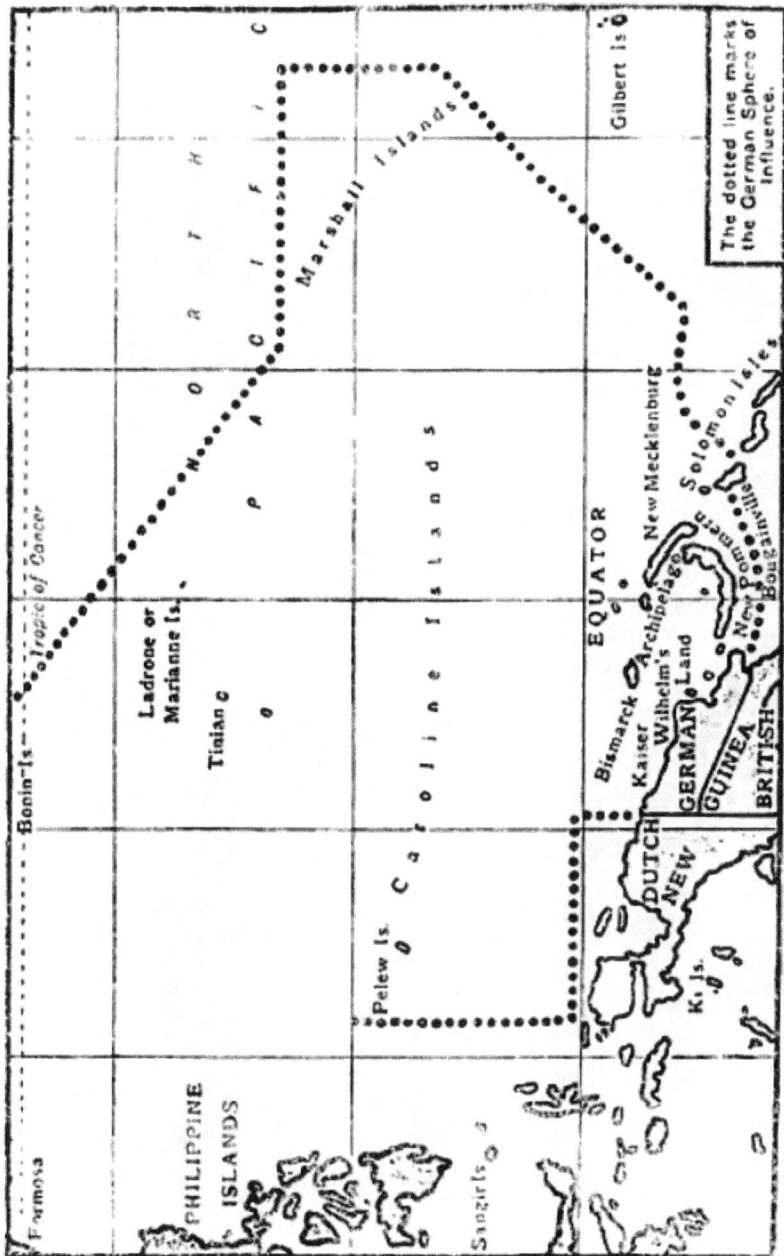

Germany's Pacific Possessions.

The dotted line marks the German Sphere of Influence.

Formosa
Bonin Is.
Tropic of Cancer
PHILIPPINE ISLANDS
Ladrone or Marianne Is.
Tinian
Sangir Is.
Pelew Is.
Caroline Islands
Marshall Islands
Gilbert Is.
NORTH PACIFIC
EQUATOR
DUTCH NEW
K. Is.
Bismarck Archipelago
Kaiser Wilhelm's Land
New Mecklenburg
New Pomerania
Bougainville
Solomon Isles
GERMAN GUINEA
BRITISH

New Zealanders in Samoa: The 5th, Wellington, Regimental Band at Apia.
Lieutenant–Colonel C. H. Turner, Infantry Commander in the centre

A little to the east lay the Solomon Islands, that archipelago of high wooded mountains and cannibal tribes which Germany shared with Britain, owning the two chief western islands, Bougainville and Buka. North of New Guinea, but still forming part of the protectorate, were three groups midway between Australia and Japan—the Carolines, the Pelew, and the Marianne or Ladrone Islands. They were bought from Spain in 1889, and consisted of some six hundred coral reefs, divided into an eastern and a western group for the purposes of administration, and yielding little but copra. Detached to the east lay the Marshall Islands, twenty-four in number, whose chief product was phosphates.

Germany's remaining possession in the South Seas was Samoa, and the tale of her doings there may be read in Stevenson's *A Footnote to History*. The group consists of the two large islands, Savaii and Upolu, with Apia, the chief port, on the latter. Some 500 Europeans, chiefly British and German, resided there, about 1,500 Chinese, and a dwindling native population of about 15,000. From Samoa came copra in large quantities, and of late a fair amount of rubber.

Lastly, far to the north on the China coast, in the province of Shantung, lay the important German possession of Kiao-chau, the history of whose acquisition has already been told in these pages. It is a district of some 200 square miles in extent, situated on a sheltered bay, and surrounded by a neutral zone. The town of Tsing-tau was a naval station, and most of its 5,000 German inhabitants were marines. The place was strongly fortified both by land and sea Germany had spent 20,000,000 on it and was connected by rail with the Chinese lines. Its importance was due to its contiguity to the Japanese Port Arthur and the British Wei-hei-wei, and to the excellence of its harbour, which made it an ideal base for the German Pacific Squadron.

The German Pacific possessions had long been a grievance to the Australian Commonwealth, and the first blow was struck by the adjacent British dominions. The Australian Squadron, assisted by the China Squadron, patrolled the Pacific for German cruisers. The initial attack was made on Samoa. On 15th August a New Zealand Expeditionary Force, some 1,500 strong, left Wellington in troopships, and sailed for Samoa under the escort of H.M.S. *Australia*, H.M.S. *Melbourne*, and the French cruiser *Montcalm*. On 28th August it reached Apia, and the commanding officer, Colonel Logan, took possession of the islands without resistance. The German officials came in and swore fealty, and were confirmed in their posts.

GERMAN RESERVISTS IN SAMOA

BRITISH TROOPS ARRIVE AT TSING-TAU

Then came the turn of New Pomerania, which had already been reconnoitred. On 11th September an expeditionary force arrived at Herbertshohe, the port at the north-eastern extremity of the island. A party of sailors, under Commander J. A. H. Beresford, landed at dawn, and proceeded through the bush towards the wireless station. The advance was not unopposed, for the Germans seem to have concentrated here most of the troops which they possessed in their New Guinea Protectorate. In several places the road was mined, while rifle-pits had been dug along the edge, and snipers placed in the neighbouring trees. The sailors fought their way for six miles to the wireless station, where the German defence surrendered. Our casualties were ten officers and four seamen, and the whole German force fell into our hands. At the same time the ports of Herbertshohe and Simpsonhafen, and the capital, Rabaul, were occupied without trouble.

Two days later our troops sailed for the Solomon Islands, and secured without difficulty the surrender of Bougainville. We then turned our attention to Kaiser Wilhelm's Land, where we expected a more serious opposition. But again we won a bloodless victory. The British flag was hoisted in Friedrich Wilhelmshafen, and a garrison left behind. The Australian Navy had done its work with admirable precision and dispatch, covering great distances in a very short time. H.M.S. *Melbourne*, for example, sailed 11,000 miles in the first six weeks of war. At the end of September one or two small islands were still nominally German, but for all serious purposes the *Kaiser's* dominions in the Pacific had disappeared. The important German wireless stations at Yap (Caroline Islands), Namu (Gilbert Islands), and Rabaul (New Pomerania) had been destroyed. Early in November the Japanese occupied the Marshall Islands and the other northern groups, which they handed over to Australia.

The German Pacific Squadron, based on Kiaochau, did not attempt to defend the Pacific islands. The bulk of it, under Admiral von Spee, sailed for the western shores of South America, with what consequences we shall presently learn. Two smaller cruisers, the *Emden* and the *Koenigsberg*, betook themselves to the Indian Ocean, and, as we have already recorded, did considerable damage to our commerce. The *Koenigsberg*, after her easy destruction of the *Pegasus* in Zanzibar roads, gave little more trouble, and proved unable to play the part allotted to her in the attack on Mombasa. Her end came about 10th November, when she was found by H.M.S. *Chatham* hiding in shoal water about six miles up the Rufigi River. Here she was sealed up

THE CRUISER "EMDEN"

THE WRECK OF THE "EMDEN"

and disposed of at our leisure, the fairway being blocked by sunken colliers.

The *Emden* had also a short life, but, in the language of the turf, she had a good run for her money. We last saw her off the Malabar coast of India on the last day of September. Then she turned south-eastward, and captured five merchantmen in the Indian Ocean, of which she sank four and sent one, the *Gryfedale*, into Colombo. She was next heard of off the north end of Sumatra, where our cruisers captured her collier and her attendant steamer, the *Markomannia*. The loss of her colliers made her task difficult, but it did not weaken her boldness. On 30th October she entered the roadstead of Penang, flying a neutral flag and rigging up a dummy funnel, with the result that she succeeded in torpedoing a Russian cruiser and a French destroyer. Once more this new "Flying Dutchman" vanished, but her course was near its end. On 9th November she appeared off the Cocos (or Keeling) Islands with the intention of destroying the wireless station and cutting the cable.

A wireless message was, however got off, which was picked up by the cruiser *Sydney* of the Australian Navy about fifty miles to the east. This message, which was much mutilated, ran, "Strange warship off entrance," and the presence of the *Emden* was at once conjectured. The *Sydney* sighted the feathery cocoanut trees on the Keeling Islands about 9.15 a.m. on the 9th, and shortly after saw the top of the *Emden's* funnels. She was lying off Direction Island, where she had landed a party to destroy the cable station. The *Emden* opened fire at long range, and then steered a northerly course, fighting all the while a running battle with the *Sydney*. One hour and forty minutes later she ran ashore on North Keeling Island, a burning wreck, with her funnels shot away and her decks a shambles. It was an unequal contest. The *Sydney's* 6-inch guns had an easy mastery over the 4.1-inch guns of the *Emden*, and while the latter had 230 killed and wounded, the former had only 18 casualties.

Captain Karl von Müller was captured and his sword returned to him, for he had proved a gallant enemy. If he sent out S.O.S. signals to entice our merchantmen, then indeed he was guilty of a grave breach of the laws of war; but there was no objection to his disguise at Penang, provided he flew the German flag before taking hostile action. He treated the crews of his captures with generosity, and no act of brutality was ever brought against him.

The *Emden* was an expensive ship to our commerce. In two months she captured seventeen merchantmen, which made up about half the

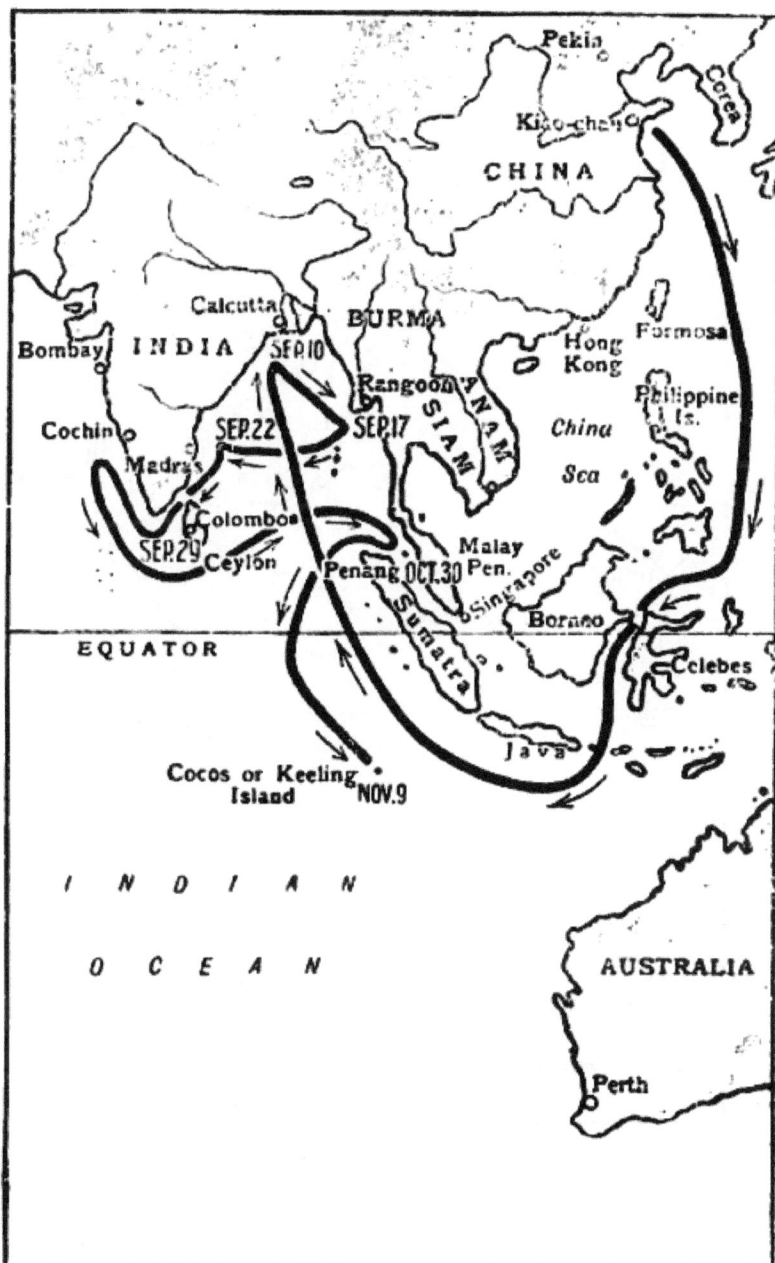

The Route of the "Emden."

TSING-TAU
AND
ENVIRONS

Scale of Miles

Sy Fang
Barracks
Great Harbour
Pump Ho
Sau tschau-tan
Tai tung tschen
Yang tschia tsun
Barracks
Berk
Little Harbour
Ta pau tau
Signal Hill
Bismarck Berg
Stn
Artillery Lager
Reservoir
To Lao shan
Barracks
Achona
Auguste Victoria Bay
Outer Roads
Iltis Bay

's Environs

total loss to that date of our mercantile marine. One way and another she cost us rather more than the price of a Dreadnought. In her short life she did far more damage proportionately than the *Alabama*, which destroyed about sixty-eight ships, valued at some three millions sterling, but took two years to do it, as against the *Emden's* two months. On the other hand, it should be said that the *Emden* was more than three times the size of the Confederate privateer. Both vessels made a stout fight at the last, and Captain Semmes, like Captain von Müller, was saved, and became something of a hero in the popular esteem of his enemies.

We must turn next to the chief episode in the Eastern Seas, the siege and capture of the fortress of Tsing-tau. This was the only German fortress to be carried in the early months of the war. It was an elaborate entrenched camp, strong both by land and sea, and equipped with the latest type of fort, with concrete and steel cupolas, and all the other modern refinements upon Brialmont. Japan, as we have seen, delivered her ultimatum to Germany on 15th August, and the days of grace came to an end on 23rd August. She entered upon war partly out of general considerations of policy, and partly from an old and well-founded national antipathy. But she entered upon it at the request of Britain, who, as Baron Kato informed the Japanese Parliament, asked her to free their joint commerce from the German menace in Eastern waters.

The Japanese Army was largely modelled on the German; it was from German instructors that she had learned much of that art of war which had given her the Manchurian victory; and there was much in the German military temperament with which she sympathized. At the outbreak of war the best opinion in Japan believed that Germany would win, but it nevertheless abided by the terms of its alliance.

Japan had now twice the military and naval power which she had had when she began the war with Russia. This is not the place to enlarge on her armed strength; suffice it to say that she had an army with a peace strength of 250,000, which in war would be increased to 1,000,000; she had made a speciality of artillery, especially the heavier guns; her navy comprised six Dreadnoughts, six other battleships, four first-class battle-cruisers, and large classes of cruisers, destroyers, and coast-defence ships. In tonnage her fleet was nearly double the size of that which she had possessed at the date of the Treaty of Portsmouth. For the assault of Tsing-tau she organised a special siege force, under the command of Lieutenant-General Kamio. It embraced a division of infantry, and three additional brigades—a corps of siege artillery, a flying detachment, and detachments of engineers and marine artillery. A squadron from her fleet, under Vice-Admiral Kato, which was assisted by several British warships belonging to the China station, co-operated by sea.

The map will show the nature of the Tsing-tau fortress. It stood near the end of the Tsing-tau peninsula, which formed the eastern containing shore of Kiao-chau Bay. To the north-east of the town were a number of low heights—Bismarck Hill, Moltke Hill, Iltis Hill—which the Germans had heavily fortified. Beyond the peninsula lay marshy coastland, much liable to flooding, through which the railway ran west to the town of Kiao-chau, within the German sphere of influence, but outside the leased territory. The German governor, Admiral Meyer Waldeck, and his garrison of 5,000 were bidden by the *Kaiser* to defend the fortress as long as breath remained in their bodies. The German squadron, under Admiral von Spee, had very properly sailed away, for a besieged harbour is not the place for a fleet in being, but several of the smaller warships remained behind.

On 27th August, the Japanese took the first step by occupying as a base some of the small islands which cluster around the mouth of the harbour. From these they instituted a series of mine-sweeping operations, a wise precaution, for the Germans had relied much upon that peril of the seas. So thorough was the Japanese work that only one vessel of their fleet was mined during the siege. On 2nd September they landed troops at the northern base of the peninsula, their object being to cut off the fortress by a movement against it from the mainland. But the autumn rains, very heavy in Shantung, put a bar to this enterprise. All the rivers, which descended from the hills, rose in high flood, and spread out in lagoons over the coastlands.

General Kamio had to content himself with sending aeroplanes over the fortress, which dropped bombs successfully on the wireless station, the electric-power station, and on the ships in the harbour, and with an assault upon the railway station of Kiao-chau, at the head of the bay, which he took on 13th September. He was then some twenty-two miles from Tsing-tau itself, and had the railway line to aid his advance. By the 27th he had reached the chief of the outer defences of the place, Prince Heinrich Hill, and next day captured it without serious opposition. This gave him a gun position from which he could dominate all the inner forts, much as the fall of the trans-Nethe forts gave the Germans command over the inner lines of Antwerp.

TROOPS LANDING IN SAMOA

On the 23rd, a small British force arrived from Wei-hei-wei to co-operate with the Japanese. It consisted of the 2nd battalion of the South Wales Borderers, and about half a battalion of the 36th Sikhs, and was under Brigadier-General Barnardiston, who commanded the British troops in North China. It landed at Laoshan Bay, on the seaward side of the peninsula, and, having only a short way to march, joined hands with the Japanese on 28th September, just after the capture of Prince Heinrich Hill. Since the floods were now falling, advance was easier, and the invaders were soon only five miles from Tsing-tau, and had drawn the cordon tight across the peninsula. German warships in the bay attempted to bombard the Japanese right, but were driven off by Japanese aeroplanes, which showed extraordinary boldness and skill during the whole operations.

Meanwhile a vigorous bombardment was going on from the Japanese squadron lying in the mouth of the harbour, and on 30th September a German counter-attack both by sea and land was quickly beaten off. Slowly General Kamio was coming to the conclusion that the enemy either did not mean to obey their *Kaiser* and fight to the last breath, or had very doubtful fighting ability. They were enormously wasteful of shells, which did not look as if they contemplated a long resistance. The Japanese general was convinced that a fierce assault was more desirable than a slow investment. But first he gave the non-combatants in Tsing-tau a chance to leave, and on 15th October a party of women and children and a number of Chinese were conducted through the Japanese lines.

General Kamio had now his big guns in position, and the bombardment began in earnest. He had practically no field artillery, but he had a heavy siege train of 140 guns, including six 11-inch howitzers, and a large number of 6-inch and 8-inch pieces. The Germans seem to have had nothing larger than 8-inch. The first general bombardment was from the sea, when considerable damage was done to the forts on Kaiser Hill and Iltis Hill. On the 31st of October, the birthday of the Emperor of Japan, the first land bombardment began. On that day most of the inner forts were silenced, and, as at Antwerp, the skies were black with the smoke of burning oil-tanks.

On 1st November, H.M.S. *Triangle* silenced the forts on Bismarck Hill, and presently only one fort, Huichuan, was left in action. Next day, the Austrian cruiser, *Kaiserin Elizabeth*, was sunk in the harbour, and the floating dock disappeared, having probably been blown up by the defenders. Meantime the army was pushing its way down the peninsula, driving back the German infantry, and making large captures of guns and prisoners. By the night of 6th November, the Allies were through the inner forts, with their trenches up to the edge of the last redoubts, and the outworks to east and west were taken during the night. Early on the morning of the 7th the hour had come for the final attack in mass.

That attack was never delivered. At six o'clock white flags fluttered from the central forts and from the tower of the Observatory. That day representatives of the two armies met, and at 7.30 in the evening Admiral Meyer Waldeck signed the terms at of capitulation. At ten on the morning of the 10th, the Germans formally transferred Tsing-tau to General Kamio, and Germany's much-debated foothold on the continent of Asia had gone. The German casualties were heavy, and the survivors, nearly 3,000 in number, were sent as prisoners to Japan, Admiral Meyer Waldeck and his staff being allowed to retain their swords. The Japanese losses, out of a total of 22,980, were 236 killed and 1,282 wounded, and the British losses, out of a force of 1,500, were 12 killed and 61 wounded. In addition, Japan lost one third-class cruiser, the *Takachiho*, one third-class destroyer, the *Shirotae*, torpedo boat No. 23, and three minesweepers.

The capture of Tsing-tau, seventy-six days after the declaration of war, and little more than a month after the investment was complete, came as a surprise to Japan, who had made preparations for a struggle till Christmas, and to Germany, who had not realized that the fate which had befallen Namur and Maubeuge would, under similar circumstances, befall her own fortresses. General Kamio handled the expedition with perfect judgment, and provided brilliantly for co-operation between the sea and land forces. It was an achievement of which Japan might well be proud, for it was to her armies that Tsing-tau yielded, since, though the British contingent had done well, it was only one-fourteenth of the investing force. When General Barnardiston reached Tokio, he was given a popular reception, such as had never in the history of Japan been accorded to any stranger. It appeared that the Japanese had entered upon the war not for their own interests alone, and that they were mindful of the ties which bound them to their allies.

The South African Rebellion

The grant of self-government to the Transvaal and Orange Free State in 1906, four years after the conclusion of the South African War, was a bold step, which occasioned much uneasiness to those who were most familiar with the temper of the back-*veld*. A strong people like the Boers do not surrender readily their dreams, and their tenacity of purpose was kept alive by certain sections of the Dutch Church, and by the ignorance and remoteness from modern life of the rural population. That the venture did not end in disaster was due to two events which could not have been foreseen. One was the movement towards a Union of South Africa, the foundations of which had been laid by Lord Milner's reconstruction after the war, and which Lord Selborne, aided by a brilliant band of young Englishmen, brought to a successful conclusion. The second was the appearance of two Dutch statesmen of the first quality. The old Afrikander leaders, like Mr. Hofmeyer, had often been men of great ability and foresight, but they had lacked the accommodating temper of statesmanship.

General Botha, the first Prime Minister of the Union, had been the ablest of the Boer generals, and his subsequent work entitles him to a high place among Imperial statesmen. He had the large simplicity of character and the natural magnetism which makes the born leader of men; his record in the field gave him the devoted allegiance of the old commandos; he was a sincere patriot, both of South Africa and of the Empire, for, while abating nothing of his loyalty towards the land of his birth, he saw that the fortunes of South Africa were bound up inextricably with the fortunes of the Empire as a whole; while he had that noble opportunism, that wide practical sagacity, which enabled him to move by slow degrees and to conciliate divergent interests by sheer tact and goodwill. His lieutenant, General Smuts, had won fame alike as a scholar, a lawyer, and a commander in the field. With greater knowledge and a keener intellect than his chief, he had not General Botha's gift of popularity and popular leadership; but between them the two showed a combination of talents which it would be hard to parallel from any other part of the British dominions.

General Botha had not an easy part to play. The Unionist Party, led first by Sir Starr Jameson and then by Sir Thomas Smartt, while remaining the official Opposition, might be trusted to cooperate in all reasonable legislation. But among the Dutch there was a section, led by General Herzog, and drawing its support chiefly from the Orange Free State, which was definitely anti-British, and aimed not at racial union but at Dutch ascendancy. It was a true party of reaction, narrow and sectional in its aims, and bitter in its spirit. There was also growing up on the Rand and in the industrial centres a Labour Party, largely officered by professional agitators from overseas, which realized the delicacy of South African economic conditions, and aimed at a "hold-up" in the interests of a class.

It will thus be seen that South African politics showed few affinities with those of other British countries. The party in power, General Botha's, was a Conservative Party, composed mainly of landowners and farmers, and representing landed capital; the Opposition, mainly British in blood, contained most of the industrial capitalists, and was mildly progressive in character; the Labour Party was not such as we are familiar with in Britain, but in the main rigidly "class" in its aims and anarchical in its methods; while the Herzogites were nakedly reactionary and obscurantist. As usually happens, the two extremes tended to form a working alliance, and we had the extraordinary spectacle of the Rand agitator and the *taakhaar* from the wilds meeting on the same platform.

General Botha before the war began had cleared the air by two bold steps. He had dismissed General Herzog from the Ministry, and definitely dissociated himself from his aims, thereby driving the Herzogites into violent opposition. Then he had dealt faithfully with the Labour Party. The first great strike on the Rand in 1913 had been a success, for the government were unprepared, and the strike leaders dictated their own terms. The second attempt was a complete fiasco. The government called out all its forces, the reign of terror was broken in three days, and ten of the leaders were summarily deported under martial law. The result was to bring the official Opposition much closer to the government, but to array against the Prime Minister a dangerous faction made up of the Herzogites and the defeated and

94

discredited Labour Party.

The advent of war made a new division. General Herzog found that he could not collect a following, and became a trimmer. He attacked the government, but forbore to aid the rebels when the insurrection broke out. The Labour Party, considering their treatment, behaved with genuine patriotism; many of their leaders took service in the new army, the working men of the Rand hastened to enlist, and General Botha's rescinding of the deportation order was a fitting recognition of this loyalty. But meantime a very serious falling away was becoming apparent in the ranks of the Dutch. It cut across political parties, for many of the Herzogites supported General Botha's policy, and intriguers were busy among those who had never followed Herzog. The great mass of the Dutch people never wavered. Maritz's performance had offended many who would otherwise have been lukewarm on the British side, for he had in effect invaded the Cape province with foreign troops. But in certain districts a general discontent with the trend of modern politics, and dark memories of the South African War, combined with religious fanaticism to produce a dangerous temper. Presently treason found its leaders.

In the last war there was a certain *predikant* of Lichtenburg, Van Rensburg by name, who acquired a great reputation for second sight. He used to be known to our Intelligence Department as "Delarey's prophet," and was supposed to have much influence over that distinguished general. After peace he went on living in Lichtenburg, and that influence increased, while his reputation spread far and wide through the back-*veld*. When war with Germany broke out he discovered that the events foretold in the Book of Revelation were at hand, and that Germany was the agent appointed of God to purify the world. If we dared to draw the sword upon her he prophesied the blackest sorrows. He had a number of visions, one of red and blue and black bulls, and one of an angel perched on the Paardekraal monument, which he interpreted on the same lines.

The disaster at Hex River on 11th September to the troop-train carrying the Kaffrarian Rifles seemed to the superstitious a vindication of his forecast. Four days later came a second instalment. The prophet had an eye to local politics, and had announced that Generals Delarey, Beyers, and De Wet were the leaders destined to restore the old Republic. On the night of 15th September Generals Delarey and Beyers were travelling in a motorcar westward from Johannesburg, and were challenged by a police patrol which was on the look-out for a gang of desperadoes. Beyers bade the car drive on, probably fearing that his plot had been betrayed, and a shot was fired which ricocheted and killed Delarey. The true story of that night and of Delarey's intentions is still untold. It may be that he had been won over to rebellion, but it is difficult for those who shared the friendship of that high-minded gentleman to believe that he would have brought himself to violate the oath of allegiance which he had taken to the British Crown.

About Beyers's disloyalty there was soon little doubt. Early in September he had resigned his post as Commandant-General of the Union Defence Force, in a letter which revealed more than he intended, and to which General Smuts most effectively replied. He had done brilliant work in the Zoutpansberg during the South African War, and probably ranked next after Generals Botha, Delarey, and Smuts among the Dutch commanders. But for some time German agents had been working upon his vanity, while the "Prophet" played upon his sombre religion. He had visited Germany, and been received by the emperor, and from that honour he had never recovered. We need not judge him too hardly, for he paid the penalty of his folly; and it would be unreasonable to expect that rebellion would seem a heinous crime to one who, twelve years before, had been fighting against Britain.

The real gravamen of his offence is that he broke the military oath which he had sworn as commandant-general. Along with General Kemp, a former lieutenant of Delarey's and a good soldier, he proceeded to stir up disaffection in the Western Transvaal. With him was joined the famous Christian de Wet, whose name was at one time a household word among us. De Wet was not a general of the calibre of Botha, Smuts, and Delarey, and his chronic lack of discipline spoiled more than one of the last-named's movements. But as a guerilla fighter in his own countryside he had no equal. He had not Delarey's moral dignity or Beyers's knowledge of modern conditions, being a Boer of the old, stiff, narrow, back-*veld* type, with a strong vein of religious fanaticism. But his name was one to conjure with, and his accession to the ranks of the irreconcilables vastly increased the difficulty of the government's problem.

The main strength of the movement lay in the " *bywoner*," or squatter class, the "poor whites" who had been created by the Boer system of large farms and large families. For them the future held no hope. In the old days they had staffed the various treks into the wilderness, but outlets were closing, and Africa was filling up. They had little education or intelligence, but they had enough to know that their economic position was growing desperate, and they not unnaturally struck for revolution when the chance came. They made up the bulk of De Wet's men, and the rest were a few religious fanatics, a few Republican theorists, some men who still cherished bitter memories of the late war, and a number of social *déclassés* and unsuccessful politicians. Little pity need be wasted on the latter, but it is not easy to withhold a certain sympathy for the luckless *"bywoner,"* for whom the world had no longer a place.

The rebellion was not long in revealing itself. On 26th October the Union Government announced that De Wet was busy commandeering *burghers* in the north of the Orange Free State, while Beyers was at the same task in the Western Transvaal. On the 24th De Wet seized Heilbron, a little town in the north Free State, on a branch of the main line from Cape Town to Pretoria. Further, at Reitz, he had stopped a train and arrested some Union soldiers who were travelling by it. Beyers, meantime, with a commando formed chiefly of Delarey's old soldiers, was in Rustenburg, threatening Pretoria. General Botha at once summoned the burghers to put down the revolt, and to their eternal honour they responded willingly. It was no easy decision for many of them. They were called on to fight against men of their own blood, some of whom had been their comrades or their leaders in the last war.

From farm to farm went the summons, and many a farmer took down his Mauser, which had shot nothing but buck since Diamond Hill or Colesberg, and up-saddled his pony, as he had done before the great Sand River concentration. The magic name of Botha did not fail in its appeal, and in a few weeks he had over 30,000 under arms. He was now a man of fifty-two years of age, tired with heavy years of office and a sedentary life, and not in the best of health. The rebellion must have been peculiarly bitter to one who had striven beyond all others for a united South African people, and who was not likely to forget the friendships of the old strenuous days.

He did not suffer the grass to grow under his feet. Resolving to clear Beyers out of the neighbourhood of the capital before he turned to deal with De Wet, he entrained for Rustenburg on the 26th, and fell in with the enemy next day to the south of that town, about eighty miles from Pretoria, where the Zeerust road goes through the northern foothills of the Magaliesberg. There he smote Beyers and Kemp so fiercely that their commandos were scattered, eighty prisoners were taken, and the leaders fled incontinently to the south-west. Part of the rebel forces went northward into the hills of Waterberg, but the bulk of them followed their generals to Lichtenburg.

In Lichtenburg Colonel Alberts was waiting for them. His first encounter was unfortunate, for 110 of his men were cut off from the rest, and captured at Treurfontein by the rebels. A day or two later he retrieved the disaster, recovered the prisoners, and thoroughly beat Claasen, the rebel leader. Meanwhile that portion of Beyers's force which had gone north to Waterberg, and which seems to have been under the command of Muller, was busied in raiding the line that runs north from Pretoria, till Colonel van der Venter, fresh from his success in the Cape, hustled it back into the hills. On 8th November he caught the raiders at Sandfontein, near Warmbaths, some sixty miles from Pretoria, and dispersed them, with many killed, wounded, and prisoners. The remnants fled back to Rustenburg and the west.

By this time we had news of the whereabouts of Beyers and Kemp. Hunted by Colonel Lemmer, the former fled south-west to the flats of Bloemhof, crossed the Vaal River, and entered the Orange Free State. He had a sharp fight near the junction of the Vaal and the Vet, and lost about 400, as well as most of his transport, but succeeded himself in getting clear away. The men whom Colonel Alberts had already beaten were now with Kemp making for Bechuanaland and German territory. They were safe enough in that direction, for the Kalahari Desert at the end of the dry season might be trusted to take its toll of rash adventurers. On 7th November General Smuts made a speech in Johannesburg, in which, summing up the situation, he announced that the rebellion in the Cape was over, that the Transvaal rebels were now only a few scattered bands, and that in the Orange Free State alone, where De Wet was at work, had the revolt assumed any serious proportions.

De Wet had only a month of freedom, but he made good use of it so far as concerned the distance covered. Ten years before he would have made a very different sort of fight among those flats and *kopjes* of the northern Free State, where spring was beginning to tinge with green the long umber and yellow distances. But now the stars in their courses fought against him. His own countrymen had become prudent, and did not see the admirable joke of *sjamboking* a magistrate who had once fined him five shillings for whipping a native. They gave information to the government, and grudged ammunition and stores to the good cause. Once he had had fine sport in that district, slipping through blockhouse lines and eluding the clumsy British col-

THE SOUTH AFRICAN REBELLION

umns, but now he found himself being constantly brought up against that accursed thing, modern science. So long as he could trust to a good horse matters went well, but what was he to do when his pursuers took to motor cars which covered twenty miles where the British Mounted Infantry used to cover five? The times were out of joint for De Wet, and so he went *sjamboking* and commandeering through the land, perpetually losing his temper, and delivering bitter philippics against these latter days. General Botha was "ungodly," the English were "pestilential," Maritz was the only true man. Heresy, Imperialism, and negrophilism were jumbled together as the enemy. He cried, with some pathos:

> King Edward promised to protect us, but he did not keep his promise, and allowed a magistrate to be put over us.

There you have the last cry of the *ancien régime* in South Africa, which saw patriarchalism and personal government vanishing from a machine-made world.

De Wet was at Vrede on 28th October, when he had the famous interview with the magistrate already referred to. Meanwhile his lieutenant, Wessels, had looted Harrismith, near the Natal border, and damaged the railway line. Thereafter De Wet turned west, and found sanctuary in the neighbourhood of Winburg, where, on 7th November, at a place called Doornberg, he defeated a Union force under Commander Cronje, and lost his son David. At the time his army seems to have numbered 2,000 men. Next day a second rebel force was beaten at Kroonstadt by Colonel Manie Botha, who continued the pursuit for several days. By this time General Botha, having pretty well cleared the Transvaal, was on his way south, and on the 11th came in touch with De Wet at Marquard, about twenty miles east of Winburg. The rebels were in four bodies, one at Marquard, one at a place called Bantry, a third at Hoenderkop, and a fourth, with which was De Wet himself, in the Mushroom Valley.

General Botha's plan was to surround the whole rebel force, two Union armies, under Colonels Brits and Lukin, working round its flanks. Something went wrong, however, with the timing of the movement, the dispatches miscarried, and Lukin and Brits did not reach their allotted posts in time. In spite of this accident, De Wet was completely defeated. General Botha took 282 prisoners, released most of the loyalists taken by the rebels, and captured a large quantity of transport. On the 13th, it r was officially announced that the interrupted train service between Bloemfontein and Johannesburg would be resumed.

De Wet at first fled south, but presently doubled back, and on the 16th was at Virginia, on the main line. Two armoured trains on the railway managed to prevent a large part of the rebel force from crossing, and to head it eastward. Presently some of its commandants began to come in, and many who had taken up arms, attracted by the clemency of General Botha's proclamation, laid them down again. De Wet was aiming at a junction with Beyers, who was in the Hoopstad district at the time. Beyers, however, was in trouble on his own account. On the 15th, Colonel Celliers had fallen upon him at Bultfontein, and had beaten him thoroughly, and made large captures. Most of the 1,500 rebels were driven northwards, many across the Vaal.

Accordingly De Wet, fleeing from Virginia down the Sand and Vet Rivers, found Celliers ahead of him, and heard of Beyers's disaster. He saw that the game was up, and halted his force near Boshof. There seems to have been considerable disaffection in its ranks, and in a final address to them he advised all who were tired of fighting to hide their rifles and go home. Many took the advice, including two of his sons, many yielded themselves to the Union forces, but De Wet himself, with twenty-five men, made one last dash for liberty.

On 21st November he tried to cross the Vaal, and was driven back by Commandant Dutoit. In the evening, however, with a following now reduced to six, he managed to slip over the river above Bloemhof, and took the road for Vryburg and the north-west. He now picked up some fugitives, and the small commando crossed the railway line to Rhodesia, twenty miles north of Vryburg. He had, apparently, conceived the bold scheme of going through the Kalahari to German South-West Africa. But he had not allowed for the motor cars of his pursuers. For a day or two there was heavy rain, which made the roads bad, and gave the Boer ponies of his party an advantage over any motor. But by the 27th the weather had cleared, the *veldt* was hard and dry, and Colonel Brits, who had taken up the chase, began to capture the slower members of the commando.

As the fugitives penetrated into the western desert their case became more hopeless. De Wet was forced by the motors behind him to cover fifty miles at a stretch without off-saddling, a thing hateful to the Boer horse-master. The end came on 1st December, when, at a farm called Waterburg, about a hundred miles west of Mafeking, De Wet and his handful surrendered to Colonel Jordaan. He was taken to

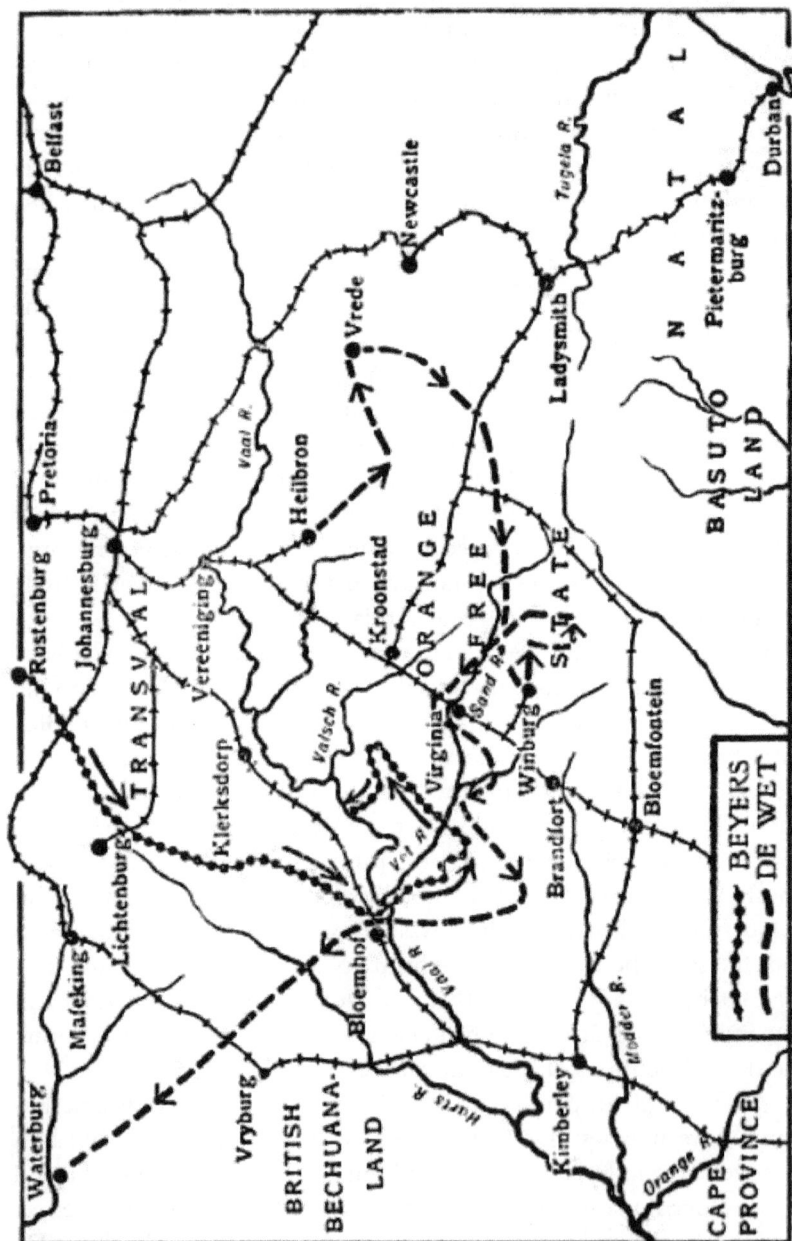

Map illustrating the wanderings of De Wet and Beyers.

Vryburg, and two days later entered Johannesburg a prisoner. He had yielded at the end with a shaggy good humour. Having decided that modern conditions were the devil, he was glad to see his own Afrikanders such adepts at the use of the powers of darkness.

With the capture of De Wet the rebellion was virtually at an end. There was a good deal of skirmishing along the south and north banks of the lower Vaal. Kemp, accompanied by the Lichtenburg "Prophet," fled west after Treurfontein to the little town of Schweizer Reneke, and thence towards Vryburg. He had some fighting at Kuruman, from which he headed south-west across the Southern Kalahari. He was engaged again north of Upington, and it was a very battered remnant which ultimately crossed the border of German South-West Africa. Early in December General Botha organised a great sweeping movement from Reitz, which ended in the surrender of Wessels with the only large body of rebels still in the field.

Beyers, with a small commando, after his defeat at Bultfontein had haunted the southern shore of the Vaal between Hoopstad and Kroonstad. On the morning of 8th December he fell in with a body of Union troops under Captain Uys, and was driven towards the river. He and some companions endeavoured to cross the Vaal, which was in high flood, and, midway in the stream, he found his horse failing, and slipped from its back to swim. His greatcoat hampered him, and he tried in vain to get rid of it. A companion heard him cry, "*Ik kan nie meer nie*" (I can do no more), as he disappeared. His body was found two days later. He had been drowned, for there was no bullet mark on him.

By the end of December the last embers of disaffection had been stamped out within the Union territory. Of the five leaders whom Maritz had named, De Wet was captured, Muller was wounded and a prisoner, Beyers was dead, Kemp was across the German border, and Herzog had never declared himself. In less than two months General Botha had harried the rebels round the points of the compass, and had taken 7,000 of them prisoners, with a total casualty list to the Union army of no more than 334. He exhibited great magnanimity and wisdom in his hour of triumph. Rebels who had been members of the Defence Force and had broken their military oath were very properly put on trial for their life. But to the rank and file he showed no harshness, and, in the interests of South Africa's future, this clemency was not misplaced.

Rebellion could not, for the country Boers, carry the moral stigma which it would bear if dabbled in by an ordinary Briton. The Empire had no sentimental claim upon them, and the case for loyalty founded on material interests required a certain level of education before it could be understood. Besides, so far as the older race of Boers was concerned, insurrection was in their bones; it had always been a recognized political expedient, and, indeed, for more than a century had been the national pastime.

There is little to tell of the rest of the fighting in Africa till the end of the year. Togoland was quiescent in our hands. In the Cameroons the French and British were slowly pushing the Germans farther into the interior, while on all the northern border there was a succession of raids and counter-raids. The Germans seem to have hoped much from a Panislamic propaganda among the Mohammedan natives, but the entry of Turkey into the war made no difference in West Africa, where the *khalif* has never been a name to conjure with. The campaign in South-West Africa had to wait till General Botha had his hands free of local rebellion. But the last months of 1914 showed a certain activity in East Africa.

In that country, as we have seen, we were compelled by the weakness of our resources to stand on the defensive, a role in which, by a mixture of skill and good fortune, we had reasonable success. But with the beginning of November our forces were largely increased, and we began a forward movement which ended in a real disaster.

On 1st November a second Indian Expeditionary Force arrived on the East African coast. It was commanded by Major-General Aitken, and consisted of one British battalion the 1st Loyal North Lancashires, the 95th and 101st Indian regiments, the 61st King George's Own Pioneers, the 1st Palamcotta Light Infantry, the 1st Kashmir Rifles, together with a few other detachments of Imperial Service troops, accompanied by two mountain batteries. On the morning of 2nd November this force, escorted by two gunboats, lay off the German port of Tanga, the coast terminus of the Moschi railway, and summoned it to surrender. The officer in charge asked for some hours' grace in order that he might communicate with the governor, who was then absent. This was granted, and the original time was largely extended, and used by the Germans to hurry down every available soldier by the Moschi line.

Towards evening the British general grew impatient, and landed one and a half battalions, who advanced through the coast scrub towards the town. There it was apparent that a strong defence had been prepared, and the invaders had to fall back towards the shore, where they could be covered by the gunboats.

The next day was occupied in landing the rest of the force, and the attack was renewed on the morning of the 4th. It proved a complete failure. The Germans had mastered the art of bush fighting. Ropes were hidden under the sand of the paths, and, when stepped on, brought down flags which gave the enemy the required range. They also adopted an old Manyumwezi trick, and hid hives of bees half-stifled with smoke beside the roads, which swarmed out when the lids were twitched off by concealed wires, and grievously stung our men. One of the North Lancashires had over a hundred stings extracted.

Yet we managed to reach the town of Tanga, where the 101st Grenadiers attacked on the left with the bayonet, and the Kashmir Rifles and the North Lancashires effected an entrance on the right. There we met a deadly enfilading fire from the housetops, and were forced back with heavy losses. There was nothing for it but to retire to the coast and re-embark. Our casualties were nearly 800, and included 141 British officers and men, so that the Tanga reverse was the most costly of the minor African battles. General Aitken's force went north to the East African Plateau, where it continued during the next months to act as a garrison and watch the borders.

The Battles of
Coronel and the Falkland Islands

In a former chapter, we carried the history of the war at sea down to the end of September, a period during which we fought one successful action and made a large number of captures, but one in which towards the close at any rate—Germany chose to fight solely with smaller craft, and all our casualties were due to the mine and the submarine. The same conditions held during October. Apart from the work of our cruisers in the outer seas, there is little to chronicle. We had one serious disaster, since one of our super-Dreadnoughts, H.M.S. *Audacious,* struck a mine off the north coast of Ireland and sank, with the loss of a single life. On 15th October, also, the old cruiser *Hawke* was torpedoed and sunk off Aberdeen, and nearly 500 men perished. We had one success, for on the afternoon of 17th October the new light cruiser *Undaunted*, Captain Cecil Fox, accompanied by the destroyers *Lance*, *Legion*, and *Loyal*, sank the four German destroyers S115, S117, S118, and S119 off the Dutch coast. Our total naval casualties during the first three months of war, leaving out of account the naval division interned in Holland, were just under 6,000, of which well over 4,000 were dead. In war by land the proportion of killed to wounded is usually about one to ten, in modern sea war it is almost ten to one.

But the opening of November saw a change in the situation. The centre of interest shifted to the Southern Pacific and the Southern Atlantic, and in two months we fought two important naval battles. To understand the events which led up to them, we must go back to what happened at the outbreak of war.

When Admiral von Spee, with the German Pacific Squadron, left Kiao-chau early in August, he succeeded in collecting seven vessels from the China and Australian stations. One of these, the *Emden*, was detached for commerce raiding in the Indian Ocean, with what success we have seen, while the light cruiser *Karlsruhe*, noted for its speed, became a privateer in the South Atlantic. There remained with him two armoured cruisers, the *Gneisenau* and the *Scharnhorst*, and three light cruisers, the *Dresden*, *Leipzig*, and *Nürnberg*. The first two were sister ships, both launched in 1906, with a tonnage of 11,400 and a speed of at least 23 knots. They carried 6-inch armour, and mounted eight 8.2-inch, six 5.9-inch, and eighteen 21-pounder guns. The *Dresden* was a sister ship of the *Emden*—3,540 tons, 24½ knots, and ten 4.1-inch guns. The *Nürnberg* was slightly smaller—3,350 tons, her armament was the same, and her speed was about half a knot quicker. Smaller still was the *Leipzig*—3,200 tons, with the same armament as the other two, and a speed of over 22 knots.

This squadron set itself to prey upon our commerce routes, remembering that the British navy was short in cruisers of the class best fitted to patrol and guard the great trade highways. Admiral von Spee sailed for the western coast of South America, and found coaling and provisioning bases on the coast of Ecuador and Colombia, and in the Galapagos Islands. The duties of neutrals were either imperfectly understood or slackly observed by some of the South American states at the beginning of the war, and the German admiral seems to have been permitted the use of wireless stations which gave him valuable information as to the enemy's movements.

Early in August a small British squadron set sail to protect the southern trade routes thus menaced. It was commanded by Rear-Admiral Sir Christopher Cradock, a capable and most popular sailor, who had served in the Sudan and at the relief of Peking, and had distinguished himself in the work of saving life at the wreck of the *Delhi*. He had in his squadron, when formed, a twelve-year-old battleship, the *Canopus*, two armoured cruisers, the *Good Hope* and the *Monmouth*, the light cruiser *Glasgow*, and an armed liner, the *Otranto*, belonging to the Orient Steam Navigation Company. None of his vessels was very strong either in speed or armament. The *Canopus* belonged to a class which had been long obsolete, her tonnage was 12,950, her speed 19 knots, and her armament four 12-inch, twelve 6-inch, and ten 12-pounder guns, all of an old-fashioned pattern. Her armour belt was only six inches thick.

The *Good Hope* was also twelve years old; her tonnage was 14,100, her speed 23 knots, and her armament two 9.2-inch, sixteen 6-inch,

H.M.S. "Glasgow"

and twelve 12-pounder guns. The *Monmouth* was a smaller vessel of 9,800 tons, with the same speed, and mounting fourteen 6-inch and eight 12-pounder guns. The *Glasgow*, which was stationed on the south-east coast of America, was a much newer vessel, and had a speed of 25 knots. Her tonnage was 4,800, and her armament two 6-inch and ten 4-inch guns.

Admiral Cradock's squadron began by sweeping the North Atlantic, and on 14th August reached Halifax, where the admiral moved his flag to the *Good Hope*. It then sailed to Bermuda, and through the West Indies to the coasts of Venezuela and Brazil. Then it cruised for a little about the Horn, and visited the Falkland Islands. By the third week of October it was in the Pacific, moving up the coast of Chile on the look-out for Admiral von Spee. The officers knew well that the enemy were the stronger, for something had happened to the *Canopus*, which had dropped behind for repairs, and the *Otranto* was, of course, no match for even a small cruiser. Reinforcements were hourly expected from Britain or the Mediterranean, but for some reason, still unexplained, these were not forthcoming. One officer wrote on 12th October:—

> From now to the end of the month is the critical time, as it will decide whether we shall have to fight a superior German force coming from the Pacific before we can get reinforcements from home or the Mediterranean. We feel that the Admiralty ought to have a better force here, and take advantage of our three to two superiority. But we shall fight cheerfully whatever odds we have to face.

And the surgeon of the *Good Hope* wrote on 25th October:—

> We think the Admiralty have forgotten their trade-route squadron 10,000 miles from London town. Five German cruisers against us. What's the betting on the field? Pray to your Penates we may prevent them concentrating.

Admiral Cradock did not fall into a trap, as was at one time suggested; he knew that when he met von Spee he would meet an enemy more than his match.

He went first to Coronel, then on to Valparaiso, and then back to Coronel to send off some cables. The *Glasgow*, to whose officers we owe the story of the fight, left Coronel at 9 o'clock on the morning of 1st November, sailing north, and about 4 o'clock in the afternoon

IN ACTION AT THE BATTLE OF CORONEL

sighted the enemy. She made out the two big armoured cruisers leading, and the light cruisers[1] following in open order, and at once sent a wireless signal to the flagship, which the Germans seem to have jammed. By 5 o'clock, however, the *Good Hope* came up, and the *Monmouth* had already joined the *Glasgow* and the *Otranto*. Both squadrons were now moving southward, the Germans having the in-shore course. The British were led by the Good Hope, with the *Monmouth*, *Glasgow*, and *Otranto* following in order; the Germans by the Scharnhorst, with the *Gneisenau*, *Dresden*, and *Nürnberg* following.

We can reconstruct something of the picture. To the east was the land, with the snowy heights of the southern Andes fired by the evening glow. To the west burned one of those flaming sunsets which the Pacific knows, and silhouetted against its crimson and orange were the British ships, like woodcuts in a naval handbook. A high sea was running from the south, and half a gale was blowing. At first some twelve miles separated the two squadrons, but the distance rapidly shrank till it was eight miles about 6.18 p.m.

About 7 o'clock the squadrons were converging, and the enemy's leading cruiser opened fire at seven miles. By this time the sun had gone down behind the horizon, but the lemon afterglow showed up the British ships, while the German were shrouded in the inshore twilight. Presently the enemy got the range, and shell after shell hit the *Good Hope* and the *Monmouth*, while the bad light and the spray from the head seas made good gunnery for them almost impossible.

At 7.50 there was a great explosion on the *Good Hope*, which had already been set on fire. The flames leaped to an enormous height in the air, and the doomed vessel, which had been drifting towards the enemy's lines, soon disappeared below the water. The *Monmouth* was also on fire and down by the head, and turned away seaward in her distress. Meantime the *Glasgow* had received only stray shots, for the battle so far had been waged between the four armoured cruisers. But as the *Good Hope* sank and the *Monmouth* was obviously near her end, the enemy cruisers fell back and began to shell the *Glasgow* at a range of two and a half miles. That the *Glasgow* escaped was something of a miracle. She was scarcely armoured at all, and was struck by five shells at the water line, but her coal seems to have saved her.

The moon was now rising, and the *Glasgow*, which had been trying to stand by the *Monmouth*, saw the whole German squadron bear-

1. The evidence of the number of German light cruisers is conflicting, but on the whole it seems probable that only the *Dresden* and the *Nürnberg* were present.

N
W — E
S

To Valparaiso

OTRANTO   NÜRNBERG
GLASGOW   DRESDEN
MONMOUTH   GNEISENAU
GOOD HOPE   SCHARNHORST
        8 Miles   (6.18 p.m.)

OTRANTO

GLASGOW   NÜRNBERG
               DRESDEN
MONMOUTH   GNEISENAU
GOOD HOPE
GLASGOW   4 Miles   SCHARNHORST (7.15 p.m.)

                         Concepcion

MOHMOUTH
out
of
action   GNEISENAU
                         Coronel
                (8 p.m.)

GOOD HOPE
out
of
action   SCHARNHORST   St. Maria
                              Is.

C H I L E

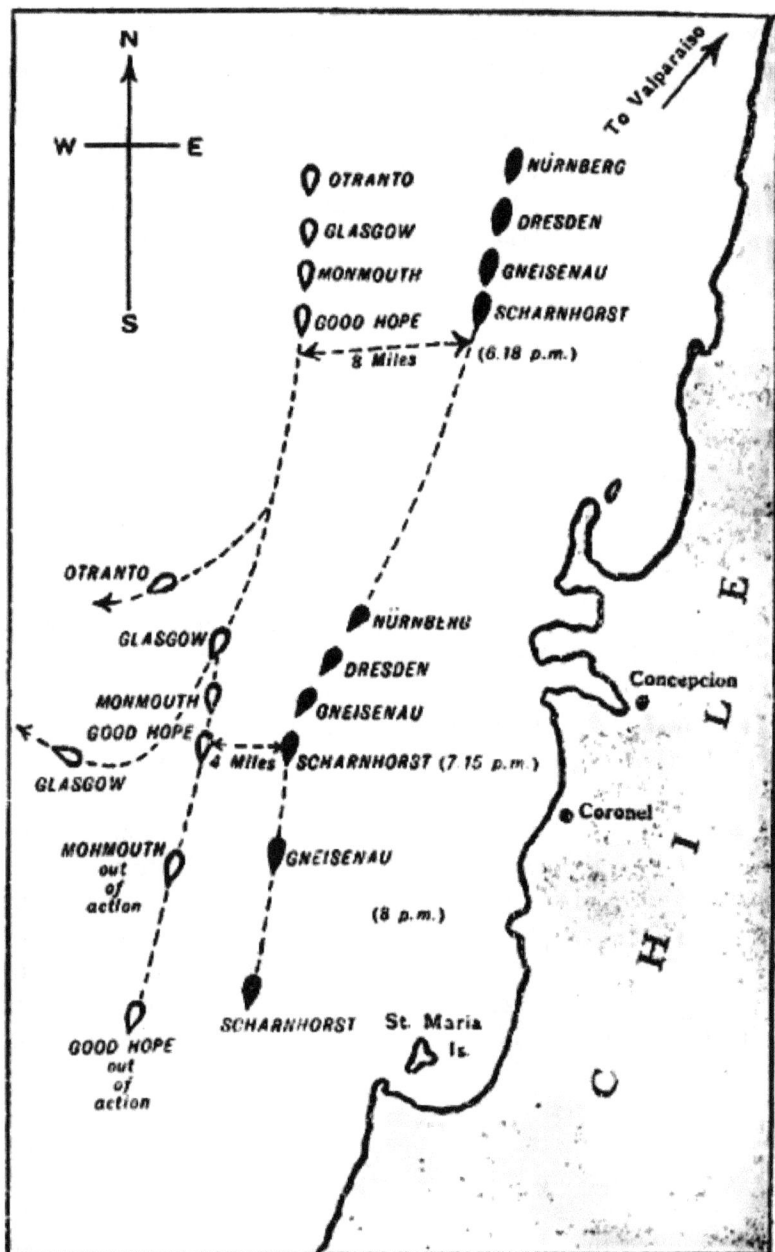

Battle of Coronel, November I.

ing down upon her. The *Monmouth* was past hope, so she did the proper thing and fled. By ten minutes to nine she was out of sight of the enemy, though she occasionally saw flashes of gun-fire and the play of searchlights, for fortunately a flurry of rain had hidden the unwelcome moon. She steered at first W.N.W., but gradually worked round to south, for she desired to warn the *Canopus*, which was coming up from the direction of Cape Horn. Next day she found that battleship, two hundred miles off, and the two proceeded towards the Straits of Magellan.

It is not for us to judge whether Admiral Cradock did rightly in entering upon this desperate battle. Probably it would have made small difference if he had waited for the Canopus, for though that vessel carried big guns, she was hopelessly slow. At any rate, he took the heroic course, and he and his 1,650 officers and men went to their death in the spirit of Drake and Grenville. The Germans had two light cruisers to our one, for the *Otranto* was negligible, but these vessels were never seriously in action, and the battle was won in the duel between the armoured cruisers. The *Good Hope* mounted two 9.2-inch guns, but these were old-fashioned, and were put out of action at the start. The 6-inch guns, which she and the *Monmouth* possessed, were no match for the broadsides of twelve 8.2-inch guns fired by the *Scharnhorst* and the *Gneisenau*. The German vessels were also far more heavily armoured, and they had the inestimable advantage of speed. They were able to get the requisite range first, and crippled Cradock before he could reply, and they had a superb target in his hulls silhouetted against the afterglow of sunset. The Battle of Coronel was fought with all conceivable odds against us.

The news woke the British Admiralty up to the necessity of dealing finally with Admiral von Spee Lord Fisher had succeeded Prince Louis of Battenberg as First Sea Lord, and one of the earliest acts of his administration was the dispatch of Rear-Admiral Sir Frederick Doveton Sturdee, who had been chief of the War Staff at the Admiralty, with a squadron to the South Atlantic. He had with him the *Invincible* and the *Inflexible*, the two first battle cruisers built by Britain. These vessels had a tonnage of 17,250, a normal speed of 25 knots, which could be increased under pressure to 28, and were each armed with eight 12-inch guns, so placed that all eight could be fired on either broadside. Their armour was 7-inch plates.

He had also three armoured cruisers, the *Carnarvon*—10,850 tons, 22-3 knots, and an armament of four 7.5-inch and six 6-inch guns;

the *Kent* and the *Cornwall*, each of 9,800 tons, 23 knots, and an armament of fourteen 6-inch and eight 12-pounder guns. At sea he was joined by the light cruiser *Bristol*, which belonged to the West Atlantic station, and was of the same class as the *Glasgow*, and he was accompanied by the armed liner *Macedonia*. Somewhere in the South Atlantic he picked up the *Glasgow*, which had made her way through the Magellan Straits.

A trap was cunningly laid for the victorious von Spee. If all tales be true, a device was employed which forms an excellent example of the "double-bluff." A wireless message was sent to the *Canopus*, bidding her proceed to Port Stanley in the Falkland Islands, where, she was informed, she would be perfectly safe, since the new guns for the forts had already arrived. This message was intercepted by the Germans, as it was meant to be, and, as was also intended, they regarded it as a ruse, designed to mislead them as to the security of the *Canopus*. They believed that all talk of forts and guns was nonsense, as it was, and that the *Canopus* lay in Port Stanley an easy prey. Admiral von Spee, therefore, resolved to make a prize of her, and at the same time to capture the wireless station at Port Stanley, which would give him a real strategic advantage.

After the Battle of Coronel, he had lingered for some time on the coast of Chile, probably waiting for his colliers, but on 15th November he left the island of Juan Fernandez, and headed for Cape Horn. The Japanese fleet was beginning to make things awkward for him in the Pacific. His intention, after he had disposed of the Canopus, was to sail across the Atlantic to the South African coast, where he might have caught the Union force which had landed at Luderitz Bay, and interfered, with disastrous effects, in the local war.

Admiral Sturdee's expedition was kept a complete secret, a wonderful achievement when we remember that our ports were full of German spies and that naval information had a knack of finding its way very speedily to the enemy. On the morning of 7th December the British squadron arrived at Port Stanley, which lies at the eastern corner of the East Island. The Falklands, with their bare brown moors shining with quartz, their endless lochans, their prevailing mists, their grey stone houses, and their population of Scots shepherds, look like a group of the Orkneys or Outer Hebrides set down in the southern seas. Port Stanley is a deeply-cut gulf leading to an inner harbour on the shores of which stands the little capital. The low shores on the south side almost give a vessel a sight of the outer sea. The entrance

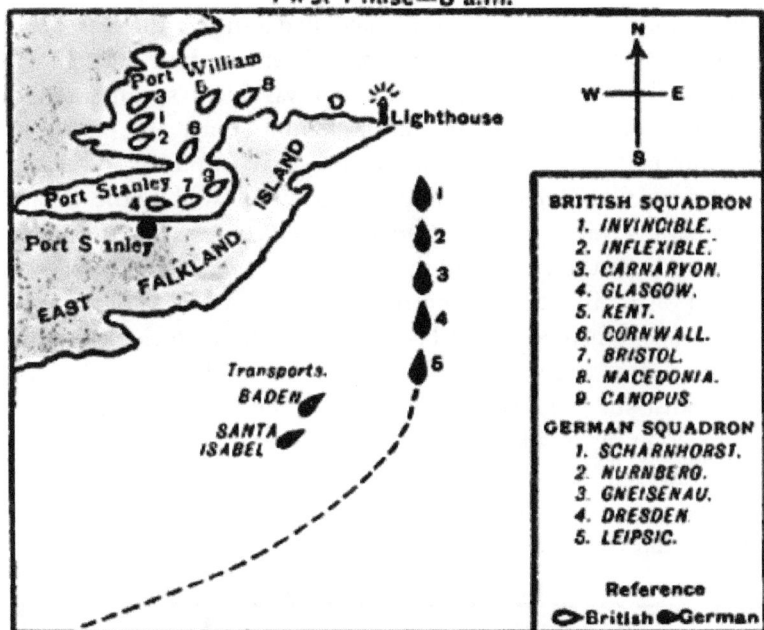

Battle of the Falkland Islands—Dec. 8.

had been defended to some extent by mines. December the 7th was spent by the British squadron in coaling. The *Canopus*, the *Glasgow*, and the *Bristol* were in the inner harbour, while the *Invincible, Inflexible, Carnarvon, Kent*, and *Cornwall* lay in the outer gulf.

About daybreak on the morning of the 8th, Admiral von Spee arrived from the direction of Cape Horn. He sent one of his light cruisers ahead to scout, and this vessel reported the presence of two British ships, probably the *Macedonia* and the *Kent*, which would be the first vessels visible to a ship rounding the islands. Upon this von Spee gave the order to prepare for battle, expecting to find only the remnants of Cradock's squadron. The Germans advanced in line, the *Gneisenau* leading, followed by the *Nürnberg*, the *Scharnhorst*, the *Dresden*, and the *Leipzig*, and steered north-east towards the entrance of the port.

At 8 o'clock the signal station announced the presence of the enemy. It was a clear fresh morning, with a bright sun, and light breezes from the north-west. All our vessels had finished coaling, except the battle cruisers, which had begun only half an hour before. Orders were at once given to get up steam for full speed. The battle cruisers raised steam with oil fuel, and made so dense a smoke that the German look-outs did not detect them. The Germans fired a shell at the wireless station about 9, and the *Canopus* had a shot at the *Scharnhorst* over the neck of land, directed by signal officers on shore. At 9.30 von Spee came abreast the harbour mouth, and was able to see the strength of the British squadron. He at once altered his course and put to sea, while Admiral Sturdee's command streamed out in pursuit.

First went the *Kent* and then the *Glasgow*, followed by the *Carnarvon*, the battle cruisers, and the *Cornwall*. The Germans had two transports with them, the *Baden* and the *Santa Isabel* , and these fell back to the south of the island, with the *Bristol* and the *Macedonia* in pursuit. The *Canopus* remained in the harbour. At about 10 o'clock the two forces were some twelve miles apart, von Spee steering about due east. The *Invincible* and the *Inflexible* quickly drew ahead, but had to slacken speed to 20 knots to allow the cruisers to keep up with them. At 11 o'clock about eleven miles separated the two forces. At five minutes to one we had drawn closer, and opened fire upon the *Leipzig*, which was last of the German line.

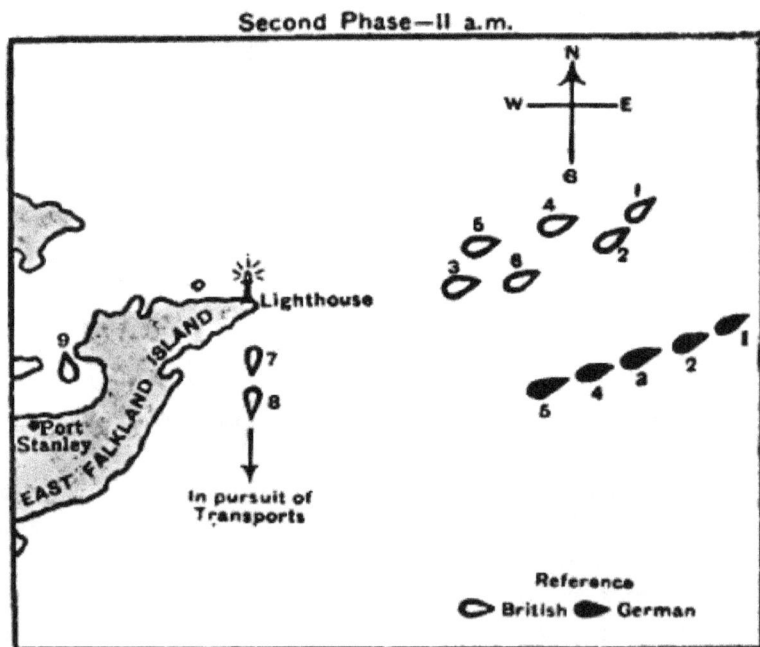

Second Phase—II a.m.

Battle of the Falkland Islands—Dec. 8.

Von Spee, seeing that flight was impossible, prepared to give battle. So far as the battle cruisers were concerned, it was a foregone conclusion, for they had the greater speed and the longer range. His

The "Scharnhorst" and the "Gneisenau"

three light cruisers turned and made off to the south, followed by the *Kent*, the *Glasgow*, and the *Cornwall*, while the *Invincible*, the *Inflexible*, and the *Carnarvon* engaged the *Scharnhorst* and the *Gneisenau*. About 2 o'clock our battle cruisers had the range of the German flagship, and a terrific artillery duel began. The smoke was getting in our way, and Admiral Sturdee used his superior speed to get to the other side of the enemy. We simply pounded the *Scharnhorst* to pieces, and just after 4 o'clock she listed to port and then turned bottom upwards with her propeller still going round. The battle cruisers and the *Carnarvon* then concentrated on the *Gneisenau*, which was sheering off to the south-east, and at 6 o'clock she too listed and went under.

Meanwhile the *Kent*, *Glasgow*, and *Cornwall* were hot in pursuit of the three light cruisers, and here was a more equally matched battle. The *Dresden*, which was farthest to the east, managed to escape. The other two had slightly the advantage of speed of the British ships, but our engineers and stokers worked magnificently, and managed to get 25 knots out of the *Kent*. It was now a thick misty day, with a drizzle of rain, and each duel had consequently the air of a separate battle. The news of the sinking of the *Scharnhorst* and the *Gneisenau* put new

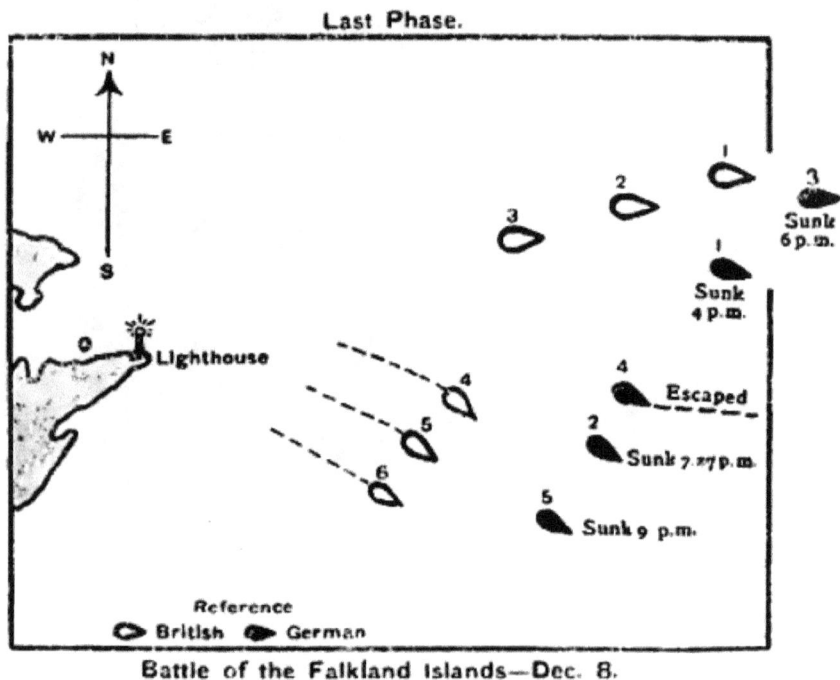

Battle of the Falkland Islands—Dec. 8.

SINKING OF THE "SCHARNHORST" AT THE BATTLE OF THE FALKLANDS

spirit into our men, and at 7.27 p.m. the *Nürnberg*, which had been set on fire by the *Kent*, went down with her guns still firing. The *Leipzig*, which had to face the *Glasgow* and the *Cornwall*, kept afloat till 9 p.m., when she too heeled over and sank.

As the wet night closed in, the battle died away. Only the *Dresden*, battered and fleeing far out in the southern waters, remained of the proud squadron which at dawn had sailed to what it believed to be an easy victory. The defeat of Cradock in the murky sunset off Coronel had been amply avenged.

The Battle of the Falkland Islands was a brilliant piece of strategy, for a plan, initiated more than a month before and involving a journey across the world, was executed with complete secrecy and precision. The honours must be divided between Sir Frederick Sturdee and the Admiralty at home, which conceived the enterprise. Technically, the sole blemish was the escape of the *Dresden*, which could scarcely have been prevented, for the *Carnarvon*, owing to her inadequate speed, could not join her sister ships in the pursuit of the lighter German vessels, and the *Glasgow*, the only ship which might have overhauled her, was busy with the *Leipzig*. The fight had a vital bearing on the position of Germany. It annihilated the one squadron left to her outside the North Sea, and it removed a formidable menace to our trade routes. After the 8th of December, the *Dresden*[2] and the *Karlsruhe* were the sole enemy cruisers left at large, for the *Bremen*, never very fortunate in her efforts, seemed to have temporarily disappeared. These, with the armoured merchantmen, the *Kronprinz Wilhelm* and the *Prince Eitel Friedrich*, were the only privateers still at work on the High Seas.

The British losses were small considering the magnitude of the victory. The *Invincible* was hit by eighteen shells, but had no casualties. The *Inflexible* was hit thrice, and had one man killed. The cruisers suffered more heavily, the *Kent*, for example, having four men killed and twelve wounded, and the *Glasgow* nine killed and four wounded. Unlike the Germans at Coronel, every effort was made by our ships to save life. The only sign of a lost vessel was at first the slightly discoloured water. Then the wreckage floated up with men clinging to it, and boats were lowered, and sailors let down the sides on bow-lines to try to rescue the survivors who floated past. The water was icy

---

2. The *Dresden* was caught off Juan Fernandez on March 14, 1915, by the *Kent* and the *Glasgow*, and sunk in five minutes. There is good reason to believe that the *Karlsruhe* was wrecked in the West Indies during the autumn of 1914.

cold—about 40 degrees—and presently many of the swimmers grew numb and went under. Albatrosses, too, attacked some of those clinging to the wreckage, pecking at their eyes and forcing them to let go. Altogether we must have saved a couple of hundred men, including the captain of the *Gneisenau*. Admiral von Spee went down, with two of his sons.

From a graphic description of the action by an officer of the *Kent*, Commander Eric Wharton, we take this extract:—

It is near dusk now, 7.30, and we have been two hours in action. Up comes every one from below, from casemates and turrets, to stare and rejoice, but they are all immediately hustled away to do what can be done to save life. All our boats are riddled, and none of them can be repaired for an hour. We do what we can with lifebuoys and lumps of wood paid astern, but it's mighty little; it's a loppy sea, and dreadfully cold. All this part was beastly. There were so many of them in sight, and we could do so little till our boats were patched. At last we could lower one cutter and the galley, and even then life-saving was no easy job. I was in the galley, and plunged about for twenty minutes to get one man. Altogether we got on board about a dozen, five of whom were really 'goners' when we hoisted them on board. The other seven have flourished and are really quite normal again now.

Early in these life-saving operations the *Nürnberg* heeled over on her side and sank. They were a brave lot; one man stood aft and held the ensign flying in his hands till the ship went under. It was strange and weird, all this aftermath, the wind rapidly arising from the westward, darkness closing in, one ship heaving to the swell, well battered, the foretop-gallant-mast gone. Of the other, nothing to be seen but floating wreckage, with here and there a man clinging, and the 'Mollyhawks' (vultures of the sea) swooping by. The wind moaned, and death was on the air. Then, see I out of the mist loomed a great four-masted barque under full canvas. A great ghost-ship she seemed. Slowly, majestically she sailed by and vanished in the night.

Let us do honour to a gallant enemy. The German admiral fought as Cradock had fought, the German sailors died as Cradock's men had died, and there can be no higher praise. They went down with colours flying, and at the last the men seem to have lined up on the decks

The Battle of the Falkland Islands

of the doomed ships. They continued to resist after their vessels had become shambles. One captured officer reported that before the end his ship had no upper deck left, every man there having been killed, and one turret blown bodily overboard by a 12-inch lyddite shell. But in all this hell of slaughter, which lasted for half a day, there was never a thought of surrender. Von Spee and Cradock lie beneath the same waters, in the final concord of those who have looked unshaken upon death.

Raids and Blockades

The war in northern waters now enters upon a singular phase which has no parallel in the conflicts of the past. An old dread took bodily form, and its embodiment proved farcical. Exasperated by failure, Germany cast from her all the ancient etiquette of war, and the result was that the law of the sea had to be largely rewritten.

The shores of Britain since the days of Paul Jones had been immune from serious hostile attentions. Very properly we regarded our navy as our defence, and paid little heed to coast fortifications, except at important naval stations such as Portsmouth and Dover. But the possibility of invasion remained in the popular mind, and was used as a goad to stir us to activity in our spasmodic fits of national stock-taking. Invasion on the grand scale was admittedly out of the question so long as our fleets held the sea; but a raid in the fog of a winter's night was conceivable, and became a favourite theme of romancers and propagandists. When the war broke out the menace was seriously regarded by the government, and during October and November, when the German guns across the Channel were almost within hearing of our southern ports, steps were taken to protect our eastern coast-line. We needed every atom of our strength for the great Flanders struggle, and if a raiding party succeeded in occupying a stretch of shore, the necessity of dislodging him might gravely handicap our major strategy.

Accordingly Yeomanry and Territorials entrenched themselves in the Eastern counties, and had the dullness of their days enlivened by many rumours. Civilians, remembering the awful warning of a recent popular drama, were perturbed by the thought of how they should conduct themselves if their homes were violated, and there was much activity in the formation of national guards, and a considerable increase in recruiting for the new service armies.

Late on the afternoon of 2nd November, eight German warships

Scale of Miles
0   50   100
Railways

Shetland Is.
Lerwich
Bergen
NORWAY
Christians
Drammen
Fair I.
Orkney Is.
Kirkwall
Scapa Flow
Stavanger
Pentland Firth
Thurso
Wick
Cromarty
Moray Firth
SKAGER RACK
Fraserburgh
Peterhead
Aalborg
SCOTLAND
Aberdeen
N   O   R   T   H
DENMARK
Dundee
Montrose
Firth of Tay
S   E   A
Esbjerg
Firth of Forth
Edinburgh
Berwick
Cromarty to Heligoland 50S m.
Carlisle
Newcastle
Sunderland
Hartlepool
Aberdeen to Heligoland 440 m.
Middlesboro
Scarborough
Rosyth to Heligoland 380 m.
Newcastle to Heligoland 360 m.
Leeds
Hull
Scarborough to Heligoland 320 m.
Heligoland
Kiel
Manchester
Grimsby
Cuxhaven
Hamburg
Wilhelmshaven
Bremerhaven
Cromer
Yarmouth to Heligoland 280 m.
Emden
Bremen
R. Weser
Birmingham
Yarmouth
Helder
Zuider
Zee
ENGLAND
Norwich
Amsterdam
The Hague
Utrecht
Hook of Holland
Rotterdam
GERMANY
R. Thames
London
Sheerness
Bristol
Chatham
Dover
Ostend
Flushing
Antwerp
Cologne
Southampton
Brighton
Folkestone
Dunkirk
Nieuport
Bruges
Brussels
Aix-la-Chapelle
Weymouth
Plymouth
Newhaven
Boulogne
Calais
Lille
Liege
BELGIUM
FRANCE

British East Coast, showing distances from German Base.

sailed from the Elbe base. They were three battle cruisers, the *Seydlitz*, the *Moltke*, and the *Von der Tann*; two armoured cruisers, the *Bluecher* and the *Yorck*; and three light cruisers, the *Kolberg*, the *Graudenz*, and the *Strassburg*. Except the *Yorck*, they were fast vessels, making at least 25 knots, and the battle cruisers carried 11-inch guns. Cleared for action, they started for the coast of England, and early in the winter dawn ran through the nets of a British fishing fleet eight miles east of Lowestoft. An old coast police boat, the *Halcyon*, was next sighted, and received a few shots, but the Germans had no time to waste on her.

About eight o'clock they were opposite Yarmouth, and proceeded to bombard the wireless station and the naval air station from a distance of about ten miles. For some reason still unknown they were afraid to venture farther inshore—probably they took their range from a line of buoys marked on the chart, and did not know that after the declaration of war these buoys had been moved 500 yards farther out to sea—so their shells only ploughed the sands and plumped in the water. In a quarter of an hour they grew tired of it, and moved away, dropping many floating mines, which later in the day caused the loss of one of our submarines and two fishing-boats. The enterprise was unlucky, for on the road back the *Yorck* struck a mine and went to the bottom with most of her crew.

The raid was a reconnaissance, and a blow aimed at the *sang-froid* of Britain. The latter purpose miscarried, for nobody in Britain gave it a second thought. To bombard the beach front of a watering-place seemed a paltry achievement. It would have been wiser had the authorities taken it more seriously, and issued instructions to civilians as to what to do in case of a repetition of such attempts. For, having found the way, the invaders were certain to return.

They came again on 16th December, when a thick, cold mist lay low on our Eastern coasts. Von Spee and his squadron had gone to their death at the Falkland Islands, and Germany was fired with a passion of revenge. Espionage had been rampant, for somehow she seemed to have learned not only the navigation of the Yorkshire coast and the topography of the coast towns, but the way through the British minefields and our own naval dispositions at the moment. The composition of the raiding force, which was under Rear-Admiral Funke, the second in command of the battle-cruiser squadron, is not yet clear; but it is almost certain that it included the *Derfflinger*, the newest of the battle cruisers, and the *Von der Tann*. The *Bluecher* was there beyond doubt, and the other two may have been the *Seydlitz* and the *Graudenz*. There were also at least two light cruisers present. Before daybreak on the 16th the squadron arrived off the mouth of the Tees, and there divided its forces. The *Derfflinger*, the *Von der Tann,* and probably the *Bluecher*, went north to raid the Hartlepools, and the other two went south against Scarborough.

A few minutes before eight o'clock those citizens of Scarborough who were out of bed saw approaching from the north four strange ships. It was a still morning, with what is called in Scotland a *haar* on the water, and something of a sea running, for the last days had been stormy. Scarborough was entirely without defences, except an old Russian 60-pounder, a Crimean relic, which was as useful as the flint arrowheads in the local museum. It had once been a garrison artillery depot, and had a battery below the castle, but Lord Haldane had altered this and made it a cavalry station. Some troops of the new service battalions were quartered in the place, and there was a wireless station behind the town. Otherwise it was an open seaside resort, as defenceless against an attack from the sea as a seal against a killer-whale.

The ships poured shells into the coastguard station and the castle grounds, where they seemed to suspect the presence of hostile batteries. Then they steamed in front of the town, approaching to some five hundred yards from the shore. Here they proceeded to a systematic bombardment, aiming at every large object within sight, including the Grand Hotel and the gasworks, while many shells were directed towards the waterworks and the wireless station in the western suburbs. Churches, public buildings, and hospitals were hit, and large areas of private houses were wrecked. For forty minutes the bombardment continued, and it is calculated that five hundred shells were fired. Midway in their course the ships swung round and began to move northwards again, while the light cruisers went out to sea and began the work of mine-dropping. The streets were crowded with puzzled and scared inhabitants, for they had no instructions what to do, and, as in every watering-place, there was a large proportion of old people, women, and invalids. At a quarter to nine all was over, and the hulls of the invaders were disappearing round the castle promontory. They left behind them eighteen dead, mostly women and children, and about seventy wounded.

About nine o'clock the coastguard at Whitby, the little town on the cliffs north of Scarborough, saw two great ships steaming up fast from the south. Ten minutes later the newcomers opened fire on the signal

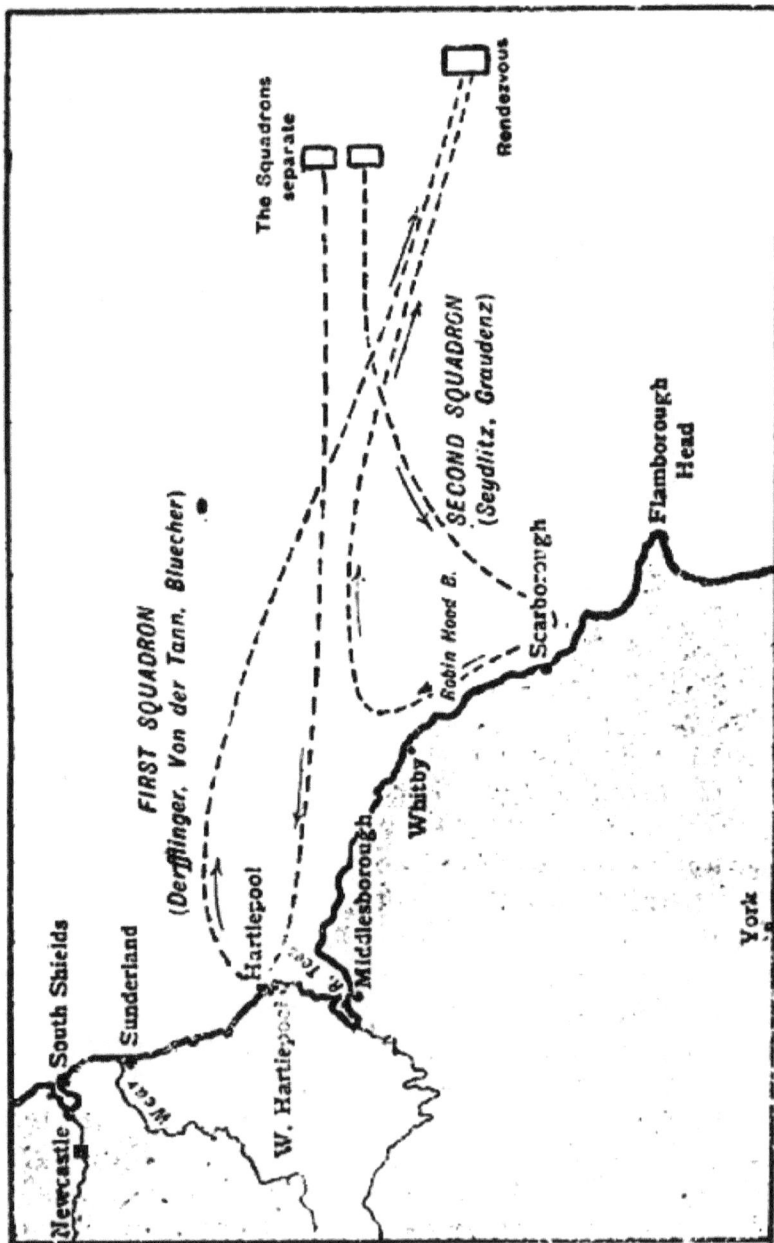

Raid on Scarborough and Hartlepool.

station on the cliff head. Several dozen shells were fired in a few minutes, many striking the cliff, and others going too high and falling behind the railway station. Some actually went four miles inland, and awakened a sleepy little village. The old Abbey of Hilda and Caedmon was struck but not seriously damaged; and on the whole, considering the number of shells it received, Whitby suffered little. The casualties were only five, three killed and two wounded. The invaders turned north-eastward and disappeared into the haze, to join their other division.

That other division had visited the Hartlepools, the only town of the three which came near to fulfilling the definition of a fortified place. It had a small fort, with a battery of small, antiquated guns. It had important docks and large shipbuilding works, which were busy at the time on Government orders, and some companies of the new service battalions were billeted in the town. Off the shore was lying a small British flotilla a gunboat, the *Patrol*, carrying 4-inch guns, and two destroyers, the *Doon* and the *Hardy*.

About the same time as the bombardment of Scarborough began, the *Derfflinger*, the *Von der Tann*, and the *Bluecher* came out of the mist upon the British flotilla and opened fire. The action took place on the north side of the peninsula on which Old Hartlepool stands. With great gallantry the small British craft tried to close and torpedo the invaders, but they were driven back with half a dozen killed and twenty-five wounded, and their only course was flight. The German ships approached the shore and fired on the battery.

Then began the first fight on English soil with a foreign foe since the French landed in Sussex in 1690—the first on British soil since the fight at Fishguard in 1797. The achievement deserves to be remembered. The battery was commanded by Lieutenant-Colonel Robson, a Territorial officer, and consisted of some Territorials of the Durham Royal Garrison Artillery and some infantry of the Durhams. The 12-inch shells of the *Derfflinger* burst in and around the battery, but the men stood to their outclassed guns without wavering, and aimed with some success at the upper decks of the invaders. For more than half an hour a furious cannonade continued, in which some 1,500 shells seem to have been fired. One ship kept close to the battery, and gave it broadside after broadside; the other two moved farther north, and shelled Old Hartlepool, and fired over the peninsula at West Hartlepool and the docks. The streets of the old town suffered terribly, the gasworks were destroyed, and one of the big shipbuilding yards damaged, but the docks and the other yards were not touched. Churches,

GERMAN RAID, DEC. 16TH, 1914, BACK OF ST. NICHOLAS
PARADE, NEAR GRAND HOTEL, SCARBOROUGH

hospitals, workhouses, and schools were all struck. Little children going to school and babies in their mothers' arms were killed. The total death-roll was 119, and the wounded over 300; six hundred houses were damaged or destroyed, and three steamers that night struck the mines which the invaders had laid off the shore, and went down with much loss of life.

The spirit in which the inhabitants of the raided towns met the crisis was worthy of the highest praise. There was dire confusion—for nobody had been told what to do; there was some panic—it would have been a miracle if there had not been; but on the whole the situation was met with admirable coolness and courage. The authorities, as soon as the last shots were fired, turned to the work of relief; the Territorials in Hartlepool behaved like veterans both during and after the bombardment; the girls in the Hartlepool Telephone Exchange worked steadily through the cannonade; and there were many instances of heroism on the part of the children who suffered so terribly. It should be remembered that we cannot compare this attack on the East Coast towns with the assaults in a land war on some city in the battle front. In the latter case the mind of the inhabitants has been attuned for weeks to danger, and preparations have been made for defence. But here the bolt came from the blue, the narrow, crowded streets of Old Hartlepool were a death-trap, and the ordinary citizen was plunged in a second from profound peace into the midst or a nerve-racking and unexpected war.

Somewhere between nine and ten on that December morning the German vessels rendezvoused and started on their homeward course. They escaped only by the skin of their teeth. Before the first shell was fired word of the attempt had reached the British Grand Fleet. Somewhere out in the *haar* two battle-cruiser squadrons were moving to intercept the raiders, and behind came half a dozen of the great battleships. But for an accident of weather the German battle-cruiser squadron would have gone to the bottom of the North Sea. But the morning *haar* thickened, till a series of blind fog-belts stretched for a hundred miles east from our shores. No dispatch has yet told the tale of that lamentable miscarriage, which was due solely to the weather, and not to any lack of skill and enterprise on the part of our admirals. Our Second Battle-Cruiser Squadron actually came within view of the enemy at a distance of eight miles, and the sight of it deflected the German course. Then, just as the trap seemed about to close, the fog thickened, speed had to be reduced, and Admiral Funke slipped through. There is reason to believe that in the flight the *Von der Tann* rammed one of the light cruisers and damaged her own bows. With this slight misadventure the raiders returned safely to the Heligoland base, to be welcomed with Iron Crosses and newspaper eulogies on this new proof of German valour.

On that same day the Admiralty issued a message pointing out that:—

Demonstrations of this character against unfortified towns or commercial ports, though not difficult to accomplish provided that a certain amount of risk is accepted, are devoid of military significance.

They must not be allowed to modify the general naval policy which is being pursued.

The first, perhaps, was a pardonable over-statement, unless we interpret the word "military" in a narrow sense. These raids had a very serious military and naval purpose, which it is well to recognise. The German aim was to create such a panic in civilian England as would prevent the dispatch of the new armies to the Continent, and to compel Sir John Jellicoe and the Grand Fleet to move his base nearer the East Coast, and undertake the duties of coast protection. The first was defeated by the excellent spirit with which England accepted the disaster. No voice was raised to clamour for the use of the new armies as a garrison for our seaboard. The second, though at first there was some natural indignation on the threatened coast and a few foolish speeches and newspaper articles, had no chance of succeeding. In vain is the net spread in sight of the bird. The only result was that more stringent measures were taken to prevent espionage, that civilians were at last given some simple emergency directions, and that recruiting received the best possible advertisement.

Germany made much of the exploit, till she discovered that neutral nations, especially America, were seriously scandalized, and then she took to lame explanations. Scarborough had been bombarded because it had a wireless station, Whitby because it had a naval signal station, Hartlepool because it had a little fort. The defence was one of those curious quibbles in which Germany delights. Technically she could make out a sort of case, and Hartlepool might fairly be said to have come within the category of a defended place. It is true that the fortifications were lamentably inadequate, but she might retort that that was our business, not hers. But the real answer is that she did not aim

GERMAN RAID, DEC. 16TH, 1914,
HOUSE IN BELVOIR TERRACE, SCARBOROUGH

at the destruction of military and naval accessories, except as an after-thought. The seafront of Scarborough and streets of Old Hartlepool were bombarded not because they were in the line of fire against a fort or a wireless station, but for their own sakes—because they contained a multitude of people who could be killed or terrorised. German espionage is wonderful and German information good. If Germany had the exact plans of the coast ports and of their condition at the time, as she certainly had, she knew very well how far they were from being fortified towns or military and naval bases.

She selected them just because they were open towns, for "frightfulness" there would have far greater moral effects upon the nation than if it had been directed against Harwich or Dover, where it might be regarded as one of the natural risks of war. Her performance was a breach not of a technicality but of the unwritten conventions of honourable campaigning.[1] The slaughter of civilians to produce an impression is one of those things repellent to any man trained in the etiquette of a great service. The German navy has been justly admired, but it was beginning to show its parvenu origin. Individual sailors might conduct themselves like gentlemen, but there was no binding tradition of gentility in the service, and, as in the army, those at the head disliked and repudiated any such weakness. The last word is with the mayor of Scarborough. He wrote:—

Some newcomers into honourable professions learn the tricks before the traditions.

The British casualties by sea, apart from the losses in battle which have been described in an earlier chapter, were not serious during the last two months of the year, but on the first day of 1915 there was a grave misfortune. On the 31st of December eight vessels of the Channel Fleet left Sheerness, and about three o'clock on the morning of 1st January, in bright moonlight, the eight were steering in single line at a moderate speed near the Start Lighthouse. There seems to have been no screen of destroyers, and the situation invited an attack from submarines, several of which had been reported in these waters. The last

---

1. "Military proceedings are not regulated solely by the stipulations of international law. There are other factors conscience, good sense. A sense of the duties which the principles of humanity impose will be the surest guide for the conduct of seamen, and will constitute the most effectual safeguard against abuse. The officers of the German Navy—I say it with emphasis—will always fulfil in the strictest manner duties which flow from the unwritten law of humanity and civilization."—Baron Marschall von Bieberstein at the Hague Conference, 1907.

GERMAN RAID, DEC. 16TH, 1914, INTERIOR OF HOUSE, NORTH MARINE DRIVE, SCARBOROUGH

of the line was the *Formidable*, Captain Loxley, a pre-Dreadnought of 15,000 tons, and a sister ship to the *Bulwark*, which had been blown up at Sheerness on 26th November. Some time after three she was struck by two torpedoes, and went down. Four boats were launched, one of which capsized, and out of a crew of some 800 only 201 were saved. Captain Loxley, one of the ablest of our younger sailors, went down with his ship. The rescue of part of the crew was due to the courage and good seamanship of Captain William Pillar, of the Brixton trawler *Providence*, who in heavy weather managed to take the inmates of the *Formidable's* cutter aboard his vessel. For this fine performance he was given a commission in the Royal Navy, and decorated by the king, who, speaking as a sailor, said:

> I realise how difficult your task must have been, because I know myself how arduous it is to gybe a vessel in a heavy gale.

The misfortune showed that the lesson of the loss of the *Cressy*, *Hogue*, and *Aboukir* had been imperfectly learned. For eight battleships to move slowly in line on a moonlit night in submarine-infested waters without destroyers was simply to court destruction.

Early on the morning of Sunday, 24th January, Rear-Admiral Hipper, who commanded the German Battle-Cruiser Squadron, left Wilhelmshaven with a strong force to repeat the exploits of Admiral Funke. The *Von der Tann* was still undergoing repairs, but he had with him the *Seydlitz*, in which he flew his flag, the *Moltke*, the *Derfflinger*, the *Bluecher*, six light cruisers, one of which was the *Kolberg*, and a destroyer flotilla. To recapitulate their strengths: the *Derfflinger* had 26,200 tons, a speed of nearly 27 knots, an armour belt of 12 inches, and eight 12-inch guns; the *Seydlitz* had 24,600 tons, the same speed, and ten 11-inch guns; the *Moltke* had 22,640 tons, 25 knots, and ten 11-inch guns; the *Bluecher* had 15,550 tons, 24 knots, and twelve 8.2-inch guns. Before starting Admiral Hipper took certain precautions. He enlarged the mine field north of Heligoland, and north of it concentrated a submarine flotilla, while he arranged for Zeppelins and seaplanes to come out from the island in certain contingencies.

It is impossible to dogmatise as to the purpose of his movements. It has been suggested that he hoped to get one or more of his battle cruisers round the north end of Scotland to attack the sea highroads of British commerce. He may have intended a new raid on our eastern coasts—the Tyne, perhaps, or the Forth. But, judging from his preparations and his subsequent tactics, it is likely that his main motive,

GERMAN RAID, DEC. 16TH, 1914, ROYAL HOTEL, SCARBOROUGH

assuming that he encountered part of the British fleet, was to retire and fight a running action, and entice our vessels within reach of his submarines or the Heligoland mine

The same morning the British Battle-Cruiser Squadron, under Vice-Admiral Sir David Beatty, put to sea. Probably some hint of the German preparations had reached the Admiralty, and developments were anticipated. He flew his flag in the *Lion*—Captain A. S. M. Chatfield a vessel of 26,350 tons, nearly 29 knots, and an armament of eight 13.5-inch guns. With him sailed five other battle cruisers: the *Tiger*—Captain Henry Pelly—28,000 tons, 28 knots, eight 13.5-inch guns; the *Princess Royal*—Captain Osmond Brock—a sister ship of the *Lion*; the *New Zealand*—Captain Lionel Halsey—18,800 tons, 25 knots, and eight 12-inch guns; the *Indomitable*—Captain Francis Kennedy—a sister ship of the *Invincible* and *Inflexible*, which were in the battle of the Falkland Islands. With the battle cruisers went four cruisers of the "town" class—the *Southampton*, the *Nottingham*, the *Birmingham*, and the *Lowestoft*; three light cruisers—the *Arethusa*, the *Aurora*, and the *Undaunted*—and destroyer flotillas, under Commander Reginald Y. Tyrwhitt. Admiral Beatty 's squadron completely outclassed Admiral Hipper's both in numbers, pace, and weight of fire, and the Germans were heavily handicapped by the presence of the *Bluecher*, whose low speed of only 24 knots marked her out as a predestined prey.

The night of Saturday, the 23rd, had been foggy, and the destroyers, scouting east of the Dogger Bank, had a difficult time. Sunday morning, however, dawned clear and sharp, for the wind had changed to the north-east, and swept the mist from the seas. About seven o'clock the *Aurora*, Captain Wilmot Nicholson, sighted the Germans off Dogger Bank, signalled the news to Admiral Beatty, and presently opened fire. Admiral Beatty steered to the direction of the flashes, and Admiral Hipper, who had been moving north-west, promptly turned round and took a course to the south-east. This sudden flight, when he could not have been informed of the enemy's strength, suggests that the German admiral's main purpose was to lure our vessels to the dangerous Heligoland area.

About eight o'clock the situation was as follows: the Germans were moving south-east in line, with the *Moltke* leading, followed by *the Seydlitz, Derfflinger*, and *Bluecher*, with the destroyers on their starboard beam, and the light cruisers ahead. Close upon them were the British destroyers and light cruisers, who presently crossed on the port side to prevent their smoke from spoiling the marksmanship of the larger vessels. Our battle cruisers did not follow directly behind, but, in order

Battle of the Dogger Bank January 1915

to avoid the mines which the enemy was certain to drop, kept on a parallel course to the westward. The *Lion* led, followed by the *Tiger*, the *Princess Royal*, the *New Zealand*, and the *Indomitable*. What followed was an extraordinary tribute to the engineers. The first three ships could easily be worked up to 30 knots, but the last two, which had normally only 25 knots, were so strenuously driven that they managed to keep in line. Our leading ships had the pace of the Germans, and no one of our squadron was seriously outclassed, while the unfortunate *Bluecher*, on the other hand, was bound to drop behind.

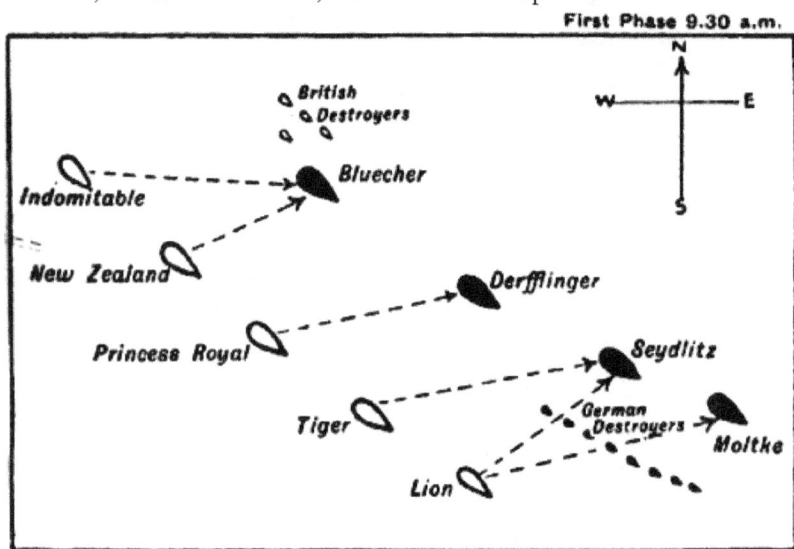

First Phase 9.30 a.m.

Battle of January 24.

Fourteen miles at first separated us from the enemy, and by nine o'clock we were within 11½ miles of the last ship. The *Lion* fired a ranging shot which fell short, but soon 9 after nine, when the squadrons were ten miles apart, she got her first blow home on the *Bluecher*. As our line began to draw level the *Tiger* continued to attack the *Bluecher*, while the *Lion* attended to the *Derfflinger*. At 9.30 the *Bluecher* had fallen so much astern that she came within range of the guns of the *New Zealand*, and the *Lion* and the *Tiger* were busy with the leading German ship, the *Seydlitz*, while the *Princess Royal* attacked the *Derfflinger*. The *Moltke*, first in the line, seems to have got off lightly, because of the smoke which obscured the range. Our destroyers and light cruisers had dropped behind, but presently, when the German destroyers threatened, the *Meteor* and "M" division, under Captain the Hon. Herbert Meade, went ahead and took up a position of great danger in the very thick of the firing.

The British gunnery was precise, shell after shell hitting a pin-point ten miles off—a pin-point, too, moving at over thirty miles an hour. It was not a broadside action, for the ships at which we aimed were stern-on. At first sight this looks like a disadvantage, but in practice it has been found to give the best results, and that for a simple reason. To get the line is an easy matter; the difficulty is to get the right elevation. In a broadside action a shell which is too high falls harmlessly beyond the vessel, because the target is only the narrow width of the deck. But in a stern-on fight the target is the whole length of the vessel, 600 feet and more, instead of 90.

By eleven o'clock the *Seydlitz* and the *Derfflinger* were on fire. The *Bluecher* had fallen behind in flames, and was being battered by the *New Zealand* and the *Indomitable*. An hour later the *Meteor* torpedoed her, and she began to sink. The crew lined up on deck, ready for death, and it was only the shouts of the *Arethusa* that made them jump into the water. With a cheer they went overboard, and none too soon, for presently the *Bluecher* turned turtle and floated bottom upwards. Our boats rescued over 120 of the swimmers, and would have saved more had not some German aircraft from Heligoland dropped bombs upon the rescue parties and killed several German sailors. The airmen clearly thought that the *Bluecher* was a sinking British cruiser, and this may have been the basis of the preposterous tale of our losses which the German Admiralty subsequently published.

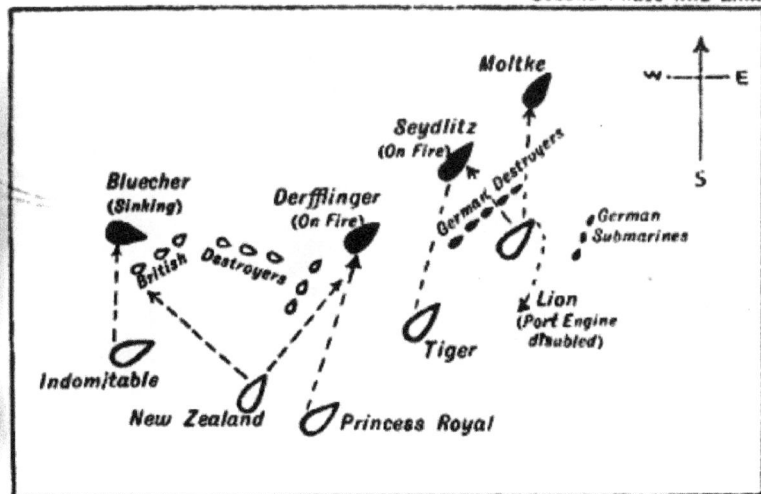

Battle of January 24.

141

H.M.S. "LION"

We must return to the doings of the three leading battle cruisers. The German destroyers managed to get between them and the enemy, and under cover of their smoke the Germans made a half turn to the north, and increased the distance. Admiral Beatty promptly altered his course to conform. The destroyers then attacked us at close quarters, hoping to torpedo, but the 4-inch guns amidships on the battle cruisers drove them off. Presently submarines were sighted, and Admiral Beatty himself saw a periscope on the starboard bow of the *Lion*. The flagship at this time was much under fire, but suffered remarkably little damage. At three minutes past eleven, however, as her bow lifted from the water it was struck by a shell which damaged the feed tank. She had to reduce her speed, and fell out of the line.

This accident had unfortunate effects on the battle, which up to now had been going strongly in the British favour. Admiral Beatty had to transfer his flag to the destroyer *Attack*, and the charge of the pursuing battle cruisers passed to the next senior officer, Rear-Admiral Moore, whose flag flew in the *New Zealand*. The *Lion* moved away to the north-west, and in the afternoon her engines began to give serious trouble. The *Indomitable*, released by the sinking of the *Bluecher*, took her in tow, and after some anxious hours she was brought safely into an English port.

The *Attack* followed hard on the battle cruisers, but it was not till twenty minutes past twelve that she overtook the *Princess Royal*, to which Admiral Beatty transferred his flag. He found that the squadron had broken off the fight and were retiring. The reasons which led Admiral Moore to this step have not yet been given to the world. According to the German report, which there is no cause to distrust, the British squadron at the moment of turning was seventy miles from Heligoland and probably at least forty from the new mine field which Admiral Hipper had laid. Admiral Moore had to make a momentous and most difficult decision, and any verdict upon its wisdom would be premature. The consequence was that what might have been a crushing victory was changed to a disappointment. The British losses were few ten men killed on the *Tiger*, four on the *Meteor*, and six wounded on the *Lion*; no British vessel was lost, and the hurt to the flagship was soon repaired. The Germans lost the *Bluecher*, the *Derfflinger* and the *Seydlitz* were seriously damaged, and many of their crews must have perished. But minor successes seem almost a failure when we were within an ace of destroying the whole German force of battle cruisers.

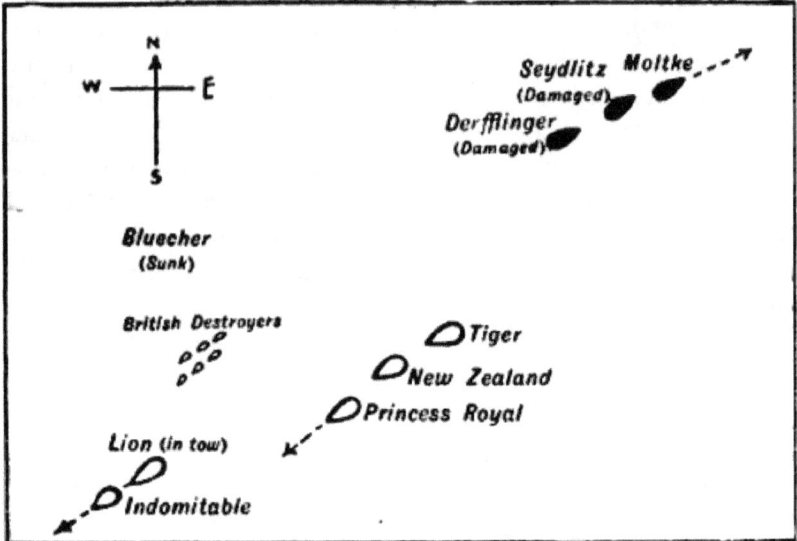

N

W —— E

S

Seydlitz Moltke _ _ ⫶
(Damaged)
Derfflinger
(Damaged)

Bluecher
(Sunk)

British Destroyers

Lion (in tow)

Indomitable

Tiger

New Zealand

Princess Royal

Battle of January 24.

To Germany the result was a grave annoyance, which was covered by a cloud of inaccurate reports. Admiral Hipper was apparently not held responsible, but Admiral von Ingenohl, for some reason still obscure, was the target of criticism. He was shortly afterwards removed from the command of the High Sea Fleet, and his place taken by Admiral von Pohl.

Three weeks later the British First Lord of the Admiralty made a statement in the House of Commons which summed up the work of the navy, and drew the attention of the nation to the lesson of the North Sea action—the power of the great guns, the excellence of British gunnery, the immense advantage of speed. From a speech of extraordinary interest we take one quotation:—

The great merit of Admiral Sir David Beatty's action is that it shows us and the world that there is at present no reason to assume that ship for ship, gun for gun, and man for man we cannot give a very good account of ourselves. It shows that at five to four in representative ships—because the quality of the ships on either side is a very fair representation of the relative qualities of the lines of battle—the Germans do not think it prudent to engage, that they accepted without doubt or hesitation their inferiority, that they thought only of flight as our men thought only of pursuit, and that they were wise in the

144

view they took, and that if they had taken any other view they would unquestionably have been destroyed. That is the cruel fact, and no falsehood—and many have been issued—no endeavour to sink by official *communiqués* vessels they could not stay to sink in war—will obscure that cruel fact. When, if ever, the great fleet sets out for the general battle, we shall hope to bring into the line a preponderance not only in quality, but in numbers, which will not be five to four, but will be something considerably greater than that.

Therefore we may consider this extra margin as an additional insurance against unexpected losses by mine and submarine, such as may at any moment occur in the preliminaries of a great sea battle. It is for these important reasons of test and trial that we must regard this action of the Dogger Bank as an important, and I think I may say satisfactory, event. The losses of the navy, although small compared to the sacrifices of the army, have been heavy. We have lost, mainly by submarines, the lives of 5,500 officers and men, and we have killed, mainly by gun fire, an equal number, which is, of course, a much larger proportion of the German forces engaged.

We have also taken in sea fighting 82 officers and 934 men prisoners of war. No British naval prisoners of war have been taken in fighting at sea by the Germans. When they had the inclination they had not the opportunity, and when they had the opportunity they had not the inclination. For the loss of these British lives we have lived through six months of this war safely and even prosperously. We have established for the time being a command of the sea such as we had never expected, such as we have never known, and such as our ancestors have never known at any other period of our history.

In the concluding words of his speech Mr. Churchill adumbrated the possibility of further naval pressure against an enemy:—

.... which, as a matter of deliberate policy, places herself outside all international obligations.

He referred especially to the imports of food, hitherto unhindered, and his prognostication was soon verified.

From the beginning of the struggle merchandise which was not contraband of war had been allowed to pass into Germany in neutral vessels. But on the 26th of January the German Government announced their intention of seizing all stocks of corn and flour, and forbade all private transactions as from that morning. This meant that grain had become a munition of war, for it was no longer possible to distinguish between imports for the civilian population and for the army in the field. Accordingly the British Government had to revise its practice. The American steamer *Wilhelmina*, laden with a cargo of food-stuffs for Germany, was stopped at Falmouth, and the case referred to the Prize Courts. In this policy Britain did not depart from the traditional principles of international practice. She did not propose to seize non-contraband goods in neutral vessels. All that happened was that certain goods, which are normally non-contraband, were now made contraband by the action of Germany.

The economic and legal bearing of these events will be discussed in a later chapter. Here it is sufficient to note the actual consequences. Germany, much perturbed by the unforeseen results of her declaration, attempted to modify it by announcing that imports of food would not be used for military purposes; but such a declaration could not be accepted by Britain, for it was not possible in practice. Then in a fit of fury Germany took the bold step of declaring war against all British merchandise—war which would follow none of the old rules, for it would be conducted by submarines, who had no facilities, even if they had the disposition, to rescue the crews. She further announced that from 18th February onward the waters around the British Isles would be considered a war region, and that any enemy merchant vessels found there "would be destroyed without its always being possible to warn the crew or passengers of the dangers threatening." The sea passage north of the Shetlands and the coastal waters of the Netherlands were declared to be exempt from this menace.

The "blockade" of Britain was not really a blockade in any technical sense. Germany merely specified certain tracts of water in which she proposed to commit acts which were forbidden by every code of naval warfare. In 1806 Napoleon had issued an earlier Berlin Decree, in which he proclaimed the British Isles to be in a state of blockade. He could not enforce it, and British trade, so far from suffering, actually increased in the ensuing years. But Napoleon, though he used the word "blockade" improperly, sought his purpose by means which were not repugnant to the ethics of civilized war. Germany, utterly incapable of a real blockade, could only succeed by jettisoning her last remnants of decency. An inferior boxer may get an advantage over a strong opponent if he gouges out his eyes.

The German announcement not unnaturally gave serious concern to neutral nations, especially to America. Germany had warned them that neutral ships might perish in the general holocaust, and their anxiety was increased by an incident which happened on 6th February. The ill-fated Cunarder *Lusitania*, which had a number of Americans on board, arrived at Liverpool flying the American flag. Such a use in emergencies is a recognised practice of war—one of Paul Jones's lieutenants passed successfully through the British Channel Fleet by hoisting British colours—and the British Foreign Office was justified in defending the custom. But clearly if it was made habitual it would greatly increase the risks of neutrals, and America had some grounds for her request that it should not be used "frequently and deliberately."

The next step of the British Government was to close absolutely to all ships of all nations the greater part of the North Channel leading from the Atlantic to the Irish Sea. Then on 1st March Mr. Asquith announced in the House of Commons that the Allies held themselves free to detain and take into port all ships carrying goods of presumed enemy origin, ownership, or destination. No neutral vessel which sailed from a German port after 1st March would be allowed to proceed, and no vessel after that date would be suffered to sail to any German port. It was not proposed to confiscate such vessels or their contents; but they would be.; detained. Such an announcement implied the strict blockade of Germany, and was defended by Mr. Asquith not as a fulfilment of, but as a departure from, international law upon the subject.

It was, in his view, a legitimate retaliation against a foe which had broken not only every international rule but every moral obligation. Clearly it could not be an "effective" blockade in the strictest sense, and this we shall consider later. But here it may be noted that it was at least as effective as the blockade proclaimed by the North in the American Civil War, when a highly-indented coast-line of 3,000 miles was watched by only twelve ships.

Before 18th February, the day of destiny, German submarines had been busy against our merchant men. They had succeeded from the beginning of the year in sinking eight, and they had been wholly unscrupulous in their proceedings, as was proved by the attack off Havre upon the hospital ship *Asturias*. By 24th February they had sunk seven more, by 10th March another four, by 17th March another eight, by 24th March another three, by 31st March another three. If we take the total arrivals and sailings of oversea steamers of all nationalities above 300 tons to and from ports in the United Kingdom during that period, we shall find that the losses work out at about three per thousand. It was not a brilliant achievement. The mountain which had been in travail with awesome possibilities brought forth an inconsiderable mouse. The "blockade" hindered the sailing of scarcely a British ship. It did not raise the price of any necessary by a farthing.

But it effectively ruined what was left of Germany's reputation in the eyes of the civilized world, and it increased, if increase were needed, the determination of the Allies to make an end of this crazy international anarchism. Some of the commanders of the German submarines—notably Captain von Weddigen, who lost his life—went about the business as decently as their orders allowed. Others, such as the miscreant who sank the *Falaba*, torpedoed the vessel before the passengers were in the boats, and jeered at the drowning. In the German Navy, as in the German Army, humanity depended upon the idiosyncrasies of individual commanders, for it had no place in the official traditions. It is a curious comment upon Baron Marschall von Bieberstein's proud boast at the Hague:—

> The officers of the German Navy, I say it with emphasis will always fulfil in the strictest manner duties which flow from the unwritten law of humanity and civilization.

The "Konigin Luise" sunk by H.M.S. "Amphion"

H.M.S. "Amphion" hitting a mine from the "Konigin Luise" it had sunk the day before.

Turkey at War

On 29th October, 1914, Turkey's many breaches of international etiquette, of which her behaviour in regard to the *Goeben* and *Breslau*, and her summary abolition of the Capitulations were the chief, culminated in definite acts of war. A horde of Bedouins invaded the Sinai Peninsula and occupied the wells of Magdala, and three Turkish torpedo boats raided Odessa, sank and damaged several ships, and bombarded the town. On the 30th the ambassadors of the Allies had interviews with the *grand vizier,* which Sir Louis Mallet described as "painful." The *sultan*, the *grand vizier*, and Djavid Bey were in favour of peace, but Enver and his colleagues overruled them. The Odessa incident was justified by a cock-and-bull story of prior Russian hostilities, and nothing remained for the ambassadors but to ask for their passports. On 1st November Sir Louis Mallet left Constantinople, and the century-old friendship of Britain and Turkey was rudely broken.

The Turkish Army was based nominally on a universal conscription, but in practice only the Mussulman population was drawn upon; not all of that, indeed, for the Arabs were more usually opposed to than incorporated in the Turkish ranks. The conscript served for twenty years—nine in the First Line (Nizam), nine in the Active Reserve (Redif), and two in the Territorial Militia (Mustafiz). The major unit was the army corps of three divisions, each division embracing ten battalions. The artillery, which had suffered severely in the Balkan wars, was patchy and largely out of date, though in recent months Germany and Austria had strengthened it with a number of heavy batteries. The peace strength of the army was, roughly, 17,000 officers and 250,000 men, and in war some total like 800,000 might have been looked for, provided equipment was forthcoming.

The commander-in-chief was Enver Bey, and the German Military Mission under General Liman von Sanders had practically taken

Peace Distribution of Turkish Army Corps.

(The 14th Corps has no Territorial Bas:)

over the duties of a General Staff. The German system of "inspections" had been instituted—four in number, with headquarters at Constantinople, Damascus, Erzhingian, and Bagdad. The fourteen army corps were distributed in peace throughout the Empire at strategic points. The 1st, 2nd, 3rd, and 4th were nominally stationed in Europe—at Constantinople, Adrianople, Kirk Kilisse, and Rodosto; but they drew most of their reserves from Asia Minor. The 5th, 6th, 7th, and 8th belonged to the Damascus "inspection;" the 9th, 10th, and 11th were in Armenia and the Caucasus, the 12th at Mosul, and the 13th at Bagdad, while the 14th Corps had no territorial basis. On the outbreak of war these corps were reshuffled, six apparently having been concentrated around the Sea of Marmora.

The Turkish infantryman had for many years a high reputation as a soldier—especially, as he showed at Plevna, in a stubborn defensive. His physique was good, his nerves steady, and his power of endurance incredible. But in recent wars his fame had suffered a certain eclipse. He had been badly led and badly armed, the commissariat and transport had been rudimentary, and successive defeats were believed to have shaken his morale. The truth seems to be that Turkey had fallen between two stools. Her ill-provided levies in the past had fought desperately under brilliant officers, because they were inspired by a simple trust in their religion and their leaders and a genuine patriotic devotion. An attempt had been made to engraft upon this tradition the mechanical perfection of the German system. But the Turk is not meant by Providence to be a soldier of the German type, and the seed of Marshal von der Goltz and General Liman von Sanders was sown in barren soil. The consequence was a machine without precision and without motive power.

The Turk had been at his best when he fought for Islam and the Padishah; but Islam was inconspicuous in the ideals of the new Committee, the old Padishah was somewhere in exile, and the new one too patently a cipher. In addition, he could have little confidence in men who had already led him to disaster, and who had caused him to endure needless and horrible privations. A perfect machine is a mighty thing, but an imperfect machine is so much scrap iron. The Turkish soldier was now an incomplete German, which is like a gun lacking the breech-block. It is impossible to withhold our sympathy from a brave race going out to battle in a cause which they neither liked nor understood, from an army in the grip of an unfamiliar and imperfect machine, from a nation sacrificed to a muddled *Weltpolitik*. Disaster loomed large in its horoscope, but courage never failed it; and the time was to come when the machine went to pieces, and, amid the snows of the Caucasus or the sands of the desert, the children of Osman, fighting once more in the old fashion, died without fear or complaint.

The beginning of war found Turkey with a curious strategical problem before her. Europe was the chief interest of her leaders. She hankered to recover the lost provinces of Thrace, and there she looked for her reward when her allies emerged victorious. But, so long as Greece and Bulgaria remained neutral, there was no room for an offensive in Europe and no need of a defensive. Accordingly she was free to move the bulk of her corps to those frontiers where she faced directly the belligerents. The chief was Transcaucasia, where, in a wild cluster of mountains, she looked across the gorges at Russia. An offensive in Transcaucasia was what Germany and Austria urgently desired. Russia, they knew, had none too many equipped men, and a diversion on her flank would draw troops from that thin line, a thousand miles long, which she held from the Niemen to the Dniester. Against Britain, too, Turkey might use her armies with effect.

An attack upon the Suez Canal would precipitate the long-expected Egyptian rebellion, and would at the worst detain the Australian and Indian troops now training there, and at the best compel Britain to send out as reinforcements some of her still scanty reserves. Further, it would bar the short road to India, and give the flame of Indian insurrection time to kindle. But the great chance of fermenting Indian trouble, in the certainty of which Germany still firmly believed, lay in the scheme now coming to a head on the Persian Gulf. German agents had been busy among the Gulf traders, and elaborate preparations had been made for undermining the virtue of the Amir of Afghanistan, and for preaching a *Jehad* among the Mussulman tribes of the Indian north-west. Turkey believed that she had little to fear in the way of attack. The Russians were too busily engaged elsewhere to penetrate far west from the frosty Caucasus, while Britain had enough to do in Flanders without attempting an advance into Syria or Mesopotamia. The one serious danger-point in a war with a great naval Power was the Dardanelles; but Enver and his colleagues were confident that the penetration of these Straits, long ago pronounced by experts a task of the utmost difficulty, had been rendered impossible for all time by the heavy guns which Krupp and Skoda had so diligently provided.

The fighting on the Suez Canal must be reserved for a later chapter. Here we propose to consider only the campaign on Turkey's eastern frontier—in Transcaucasia and in Persia. The latter comes first in order

BRITISH TROOPS ON THE ADVANCE IN MESOPOTAMIA. 1914

of time. Turkey had shown her hand since the last week of August, and Russia and Britain had anticipated the events of 30th October. On the Persian Gulf the Ottoman troops found their offensive forestalled by a British invasion.

The Persian Gulf is one of the oldest of Britain's fields of activity. Englishmen, looking for trade, visited it in the reign of Elizabeth. In its early days the East India Company established a party at Bundar Abbas, and fought stoutly with Dutch and Portuguese rivals for the better part of two centuries. The Indian navy first began the survey of the Gulf, and looked to its lighting. For fifty years we hunted down the pirates and cleared out their strongholds on the Pirate Coast. We protected Persia against those who would have deprived her of a seaboard, we policed the waters, we suppressed slavery and gun-running, we wrestled with the plague, and introduced the rudiments of sanitation in the marshy estuaries. For three hundred years we did this work for the benefit of the shipping of all nations, since we claimed no monopoly and desired no perquisites. All we took in return was a fraction of an island for a telegraph station. One thing, indeed, we asked, and that was a matter of life and death, on which compromise was impossible. No other Power should be allowed to seize territory, and no other flag should dominate those land-locked waters. For with our prestige in the Persian Gulf was bound up the future of India and of the Empire.

Before ever the Turkish crescent appeared on the shore of Arabia, Britain had shown her flag in the Gulf. In the sixteenth century Suleiman the Magnificent had captured Bagdad, but it was not till 1638 that the conquest was confirmed, and not till 1668 that Turkey reached Basra and the sea-coast. For the next two centuries the writ of Constantinople ran haltingly on the western shores or not at all. The rise of the Wahabis threatened the Turkish power, and all through the nineteenth century Eastern Arabia was the scene of a rivalry between the great Wahabi houses of Ibn Saud and Ibn Rashid, a rivalry in which the *khalif* did dare to interfere. At Koweit and at Bahrein lived independent sheikhs, and not all the efforts of Midhat Pasha could turn that coast into a Turkish province. The Gulf shores, baked and barren, and hot as a furnace, were a museum of types of incomplete sovereignty and *de facto* rule. But out on the waters lay British warships which kept the peace.

To this happy hunting-ground the eyes of Germany turned. Persia was a decrepit state, Turkey was moribund, and in Mesopotamia she saw a chance of finding a field for exploitation which would make it

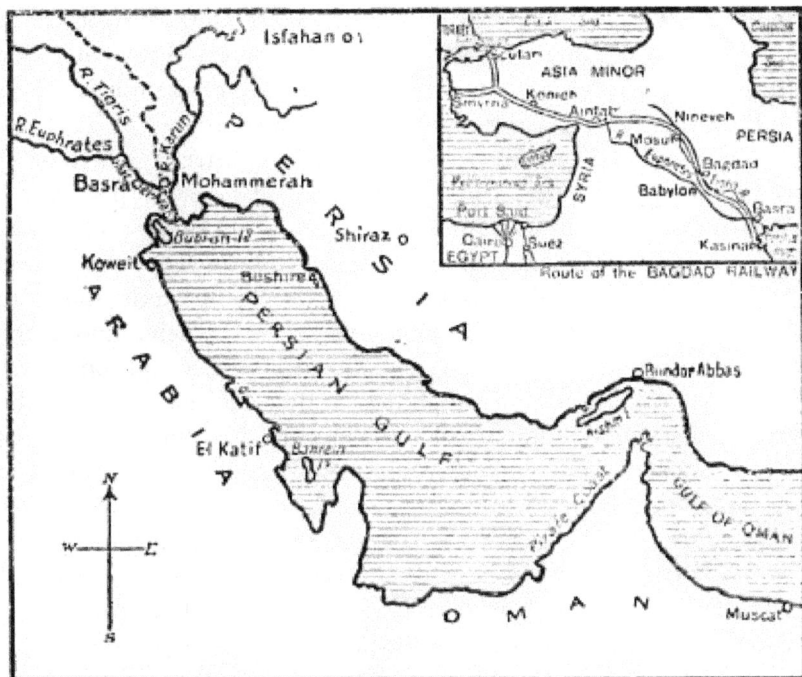

The Persian Gulf.

for Germany what Egypt was to Britain and Morocco to France. German professors told excited audiences that a thousand years ago the land had supported six million people, and that what had once been might be again. If Germany won a foothold on the Gulf, not only would she have the exploiting of Mesopotamia, but she would have weakened the British hold upon India. To secure this end Turkey must be conciliated, and the long tale of intrigue began which we have noted in previous chapters. Her trump card was the Bagdad railway, the full history of which, when it comes to be written, will fascinate the world. Suffice it to say that in 1899 a German company, backed by the Deutsche Bank, obtained a concession from the Porte to build a railway from Konieh, then the terminus of the little Anatolian railway, to Bagdad and Basra on the Persian Gulf.

The concession was made valuable by a Turkish guarantee of the interest on the cost of construction at the rate of 700 per kilometre per annum. Britain awoke somewhat late in the day to the political purport of the new railway, and a diplomatic conflict began which was still in progress at the outbreak of war. Germany had followed the practice of that Lord of Breadalbane who built his castle on the extreme confines of his land with the avowed intention of "*birsing yont.*" Her "*yont*" was Koweit, on the actual Gulf shores, and she persuaded Turkey into various pretensions to suzerainty, which the watchful eyes of the British agents detected in time and frustrated.

Meantime she was busy at her old game of "peaceful penetration." A certain firm, Wonckhaus by name,[1] played here the part which Woermann played in West Africa and Luderitz in Damaraland. A simple, spectacled gentleman in white ducks and a *topi* appears on the beach in quest of pearl shells. From a modest shanty on the foreshore he directs his operations, and spends freely money which cannot come out of his profits. Presently arrives a German consul, and soon there are little tiffs between the employees of the shell merchant and the natives, which give the consul something to do. Quickly the business grows, but not on commercial lines. Then comes the Hamburg-Amerika line, playing national airs and dispensing sweet champagne, and the spectacled gentleman is revealed as its accredited agent.

Very soon the innocent traders go concession hunting, and call upon Turkey to ratify their claims under a pretence of *suzerainty.* Then Britain interferes, reveals the hollowness of the business, and puts her veto on the game. But next week it begins all over again elsewhere. Colonel Sir Percy Cox, the British Agent and Consul-General on the Gulf, had a task scarcely less difficult than that of Lord Cromer in the early days in Egypt, and he performed it with a patience, judgment, and resolution which deserved well of his country.

By the beginning of November the British in the Gulf were ready for the offensive. The Government of India had sent the Poona Brigade,[2] under Brigadier-General W. S. Delamain, to Bahrein. On 7th November the force reached the bar of the Shat-el-Arab, where the village of Fao, with its Turkish fort, lies among the flats and palm groves. The gunboat *Odin* bombarded the fort, and troops landed and occupied the village. The brigade then sailed thirty miles up the estuary, passing the refinery of the Anglo-Persian Oil Company at Abadan, and disembarked at Sanijeh, on the Turkish bank, where it prepared an entrenched camp, and sat down to wait for the rest of the British

---

1. A brilliant account of the doings of Wonckhaus, by an authority of the first rank, will be found in Chapter LII. of the *Times' History of the War.* It should be studied by anyone who desires to realize the exceeding patience and ingenuity of German methods.

2. The brigade contained the 2nd Dorsets, the 20th (Punjab) Infantry, the 104th (Wellesley's) Rifles, the 117th Mahrattas, and the 23rd (Peshawur) and 30th Mountain Batteries.

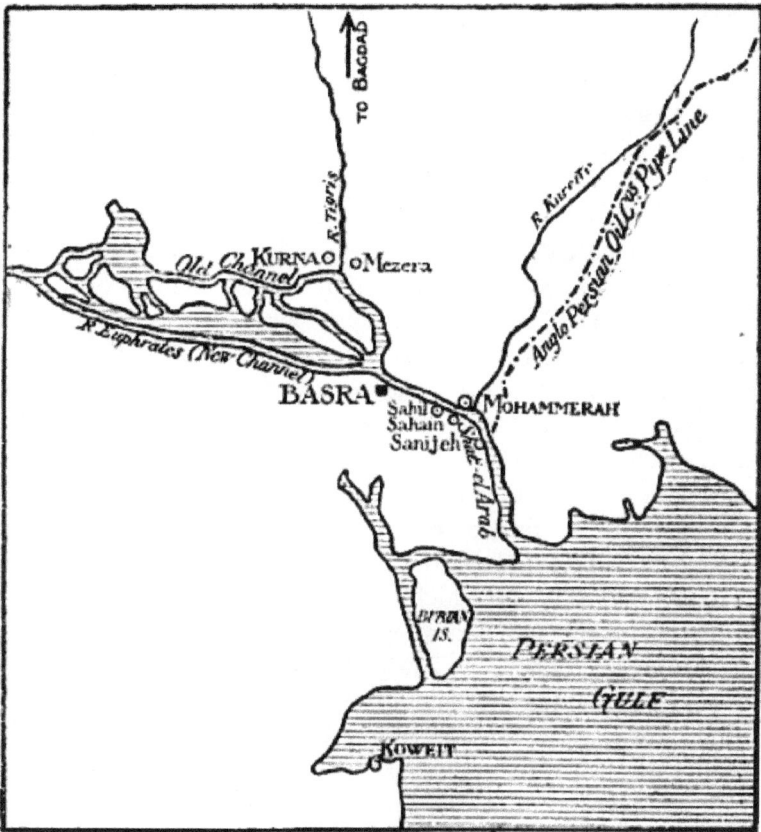

Basra and Kurna.

force. Here, on the 11th, there was some fighting with the Turks from Basra, who were dislodged from a neighbouring village by the 117th Mahrattas and the 20th Punjabis. Two days later Lieutenant-General Sir Arthur Barrett arrived with the rest of the Indian contingent—the Ahmednagar Brigade and the Belgaum Brigade.[3]

On the 15th the disembarkation of the remainder began—no light task on the soft, muddy banks of the Shat-el-Arab. Meanwhile General Delamain with the Poona Brigade was busy with a force of 2,000 Turks, who held the village of Sahain, four miles to the northward. The action was meant only as a reconnaissance in force, and Sahain

3. The Ahmednagar Brigade (Brigadier-General W. H. Bobbie) contained the 1st Oxford Light Infantry, the 119th Infantry, and the 103rd Mahrattas. The Belgaum Brigade (Brigadier-General C. I. Fry) contained the 2nd Norfolks, the 110th Mahrattas, the 7th Rajputs, and the 120th (Rajputana) Infantry. There were also the 48th Pioneers, the 3rd Sappers and Miners, and the 33rd Light Cavalry.

and the date plantation beyond it were not entirely cleared. During that day the landing was completed, and on the 16th the British force rested. News arrived that the Basra garrison was advancing to give battle; and since there were Europeans in the city whose fate might depend upon a speedy British arrival, General Barrett ordered the advance for the early morning of the 17th.

Sahain was found to be deserted, and we moved on for nine miles to a place called Sahil, near the river, where was the main Turkish force. The ground was open plain, and heavy rains in the morning had turned the deep soil into a marsh. The fight began with an artillery preparation, both from the British field guns and from gunboats on the river. The Turkish fire was bad, but they were screened by a date grove, and the country over which we advanced was as bare as a billiard table. Under a punishing fire our men never wavered, the Dorsets especially behaving with admirable coolness and decision. The enemy did not wait for the final bayonet charge, but broke and fled. Pursuit was well-nigh impossible, partly because of the heavy ground, and partly owing to a mirage which, fortunately for the enemy, appeared to screen his flight. Our losses were 353, of which 130 were in the Dorsets. Our killed were 38. The Turkish casualties were estimated at over 1,500. The action decided the fate of Basra.

On the 21st, while the bulk of our force lay at Sanijeh, news came that the Turks had evacuated Basra, and that the Arabs had begun to r loot the place. Accordingly General Barrett embarked certain troops on two river steamers, and ordered the rest of his forces to take the direct road across the desert. The Turks had sunk three steamers at one point in the Shatel-Arab, and had a battery to command the place, but after silencing the battery the river expedition managed to pass the obstruction early on the morning of the 22nd. About ten o'clock General Barrett reached Basra, where the Turkish Custom House had been set on fire, and the British flag was flown on the German consulate. The desert column, after a thirty mile march, came in about midday. Next day the British formally entered the city of Sindbad the Sailor.

During the remainder of the month we were occupied in preparing a base camp. Our position was secure, but it was certain that we would be subjected to further attack. The enemy had fled at Sahil, but he would return, and the great military station of Bagdad was little more than three hundred miles distant. Fifty miles above Basra, at the point where the former channel of the Euphrates joins the Tigris, lies the town of Kurna—a position now of less strategical importance than in former days, for the old Euphrates is little use for traffic Kurna is the point where ocean-going steamers can no longer ascend the river. On 2nd December we heard that the Turks had reassembled there, and next day a small force of Indian troops, with a detachment of the Norfolks under Lieutenant-Colonel Frazer, was sent upstream to deal with them, accompanied by three gunboats, an armed yacht, and two armed launches.

Kurna proved to be a more difficult business than was expected. The British force landed on the eastern bank four miles below the town early on the morning of the 4th, while the gunboats went ahead, shelled Kurna, and engaged the Turkish artillery on the east bank of the Tigris near Mezera, about ten miles above the town. Meanwhile the British column advanced, and about midday came abreast of Kurna, which was clearly held in force. Our men were subjected to a heavy fusillade, and since the Tigris is there three hundred yards wide, and Kurna is screened in trees, we could do little in reply. Accordingly Colonel Frazer led his troops back to the original camp, which he had strongly entrenched, and sent a message to Basra for reinforcements.

Nothing happened on the 5th, and on the 6th General Fry appeared with help—the 7th Rajputs and the rest of the Norfolks. On the 7th we advanced against Mezera, which the Turks had again occupied, took it, and drove the defenders across the water to Kurna, while our naval flotilla was busy on the river. It was now decided to take Kurna in the rear; so, early on the 8th, the 104th and 110th were marched some miles up the Tigris. A body of sappers swam the stream with a line, and with the aid of a *dhow* a kind of ferry was established, and our men crossed. By the evening the force was close to Kurna, entrenched among the trees north of the city.

But there was to be no assault. That night Turkish officers approached the British camp downstream and asked for terms. General Fry insisted upon an unconditional surrender, and just after midday next day the Turkish garrison laid down their arms. We had now obtained complete control of the whole delta, and we made entrenched camps at Kurna and Mezera on each side of the Tigris, to hold off any possible attack from the north. Turkish troops from Bagdad hovered around, and in January there were 5,000 of them seven miles from Mezera; but they offered no serious attack. We had achieved our purpose, and established a barricade against any advance upon the Gulf which might threaten India.

The Frontiers of Turkey, Persia, and Russia.

Farther north on Turkey's eastern frontier the war was with Russia alone. A glance at the map will show that the Russian Caucasian border has on the south Persia for two-thirds of its length and Turkey for one-third. Since Persia was a negligible military Power, this meant that North-western Persia gave each of the belligerents a chance of turning the flank of the other. The Persian province of Azerbaijan had, therefore, during the recent troubled years been occupied in parts by both Russian and Turkish troops, and when war broke out it was certain that this locality would be a scene of fighting. South of Lake Urmia the Turks took the offensive. A Kurdish force advanced by way of Suj Balak upon Tabriz, and meeting with no resistance from the Persian governor, took that city in the beginning of January, and moved some way northwards towards the Russian frontier. Russia, who had left no troops to speak of in Tabriz, soon repaired her omission, and having heavily defeated the invaders at Sufian, reoccupied Tabriz on 30th January.

In this unimportant section of the campaign we have to chronicle two other movements where Russia was the invader. Early in November a Russian column, assisted by the tribesmen of Maku, crossed the Turkish frontier from the extreme north-west corner of Persia, and occupied on 3rd November the ancient town of Bayazid, which lies under the snows of Ararat, on the great trade-route between Persia and the Euxine. Other columns entered Kurdistan from the east, and a movement was begun against Van. Farther north, and fifty miles west from Bayazid, another Russian column from Erivan crossed the frontier in the neighbourhood of the Alashgird valley. The town of Kara Kilisse was taken, but the Turks under Hassan ed Din Pasha—part of the Bagdad 13th Corps—showed a vigorous defensive, and held the invaders on the borders. The struggle died away towards the beginning of January, when the disaster in the Caucasus compelled a general retreat of the Turkish frontier guards upon Erzerum.

We come now to the vital part of the Eastern campaign the struggle in Transcaucasia, upon which Germany built all her hopes and Enver expended all his energy. The main features of the district are sufficiently familiar. The great range of the Caucasus, which contains the highest of European mountains, runs from the Black Sea to the Caspian, blocking the isthmus much as the Pyrenees block the neck between the Bay of Biscay and the Mediterranean. South-west of the range is a huge trough running nearly all the way to the two seas. Here stands Tiflis, the ancient capital of Georgia, and through it runs the main railway of those parts, from Batum on the Black Sea to Baku on the Caspian. On the south-west side of the trough lies the mountain tangle of Transcaucasia, midway in which comes the Russian frontier. A railway runs from Tiflis past the fortress of Kars to a terminus at Sarikamish, fifteen miles from the Turkish border, while another line runs from Alexandropol by Erivan to the Persian frontier.

Erzerum, the Turkish fortress, stands about the same distance from the frontier as Kars, but it is on no railway, and has none nearer than about five hundred miles. The mountain ranges extend north to the shores of the Black Sea, and south into Persia and Kurdistan. The whole district is one vast upland, most of the villages and towns standing at an altitude of 5,000 and 6,000 feet, and the hills rising as high again. All the passes are lofty, and in winter well-nigh impassable; none of the roads are good, and, as we have seen, there is no railway on the Turkish side, and but one that matters on the Russian. Winter campaigning there was likely to be as desperate as Xenophon's Ten Thousand had found it.

It is an old theatre of war since the days of Cyrus and Alexander, and whenever Russia and Turkey have faced each other it has been the cockpit of the struggle. There, in 1853, Shamyl led his mountaineers. There, two years later, Fenwick Williams held Kars against Muraviev in one of the greatest stands in modern history. There, in 1877, Loris Melikov and Mukhtar met, and Kars and Ardahan and Bayazid were the scenes of desperate conflicts. If Kars could be seized, the way would be open to Tiflis and the Caspian oil fields—perhaps even across the great Caucasus itself to the levels of Southern Russia. To the leaders of a race which have always been famous as mountain fighters the offensive in the Caucasus seemed the easiest way of effecting that diversion which Germany had commissioned.

Enver's strategy was ambitious to the point of madness, but it was skilful after a fashion. He resolved to entice the Russians from Sarikamish across the frontier, and to hold them at some point as far distant as possible from the railhead. Then, while thus engaged, he would swing his left centre in a wide enveloping movement against Sarikamish, and with his left push round by Ardahan and take Kars in the rear. The device has been generally described as the ordinary German enveloping movement, but it has also affinities with the Napoleonic "pivoting square." To succeed, two things were necessary. The force facing the Russian front must be strong enough to hold it while the envelopment was going on; and the operative part, the left wing, must

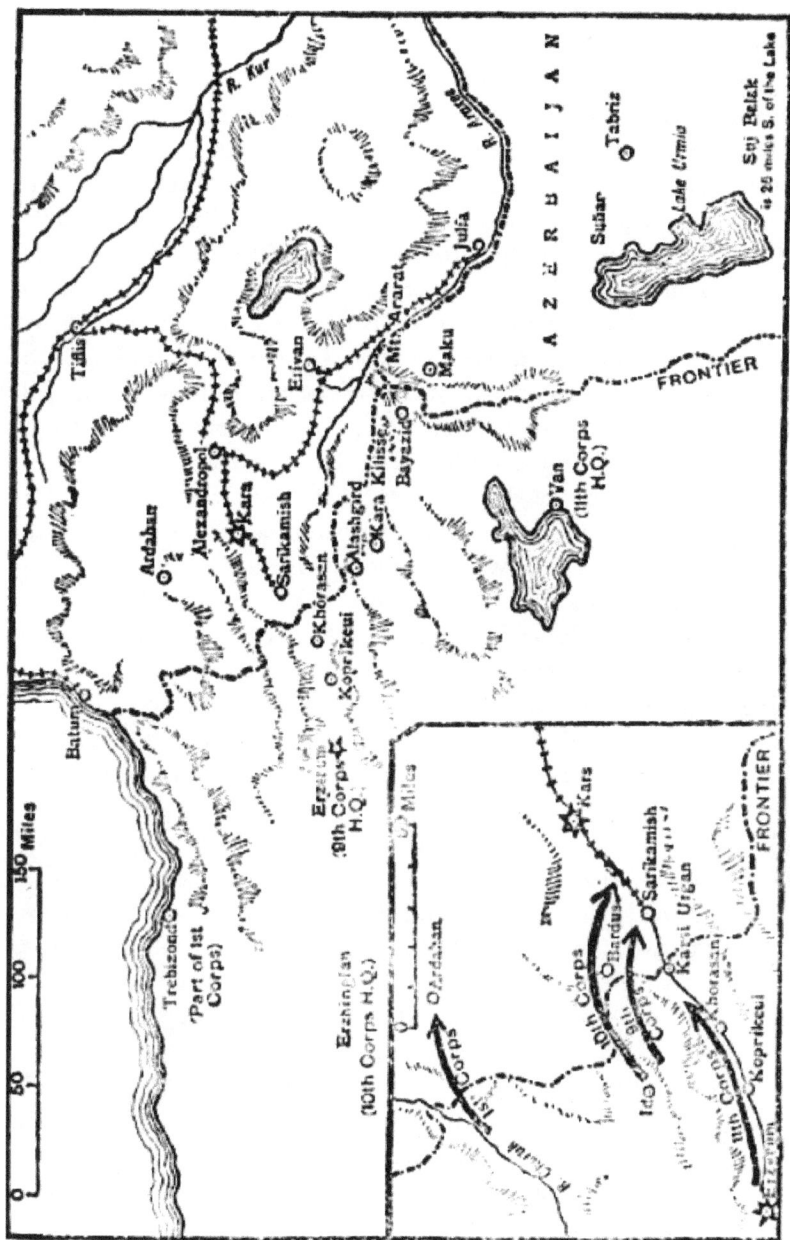

The Campaign on the Caucasian Frontier.

(Inset—The Turkish Advance.)

be correctly timed in its movements, for otherwise the Russians would be able to destroy it piecemeal. It was this "timing" which formed the real difficulty. The swing round of the left must be made by a variety of mountain paths and over necks and valleys deep in snow, where progress in winter must be tardy and precarious. To "time" such a plan accurately was beyond the wits of any mortal General Staff.

For the Caucasian campaign Turkey had the 9th, 10th, and 11th Corps—stationed in peace respectively at Erzerum, Erzhingian, and Van—which had been concentrated at Erzerum about the middle of October. To reinforce the 11th Corps, the 37th Arab division had been brought up from the 13th Bagdad Corps. For the movement on the extreme left two divisions of the 1st Corps had been brought by sea from Constantinople to Trebizond. Turkey could obviously get no reserves in case of disaster. The nearest corps, the 12th, at Mosul, had gone to Syria, and the remainder of the Bagdad Corps had its hands full with the British in the Persian Gulf. The nominal commander of the Caucasian Army was Hassan Izzet Pasha, but Enver was present as the real *generalissimo*, and he had with him a large German staff. A German, Posseld Pasha, was appointed Governor of Erzerum. The total Turkish strength was not less than 150,000, and they had against them the army of General Woronzov, which cannot at the outside have been more than three corps strong say 100,000 men.

Fighting began in the first fortnight of November, when the Russians crossed the frontier and reached Koprikeui on the Erzerum road, which, after a great deal of trouble they occupied on 20th November. The time was now ripe for Enver's plan. The 11th Corps was entrusted with the duty of holding the Russian advance on Erzerum. The 10th Corps at Id was to advance in two columns over the passes by Bardus against the road between Kars and Sarikamish, with the 9th Corps wheeling between it and the 11th. At the same time the 1st Corps, which had landed at Trebizond, was to move up the Choruk valley across a pass 8,000 feet high, take Ardahan, and advance over somewhat easier country to the railway between Kars and Alexandropol. The difficulty about the whole scheme was the roads. The only real way for an army through the Armenian heights is by the high trough in which lie Kars and Sarikamish, and thence westwards to the upper valleys of the Araxes and Euphrates. Everywhere else the paths were tracks, now blind with snow, and hopeless for artillery.

The Turkish offensive began about the middle of December. The 11th Corps pushed the Russians out of Koprikeui and forced them back a dozen miles to Khorasan, where, on Christmas Day, the retreat halted. The Russian Army was now strung out along the thirty miles of the road from Khorasan to Sarikamish. Meanwhile, in desperate weather, the 9th and 10th Corps forty miles north had struggled over the high watersheds, and by Christmas Day had descended upon Sarikamish and on the railway east of it. The 1st Corps on the extreme Turkish left was crossing in a blizzard the steeps at the head of the Choruk, and already looking down through the pauses of the storm on where Ardahan lay in its deep pocket of hills. If we take 28th December as a view-point, we find the Russian van held by the 11th Turkish Corps at Khorasan, the 9th Corps at Sarikamish, and the 10th east along the Kars railway, threatening to pierce the Russian front, and sixty miles north-east the 1st Corps descending upon Ardahan. It looked as if Enver's ambitious project had succeeded.

But the attacking force was worn out, half starved, and short of guns and ammunition, for no transport on earth could cope with such a breakneck march. The Russian general dealt first with the 10th Corps. From 28th December to 1st January there was a fierce struggle on the railway, which late on New Year's Day resulted in the defeat of the Turks and their retreat into the hills to the north. This withdrawal isolated the 9th Corps at Sarikamish, which was now enclosed between the Russian right, flung well forward in pursuit of the 10th Corps, and the Russian vanguard at Khorasan. That corps was utterly wiped out. Its general, Iskan Pasha, with all his staff, Turkish and German, surrendered after a gallant and fruitless stand. The Turks fought with their old stolidity till hunger and cold were too much for them, and they surrendered as much to the Russian field kitchens as to the Russian steel. Meanwhile the 1st Corps, which had entered Ardahan on New Year's Day, found that it could go no farther. On 3rd January a detached Russian force drove it out of the town, back over the ridges to the Choruk valley, whither the flight of the 10th Corps was also heading.

The 11th Corps at Khorasan did its best to redeem the disaster. It could not save the 9th Corps, but it might cover the retreat of the 10th, and accordingly it pushed back the Russian van from Khorasan, and advanced as far as Karai Urgan, some twenty miles from Sarikamish. It achieved its purpose, for the pursuit of the 10th Corps was relaxed, and the bulk of the Russian Army went westwards to reinforce the van. At Karai Urgan a three days' battle was fought among snowdrifts, and by the 17th the 11th Corps had been broken also, and, with heavy losses in men and guns, was retreating upon Erzerum. Meanwhile the 1st Corps and the remnant of the 10th were cleared from the Choruk valley by the Russian right, and driven towards Trebizond. The Turkish navy, which attempted to send stores and reinforcements by sea, was no more fortunate, for the several transports and provision boats were sunk along the coast by Russian warships, and the *Breslau* and the *Hamidieh* were hunted home by the Black Sea Fleet. The *Goeben* had been for some weeks out of action.

So ended Enver's bold diversion. It had failed signally because his reach exceeded his grasp, as has happened before with adventurers. The three weeks of desperate conflict amid snowdrifts and blizzards— for the battlefields were scarcely less than 8,000 feet high—must have accounted for not less than 50,000 of Turkey's strength. Badly led and ill equipped, the starving Turkish levies had fought like heroes, and their sufferings were among the most terrible of the war. The Battle of Sarikamish—to localise the series of engagements—made certain that Russia would not be menaced from the Caucasus. Turkey must look elsewhere to find the joint in the armour of the Allies.

The Situation in Egypt

The story of Egypt is the romance of politics; but this is not the place to describe at length its slow and varied drama. For that the reader must consult the works of Lord Cromer and Lord Milner, the men who were the chief actors in the piece. In 1517, forty-eight years before the Turkish invasion of Europe spent itself on the fortifications of Malta and the gallantry of the Knights of St. John, the Sultan Selim acquired Egypt by conquest; and in spite of many vicissitudes, of the weakness of Turkish rule, the ambitions of Napoleon, and the boldness of Mehemet Ali, the suzerainty of Constantinople continued. The misgovernment of Ismail and the precarious position of the Egyptian bondholders brought in the Western Powers, France and Britain, and a dual control was established over administration.

Then came the deposition of Ismail, followed by the Nationalist rising under Arabi, the bombardment of Alexandria, and the Battle of Tel-el-Kebir. To Britain fell the task of restoring order, and British occupation began. There succeeded the menace from the Sudan, the devastating advance of the *Mahdi* and his fanatical armies, the loss of the southern provinces, and the death of Gordon. *Quae caret ora cruore nostro?* is more true of Britain than of Rome, and the sands of the Nile have had the best of our British blood.

From 1885 onwards the task of the *de facto* rulers of Egypt was twofold—the reconquest of the Sudan, and the elevation of the Nile valley from bankruptcy to prosperity. The first was accomplished in 1898, when Lord Kitchener, at the Battles of the Atbara and Omdurman, shattered the Dervish levies. The second, in the hands of Lord Cromer, progressed yearly, in spite of international bickerings, Court intrigues, and a preposterous dualism in finance. In a multiplicity of problems there is usually, as Lord Cromer saw, one master question, the settlement of which involves the others. In the case of Egypt this was finance; and with infinite patience and perfect judgment the greatest of modern administrators first of all reduced taxation, then from his scanty balances spent wisely on reproductive works, till he had given Egypt the water which is her life, and raised the peasants from a condition of economic slavery to a comfort unknown in the Nile valley since the days of the Pharaohs. In 1904 the British occupation was formally recognized by the Powers of Europe, and the Egyptian finances were released from the bondage of international control.

With prosperity came political activity, and with political activity its degenerate offspring, the demagogue. Lord Cromer handled the thing discreetly, providing means for the expression of popular opinion, and giving to the Egyptians as large a share in the administration of their land as was compatible with efficiency. He devoted himself, too, to educational schemes, with excellent results. His successor, Sir Eldon Gorst, came at a time when, both in Turkey and Persia, Liberal movements were beginning, and it fell to him to make a further experiment in meeting the wishes of Egyptian Nationalists. British control was reduced to a minimum, and Egyptian ministers were given a large responsibility. The venture was not altogether successful, for the *khedive* was there to turn Nationalism into a Court intrigue, and the attempt to "Liberalise" Egypt resulted in the reappearance of some of the old abuses.

The advent of Lord Kitchener found the Nationalist movement a good deal discredited, and his brilliant years of office represented a return to something like paternal government. He knew the East as few living men knew it, and he speedily acquired the confidence and admiration of all classes of the population. Under him there was no sudden attempt to Westernize institutions, but a continuation of the patient and gradual adjustment and remodelling which had been Lord Cromer's policy:

> The counsels to which Time hath not been called, Time will not ratify.

Germany, as we have seen, looked on Egypt as a nursery of sedition. She had considered carefully events like that at Denshawai and the wilder speeches of the demagogues; and with her curious inability to look below the surface of things, she had jumped to the conclusion that democracy and Islam and Chauvinism would combine to produce an explosion. But the truth was that the ordinary Egyptian was perfectly content, and had no grievance; while in the Sudan the war awoke an extraordinary enthusiasm for the British cause, led by a descendant of the Prophet and the eldest son of the *Mahdi*. Let Lord Cromer speak:—

> Why is it that the appeals to religious zeal and fanaticism made by the Turkish militarists and their German fellow-conspirators have been wholly unproductive of result, and have been answered both in Egypt and in the Sudan by the most remarkable expressions of loyalty and friendship towards the British Government? The presence of British garrisons in Cairo, Alexandria, and Khartum unquestionably counts for much in explanation of these very singular political phenomena. Something also may possibly be attributed to the fact that the more educated classes may have recognised that the Turco-Prussian regime with which they were threatened would assuredly combine many of the worst features both of Western and Eastern administration. But amongst contributory causes I have no hesitation in assigning the foremost place to the fact that no general discontent prevailed of which the agitator, the religious fanatic, or the political intriguer could make use as the lever to further his own designs.
>
> In spite of the most positive assurances that they were the victims of ruthless tyranny and oppression, the population both of Egypt and the Sudan refused to believe that they were misgoverned. And why was it that no general discontent prevailed? ... The true reason ... is, I believe, that State expenditure has been carefully controlled, and has been adapted to the financial resources of the two countries concerned, with the result that taxation has been low. It was futile to expect that the Egyptian *fellah*, or the Sudanese tribesman, would believe that he was oppressed and maltreated when the demands of the tax-gatherer not only ceased to be capricious, but were far more moderate than either he or his immediate progenitors had ever dreamed to be possible. [1]

On 17th December the Khedive Abbas II., having thrown in his lot with Turkey, ceased to reign in Egypt, which, with the assent of France, was formally proclaimed a British Protectorate. Lieutenant-Colonel Sir Arthur Henry MacMahon, a distinguished Indian political officer, was appointed High Commissioner. The title of *Khedive*,

---

1. *Abbas II.*, In the same work will be found an interesting study of the late *khedive*,

TURKISH TROOPS MUSTERING, PREPERATORY TO AN ATTACK ON THE CANAL

first adopted by Ismail, disappeared; and the throne of Egypt, with the title of Sultan, was offered to Prince Hussein Kamel Pasha, the second son of Ismail, and therefore the eldest living prince of the house of Mehemet Ali—an able and enlightened man, who had done great services to Egyptian agriculture. The change thus made was the smallest which the circumstances permitted. There was no annexation; the shadowy suzerainty of Turkey disappeared; but otherwise things remained as before.

Apparently the tribute to Constantinople still continued, since that tribute had been ear-marked for the interest on the Ottoman debt, and was paid direct to the bondholders. Protectorate is the vaguest of political terms, and may involve anything from virtual sovereignty to an almost complete detachment. In this case it meant that Britain was now wholly responsible for the defence of Egypt and for her foreign relations. The very vagueness of the arrangement had its merits, for nothing was laid down as to the order of succession to the *sultanate*, and the hands of the British Government were left free for some future revision of the whole arrangement. In the meantime it regularized an anomalous international status.

The first object of a belligerent Turkey would naturally be the Suez Canal. The Turkish force in Syria in peace time consisted of the 8th Corps of three divisions, whose headquarters were Damascus. But during November there was a large concentration in Syria, which included the bulk of the 12th Corps from Mosul, part of the 4th Corps from Adrianople, and apparently the Anatolian division normally stationed at Smyrna. Out of this force, which cannot have been less than 90,000, an Expeditionary Army of 65,000 men was created. Its commander was Djemal Pasha, the Turkish Minister of Marine, a vehement Pan-Islamist, and an inveterate enemy of Britain. The seizure of the two Ottoman Dreadnoughts building in England had embittered his mind, and he burned to wipe off the score by a blow at the Suez Canal, one of the channels by which Britain exerted her naval supremacy. He had been Governor of Bagdad and of Basra, and had been at the head of an army corps in the Balkan war. He had no particular military reputation, having won his power rather as an energetic leader of the Committee of Union and Progress than as a general in the field.

The advantages of a blow at the Suez Canal were obvious. If the eastern bank could be held the use of the canal by shipping would be endangered, and Britain cut off from one of her most vital sea routes.

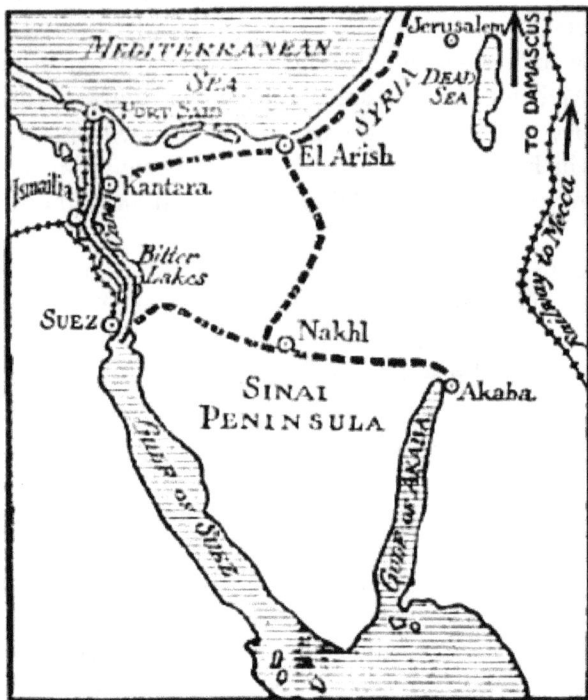

The Suez Canal and the Sinai District.

If the Canal could be crossed in force, then there was the chance of
that Egyptian rising for which the faithful of Turkey and Germany
hoped. But the difficulties were no less conspicuous. To reach the Canal from Syria an all but waterless desert had to be traversed, a stretch
varying from 120 to 150 miles in width. Across this tract of rock and
sand there were three routes, all of them hard. The first, which we may
call the northern, touched the Mediterranean coast at El Arish, and
ran across the desert to El Kantara, on the Canal, twenty-five miles
south of Port Said. It was 120 miles long, and had on its course only
a few muddy wells, quite insufficient to water an army. The southern
road ran from Akaba, at the head of the gulf of that name on the Red
Sea, across the base of the peninsula of Sinai to a point on the Canal
a little north of Suez.

This route was the old Pilgrims' Road from Egypt to Mecca; it was
150 miles long, and, like the other, ill supplied with wells. Between
the two was a possible variant which we may call the Central Route.
Leaving the Mediterranean coast at El Arish, it ran up the dry valley

Battle of the Suez Canal

called the Wady el Arish to where the upper part of that depression touched the Pilgrims' Road. Now, from the Turkish bases of Gaza and Beer-sheba there was no railway to assist an advance, and no route for motor transport; and, since an army must carry its own water, it seemed impossible for the invaders to move in force unless they laid down some sort of light railway, or so improved the roads as to make them possible for motors. The Mecca Railway, which ran to the east of Akaba, gave them no help, for between it and the escarpment of the Sinai peninsula lay two rugged limestone ridges, enclosing a trench 3,000 feet deep. The best route—indeed the only possible—for a light railway was up the Wady el Arish, but this had the disadvantage that at its debouchment on the coast it would come under fire from the sea.

The difficulties of Turkey's strategical problem were enhanced by the nature of her object of attack. The Suez Canal is not only the equivalent of a broad and deep river, but it is navigable for warships, and its banks provide superb opportunities for defence. It cannot be turned, for it runs from sea to sea. It has a width of over 200 feet, and the banks in most places rise at an angle of thirty degrees to a height of 40 feet. On its western shore a lateral railway runs the whole way from Port Said to Suez, connecting at Ismailia with the line to Cairo, and a fresh-water canal follows the same bank for three-quarters of its length, from Suez to El Kantara. Again, most of the ground to the east is flat, and offers a good field of fire to the defenders on the west bank, or to ships in the channel.

In a few places there are dunes on the east side which might give cover to an invader. Such a place is just south of El Kantara, several others are to be found south of Ismailia, and there is a small rise south of the Bitter Lakes. Any Turkish attack might therefore be looked for in the Ismailia-Bitter Lakes section. The size and composition of the British forces in Egypt at the time were rightly kept secret, for they were largely a reserve for the Allies in Western Europe. They included detachments of Indian cavalry and infantry, the Australian and New Zealand contingents under Major-General Birdwood, a number of British Territorials, among them the East Lancashire Division, as well as the regular Egyptian Army. The whole force was under the command of Major-General Sir John Maxwell, a soldier with a long experience of the Nile valley wars.

At the end of October it was reported that a force of 2,000 Bedouins was marching on Egypt, and on November 21st there was a skirmish at Katiyeh, east of the Canal, between this force or a part of it, and some of the Bikanir Camel Corps under Captain Chope. Previous to this the Anglo-Egyptian posts had been withdrawn from El Arish and from the Sinai Peninsula. Nothing more was heard of the invasion for more than two months. There were many rumours that Djemal Pasha was having difficulties with his Syrian command, and was impressing for his expeditionary force a variety of unwarlike Syrians from peasants in the Jordan valley to cab drivers in Jerusalem.

On January 28, 1915, small advanced parties had crossed the desert. One coming by the El Arish route reached Katiyeh, and was beaten back by a Gurkha post east of El Kantara. Another party coming by the Akaba route was driven back at Kubri, just east of Suez. The desert was well scouted by British airmen, and about that time we landed a party at Alexandretta Bay, in North Syria, and cut the telegraph wires. On the 29th it was announced that the Turks had occupied Katiyeh, and had several posts to the west of that place. Four days later, on 2nd February, came the main attack, for which these proceedings had been reconnaissances.

The Turks officially described the main attack as a reconnaissance, and we may accept the description, for it cannot be regarded as a serious invasion. But it seems likely that it was a reconnaissance, not of design but by compulsion, and that Djemal Pasha found, when he began the attempt, that to transport even one army corps across the desert was wholly beyond his power, and that of his German Chief of Staff, von Kressenstein. The troops numbered about 12,000, and advanced by the central route up the Wady el Arish. Four hours' journey from the Canal they split into two detachments. One moved against Ismailia, to the south of which the east bank gives a certain cover. A second, and much the strongest, advanced to a point opposite Toussum, just south of Lake Timseh, where a patch of ground on the east is high and broken. A small flanking attack was made from the northern route against El Kantara. The Mosul and Smyrna divisions had been left behind, and the troops were the 25th or Damascus division of the 8th Corps, with a few of the 4th (Adrianople) Corps, a remnant of the old Tripoli field force, known as the Champions of Islam, and a number of Bedouin irregulars under Mumtaz Bey.

The first movement was made on the night of 2nd February. A feint against Ismailia that evening had been spoiled by a dust storm, but in the darkness our sentries on the Canal saw and fired at shadowy figures on the side opposite Toussum. The Turks had brought a number of pontoon boats in carts across the desert, and these they attempted to launch, along with several rafts made of kerosene tins. They never had a chance of succeeding. Crowded on the shore, with a high, steep bank behind them, our men mowed them down with rifle fire and Maxims. A few of the vessels were launched, but they were soon riddled and sunk. The enemy then lined the high banks, and tried to silence our fire, and the duel went on till morning broke. With daylight the battle became general all along the stretch from Ismailia to the Bitter Lakes. We had a small flotilla on the Canal—several torpedo boats, the old Indian Marine transport *Hardinge*, and the French

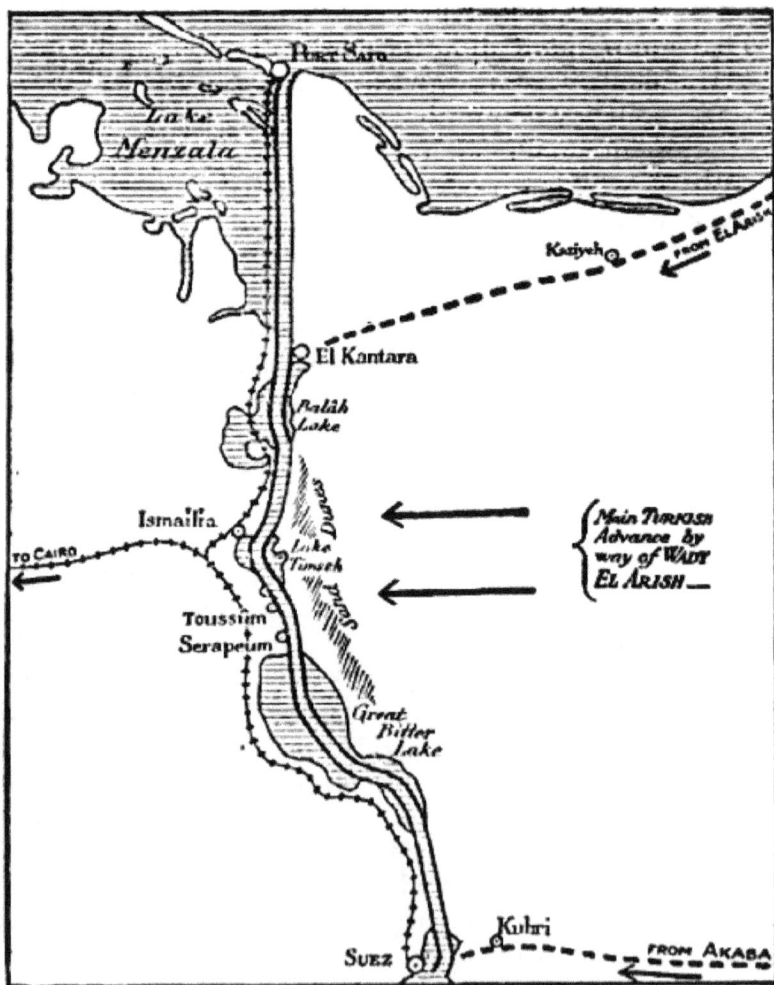

Fighting at the Suez Canal, February 2-4.

guardships *Requin* and *d'Entrecasteaux*.

The Turks had a number of field batteries and two 6-inch guns, which one of the French ships promptly silenced. The torpedo boats made short work of the remaining pontoons, and the crew of one landed on the eastern bank, and raided a trench of the enemy. A few Champions of Islam had got across in the night—a score, perhaps, in all—and sniped our men in the rear; but they were speedily disposed of, and those who swam over later were deserters.

In the afternoon our Indian troops from Serapeum and Toussum took the offensive, and, supported by artillery, drove the enemy from a large part of the eastern bank; Meanwhile the Ismailian garrison also moved forward, and cleared their front. About the same time the half-hearted attacks on our flank near El Kantara and Suez had also failed. By the evening of the 3rd the fiasco was over, and early next morning we crossed the Canal in force and began the work of rounding up the enemy. We counted 400 killed and made 600 prisoners during the two days' fighting, so we may estimate the total Turkish casualty list for the battle of the Canal at well over 2,000. The list grew rapidly in the succeeding days, as deserters began to drift in.

By 8th February there were no Turks within twenty miles of the Canal, and beyond that only a few scattered rearguards, the main force being in full retreat for the borders. It should never have been allowed to return. With 130 waterless miles to cover, there was no reason why a beaten and dispirited force should ever succeed in reaching Beersheba. That it did, and with all its guns, detracts considerably from the British success. The cause of this escape seems to have been a heavy sandstorm, which made it impossible to use our camel corps. It is believed, however, that the Turks suffered heavily in the retreat from their Bedouin allies, who, baffled of the plunder of Egypt, took what they pleased from their friends.

It remains to notice one or two further incidents in the Turkish campaign. Cyprus, which had been administered by Britain since 1878, was formally annexed to the British Empire. The town of Akaba on the Red Sea, which was apparently being used as a station for mine-laying, was visited by H.M.S. *Minerva*, who found the place occupied by soldiers, including one German officer. The *Minerva*, being unable to get satisfaction, shelled the fort and destroyed the barracks and Government buildings, but did no harm to private dwellings. A British cruiser, with a landing party of Indian troops, captured the Turkish fort at Sheik Said, opposite Perim, at the southern end of the

Red Sea. In South-Eastern Arabia our Indian troops had some fighting around Muscat, but this was only indirectly traceable to the war with Turkey. The Sultan of Oman had for two years been at strife with certain of his lieges, and since all men were fighting, the rebels were resolved to follow the fashion and join in on his own account.

★★★★★★

Publisher's Note

The close of 1914 had 'set the stage' for a world at war. The principal protagonists had spread their influence all over the globe and, inevitably, the fires of the great conflagration burst into being accordingly. Few of the theatres of war would see immediate resolutions and those events that 1914 had seen set into motion would virtually, in every way, grind on in escalation in the months and years to come.

Appendices

DISPATCHES DEALING WITH THE BATTLE

OF THE BIGHT OF HELIGOLAND.

Admiralty, 21st October 1914.

The following dispatches have been received from Vice-Admiral (Acting) Sir David Beatty, K.C.B., M.V.O., D.S.O., H.M.S. *Lion*; Rear-Admiral Arthur H. Christian, M.V.O., H.M.S. *Euryalus*; Commodore Reginald Y. Tyrwhitt, Commodore (T), H.M.S. *Arethusa*; and Commodore Roger J. B. Keyes, C.B., M.V.O., Commodore (S), reporting the engagement off Heligoland on Friday, the 28th August:—

1. *Dispatch from Vice-Admiral Sir David Beatty, Commanding the Battle Cruiser Squadron.*

H.M.S. *Lion*, 1st September 1914.

Sir, I have the honour to report that on Thursday, 27th August, at 5 a.m., I proceeded with the First Battle Cruiser Squadron and First Light Cruiser Squadron in company, to rendezvous with the Rear-Admiral, *Invincible*.

At 4 a.m., 28th August, the movements of the Flotillas commenced as previously arranged, the Battle Cruiser Squadron and Light Cruiser Squadron supporting. The Rear-Admiral, *Invincible*, with *New Zealand* and four destroyers having joined my flag, the squadron passed through the prearranged rendezvous.

At 8.10 a.m. I received a signal from the Commodore (T), informing me that the flotilla was in action with the enemy. This was presumably in the vicinity of their prearranged rendezvous. From this time until 11 a.m. I remained about the vicinity ready to support as necessary, intercepting various signals, which contained no information on which I could act.

At 11 a.m. the squadron was attacked by three submarines. The attack was frustrated by rapid manoeuvring, and the four destroyers were ordered to attack them. Shortly after 11 a.m., various signals having been received indicating that the Commodore (T) and Commodore (S) were both in need of assistance, I ordered the Light Cruiser Squadron to support the torpedo flotillas.

Later I received a signal from the Commodore (T), stating that he was being attacked by a large cruiser, and a further signal informing me that he was being hard pressed and asking for assistance. The Captain (D), First Flotilla, also signalled that he was in need of help.

From the foregoing the situation appeared to me critical. The flotillas had advanced only ten miles since 8 a.m., and were only about twenty-five miles from two enemy bases on their flank and rear respectively. Commodore Goodenough had detached two of his light cruisers to assist some destroyers earlier in the day, and these had not yet rejoined. (They rejoined at 2.30 p.m.) As the reports indicated the presence of many enemy ships—one a large cruiser—I considered that his force might not be strong enough to deal with the situation sufficiently rapidly, so at 11.30 a.m. the battle cruisers turned to E.S.E., and worked up to full speed. It was evident that to be of any value the support must be overwhelming and carried out at the highest speed possible.

I had not lost sight of the risk of submarines, and possible sortie in force from the enemy's base, especially in view of the mist to the South-East.

Our high speed, however, made submarine attack difficult, and the smoothness of the sea made their detection comparatively easy. I considered that we were powerful enough to deal with any sortie except by a battle squadron, which was unlikely to come out in time, provided our stroke was sufficiently rapid.

At 12.15 p.m. *Fearless* and First Flotilla were sighted retiring west. At the same time the Light Cruiser Squadron was observed to be engaging an enemy ship ahead. They appeared to have her beat.

I then steered N.E. to sounds of firing ahead, and at 12.30 p.m. sighted *Arethusa* and Third Flotilla retiring to the westward engaging a cruiser of the *Kolberg* class on our port bow. I steered to cut her off from Heligoland, and at 12.37 p.m. opened fire. At 12.42 the enemy turned to N.E., and we chased at 27 knots.

At 12.56 p.m. sighted and engaged a two-funnelled cruiser ahead. *Lion* fired two salvos at her, which took effect, and she disappeared into the mist, burning furiously and in a sinking condition. In view of the mist and that she was steering at high speed at right angles to *Lion*, who was herself steaming at 28 knots, the *Lion's* firing was very creditable.

Our destroyers had reported the presence of floating mines to the eastward, and I considered it inadvisable to pursue her. It was also essential that the squadrons should remain concentrated, and I accordingly ordered a withdrawal. The battle cruisers turned north and circled to port to complete the destruction of the vessel first engaged. She was sighted again at 1.25 p.m. steaming S.E. with colours still flying. *Lion* opened fire with two turrets, and at 1.35 p.m., after receiving two salvos, she sank.

The four attached destroyers were sent to pick up survivors, but I deeply regret that they subsequently reported that they searched the area but found none.

At 1.40 p.m. the battle cruisers turned to the northward, and *Queen Mary* was again attacked by a submarine. The attack was avoided by the use of the helm. *Lowestoft* was also unsuccessfully attacked. The battle cruisers covered the retirement until nightfall. By 6 p.m., the retirement having been well executed and all destroyers accounted for, I altered course, spread the light cruisers, and swept northwards in accordance with the commander-in chief's orders. At 7.45 p.m. I detached *Liverpool* to Rosyth with German prisoners—7 officers and 79 men, survivors from *Mainz*. No further incident occurred.—I have the honour to be, Sir, your obedient Servant,

(Signed)

David Beatty,
Vice-Admiral.

The Secretary of the Admiralty.

2. *Dispatch from Rear-Admiral Christian, commanding the Seventh Cruiser Squadron.*

Euryalus 28th September 1914.

Sir, I have the honour to report that in accordance with your orders a reconnaissance in force was carried out in the Heligoland Bight on the 28th August, with the object of attacking the enemy's light cruisers and destroyers.

The forces under my orders (*viz.*, the Cruiser Force, under Rear-

Admiral H. H. Campbell, C.V.O., *Euryalus*, *Amethyst*, First and Third Destroyer Flotillas and the submarines) took up the positions assigned to them on the evening of the 27th August, and, in accordance with directions given, proceeded during the night to approach the Heligoland Bight.

The cruiser force under Rear-Admiral Campbell, with *Euryalus* (my flagship) and *Amethyst*, was stationed to intercept any enemy vessels chased to the westward. At 4.30 p.m. on the 28th August these cruisers, having proceeded to the eastward, fell in with *Lurcher* and three other destroyers, and the wounded and prisoners in these vessels were transferred in boats to *Bacchante* and *Cressy*, which left for the Nore. *Amethyst* took *Laurel* in tow, and at 9.30 p.m. *Hogue* was detached to take *Arethusa* in tow. This latter is referred to in Commodore R.Y. Tyrwhitt's report, and I quite concur in his remarks as to the skill and rapidity with which this was done in the dark with no lights permissible.

Commodore Reginald Y. Tyrwhitt was in command of the destroyer flotillas, and his report is enclosed herewith. His attack was delivered with great skill and gallantry, and he was most ably seconded by Captain William F. Blunt, in *Fearless*, and the officers in command of the destroyers, who handled their vessels in a manner worthy of the best traditions of the British navy.

Commodore Roger J. B. Keyes, in *Lurcher*, had, on the 27th August, escorted some Submarines into positions allotted to them in the immediate vicinity of the enemy's coast. On the morning of the 28th August, in company with *Firedrake*, he searched the area to the southward of the battle cruisers for the enemy's submarines, and subsequently, having been detached, was present at the sinking of the German Cruiser *Mainz*, when he gallantly proceeded alongside her and rescued 220 of her crew, many of whom were wounded. Subsequently he escorted *Laurel* and *Liberty* out of action, and kept them company till Rear-Admiral Campbell's cruisers were sighted.

As regards the submarines officers, I would specially mention the names of:—

(a) Lieutenant-Commander Ernest W. Leir. His coolness and resource in rescuing the crews of the *Goshawk's* and *Defender's* boats at a critical time of the action were admirable.

(b) Lieutenant-Commander Cecil P. Talbot. In my opinion, the bravery and resource of the Officers in command of Submarines since the war commenced are worthy of the highest commendation.

I have the honour to be, Sir,

Your obedient Servant,

A. H. Christian,

Rear-Admiral.

The Secretary, Admiralty.

3. *Dispatch from Commander R. Y. Tyrwhitt, commanding the Destroyer Flotillas.*

H.M.S. *Lowestoft*, 26th September 1914.

Sir, I have the honour to report that at 5 a.m. on Thursday, 27th August, in accordance with orders received from Their Lordships, I sailed in *Arethusa*, in company with the First and Third Flotillas, except *Hornet*, *Tigress*, *Hydra*, and *Loyal*, to carry out the prearranged operations. H.M.S. *Fearless* joined the Flotillas at sea that afternoon.

At 6.53 a.m. on Friday, 28th August, an enemy's destroyer was sighted, and was chased by the 4th Division of the Third Flotilla.

From 7.20 to 7.57 a.m. *Arethusa* and the Third Flotilla were engaged with numerous destroyers and torpedo boats which were making for Heligoland; course was altered to port to cut them off.

Two cruisers, with 4 and 2 funnels respectively, were sighted on the port bow at 7.57 a.m., the nearest of which was engaged. *Arethusa* received a heavy fire from both cruisers and several destroyers until 8.15 a.m., when the four-funnelled cruiser transferred her fire to *Fearless*.

Close action was continued with the two-funnelled cruiser on converging courses until 8.25 a.m., when a 6-inch projectile from *Arethusa* wrecked the fore bridge of the enemy, who at once turned away in the direction of Heligoland, which was sighted slightly on the starboard bow at about the same time.

All ships were at once ordered to turn to the westward, and shortly afterwards speed was reduced to 20 knots.

During this action *Arethusa* had been hit many times, and was considerably damaged; only one 6-inch gun remained in action, all other guns and torpedo tubes having been temporarily

185

disabled.

Lieutenant Eric W. P. Westmacott (signal officer) was killed at my side during this action. I cannot refrain from adding that he carried out his duties calmly and collectedly, and was of the greatest assistance to me.

A fire occurred opposite No. 2 gun port side caused by a shell exploding some ammunition, resulting in a terrific blaze for a short period and leaving the deck burning. This was very promptly dealt with and extinguished by Chief Petty Officer Frederick W. Wrench, O.N. 158630.

The flotillas were reformed in divisions and proceeded at 20 knots. It was now noticed that *Arethusa's* speed had been reduced.

Fearless reported that the 3rd and 5th Divisions of the First Flotilla had sunk the German commodore's destroyer and that two boats' crews belonging to *Defender* had been left behind, as our destroyers had been fired upon by a German cruiser during their act of mercy in saving the survivors of the German destroyer.

At 10 a.m., hearing that Commodore (S) in *Lurcher* and *Firedrake* were being chased by light cruisers, I proceeded to his assistance with *Fearless* and the First Flotilla until 10.37 a.m., when, having received no news, and being in the vicinity of Heligoland, I ordered the ships in company to turn to the westward.

All guns except two 4-inch were again in working order, and the upper deck supply of ammunition was replenished.

At 10.55 a m a four-funnelled German cruiser was sighted, and opened a very heavy fire at about 11 o'clock.

Our position being somewhat critical, I ordered *Fearless* to attack, and the First Flotilla to attack with torpedoes, which they proceeded to do with great spirit. The cruiser at once turned away, disappeared in the haze, and evaded the attack.

About 10 minutes later the same cruiser appeared on our starboard quarter. Opened fire on her with both 6-inch guns; *Fearless* also engaged her, and one division of destroyers attacked her with torpedoes without success.

The state of affairs and our position was then reported to the Admiral Commanding Battle Cruiser Squadron.

We received a very severe and almost accurate fire from this cruiser; salvo after salvo was falling between 10 and 30 yards short, but not a single shell struck; two torpedoes were also fired at us, being well directed, but short.

The cruiser was badly damaged by *Arethusa's* 6-inch guns and a splendidly directed fire from *Fearless*, and she shortly afterwards turned away in the direction of Heligoland.

Proceeded, and four minutes later sighted the three-funnelled cruiser *Mainz*. She endured a heavy fire from *Arethusa* and *Fearless* and many destroyers. After an action of approximately 25 minutes she was seen to be sinking by the head, her engines stopped, besides being on fire.

At this moment the Light Cruiser Squadron appeared, and they very speedily reduced the *Mainz* to a *condition* which must have been indescribable.

I then recalled *Fearless* and the destroyers, and ordered cease fire.

We then exchanged broadsides with a large, four-funnelled cruiser on the starboard quarter at long range, without visible effect.

The Battle Cruiser Squadron now arrived, and I pointed out this cruiser to the admiral commanding, and was shortly afterwards informed by him that the cruiser in question had been sunk and another set on fire.

The weather during the day was fine, sea calm, but visibility poor, not more than 3 miles at any time when the various actions were taking place, and was such that ranging and spotting were rendered difficult.

I then proceeded with 14 destroyers of the Third Flotilla, and 9 of the First Flotilla.

Arethusa's speed was about 6 knots until 7 p.m., when it was impossible to proceed any further, and fires were drawn in all boilers except two, and assistance called for.

At 9.30 p.m. Captain Wilmot S. Nicholson, of the *Hogue*, took my ship in tow in a most seamanlike manner, and, observing that the night was pitch dark and the only lights showing were two small hand lanterns, I consider his action was one which deserves special notice from Their Lordships.

I would also specially recommend Lieutenant-Commander Arthur P. N. Thorowgood, of *Arethusa*, for the able manner he prepared the ship for being towed in the dark.

H.M. Ship under my command was then towed to the Nore,

187

arriving at 5 p.m. on the 29th August. Steam was then available for slow speed, and the ship was able to proceed to Chatham under her own steam.

I beg again to call attention to the services rendered by Captain W. F. Blunt, of H.M.S. *Fearless*, and the commanding officers of the destroyers of the First and Third Flotillas, whose gallant attacks on the German cruisers at critical moments undoubtedly saved Arethusa from more severe punishment and possible capture.

I cannot adequately express my satisfaction and pride at the spirit and ardour of my officers and ship's company, who carried out their orders with the greatest alacrity under the most trying conditions, especially in view of the fact that the ship, newly built, had not been 48 hours out of the dockyard before she was in action.

It is difficult to specially pick out individuals, but the following came under my special observation:—

H.M.S. *Arethusa.*

Lieutenant-Commander Arthur P. N. Thorowgood, first lieutenant, and in charge of the after control.

Lieutenant-Commander Ernest K. Arbuthnot (G.), in charge of the fore control.

Sub-Lieutenant Clive A. Robinson, who worked the rangefinder throughout the entire action with extraordinary coolness.

Assistant Paymaster Kenneth E. Badcock, my secretary, who attended me on the bridge throughout the entire action.

Mr. James D. Godfrey, Gunner (T.), who was in charge of the torpedo tubes.

The following men were specially noted:—

Armourer Arthur F. Hayes, O.N. 342026 (Ch.).

Second Sick Berth Steward George Trolley, O.N. M.2Q6 (Ch.).

Chief Yeoman of Signals Albert Fox, O.N. 194656 (Po.), on fore bridge during entire action.

Chief Petty Officer Frederick W. Wrench, O.N. 158630 (Ch.) (for ready resource in extinguishing fire caused by explosion of cordite).

Private Thomas Millington, R.M.L.I., No. Ch. 17417.

Private William J. Beirne, R.M.L.I., No. Ch. 13540.

First Writer Albert W. Stone, O.N. 346080 (Po.).

I also beg to record the services rendered by the following officers and men of H.M. Ships under my orders:—

H.M.S. *Fearless.*

Mr. Robert M. Taylor, gunner, for coolness in action under heavy fire.

The following officers also displayed great resource and energy in effecting repairs to *Fearless* after her return to harbour, and they were ably seconded by the whole of their staffs:—

Engineer Lieutenant-Commander Charles de F. Messervy.

Mr. William Morrissey, Carpenter.

H.M.S. *Goshawk.*

Commander the Hon. Herbert Meade, who took his division into action with great coolness and nerve, and was instrumental in sinking the German destroyer 187, and, with the boats of his division, saved the survivors in a most chivalrous manner.

H.M.S. *Ferret.*

Commander Geoffrey Mackworth, who, with his division, most gallantly seconded Commander Meade, of *Goshawk.*

H.M.S. *Laertes.*

Lieutenant Commander Malcolm L. Goldsmith, whose ship was seriously damaged, taken in tow, and towed out of action by *Fearless.*

Engineer Lieutenant-Commander Alexander Hill, for repairing steering gear and engines under fire.

Sub-Lieutenant George H. Faulkner, who continued to fight his gun after being wounded.

Mr. Charles Powell, Acting Boatswain, O.N. 209388, who was gunlayer of the centre gun, which made many hits. He behaved very coolly, and set a good example when getting in tow and clearing away the wreckage after the action.

Edward Naylor, Petty Officer, Torpedo Gunner's Mate, O.N. 189136, who fired a torpedo which the commanding officer of *Laertes* reports undoubtedly hit the *Mainz,* and so helped materially to put her out of action.

Stephen Pritchard, Stoker Petty Officer, O.N. 285152, who very gallantly dived into the cabin flat immediately after a shell had exploded there, and worked a fire hose.

Frederick Pierce, Stoker Petty Officer, O.N. 307943, who was on watch in the engine room and behaved with conspicuous coolness and resource when a shell exploded in No. 2 boiler.

H.M.S. *Laurel.*

Commander Frank F. Rose, who most ably commanded his vessel throughout the early part of the action, and after having been wounded in both legs, remained on the bridge until 6 p.m., displaying great devotion to duty.

Lieutenant Charles R. Peploe, first lieutenant, who took command after Commander Rose was wounded, and continued the action till its close, bringing his Destroyer out in an able and gallant manner under most trying conditions.

Engineer Lieutenant-Commander Edward H. T. Meeson, who behaved with great coolness during the action, and steamed the ship out of action, although she had been very severely damaged by explosion of her own lyddite, by which the after funnel was nearly demolished. He subsequently assisted to carry out repairs to the vessel.

Sam Palmer, Leading Seaman (G.L. 2) O.N. 179529, who continued to fight his gun until the end of the action, although severely wounded in the leg.

Albert Edmund Sellens, Able Seaman (L.T.O.) O.N. 217245, who was stationed at the fore torpedo tubes; he remained at his post throughout the entire action, although wounded in the arm, and then rendered first aid in a very able manner before being attended to himself.

George H. Sturdy, Chief Stoker, O.N. 285547, and

Alfred Britton, Stoker Petty Officer, O.N. 289893, who both showed great coolness in putting out a fire near the centre gun after an explosion had occurred there; several lyddite shells were lying in the immediate vicinity.

William R. Boiston, Engine Room Artificer, 3rd class, O.N. M.I369, who showed great ability and coolness in taking charge of the after boiler room during the action, when an explosion blew in the after funnel and a shell carried away pipes and seriously damaged the main steam pipe.

William H. Gorst, Stoker Petty Officer, O.N. 305616.

Edward Crane, Stoker Petty Officer, O.N. 307275.

Harry Wilfred Hawkes, Stoker 1st class, O.N. K. 12086.

John W. Bateman, Stoker 1st class, O.N., K. 12100.

These men were stationed in the after boiler room, and conducted themselves with great coolness during the action, when an explosion blew in the after funnel, and shell carried away pipes and seriously damaged the main steam pipe.

H.MS. *Liberty*.

The late Lieutenant-Commander Nigel K. W. Barttelot commanded the *Liberty* with great skill and gallantry throughout the action. He was a most promising and able officer, and I consider his death is a great loss to the navy.

Engineer-Lieutenant-Commander Frank A. Butler, who showed much resource in effecting repairs during the action.

Lieutenant Henry E. Horan, first lieutenant, who took command after the death of Lieutenant-Commander Barttelot, and brought his ship out of action in extremely able and gallant manner under most trying conditions.

Mr. Harry Morgan, Gunner (T), who carried out his duties with exceptional coolness under fire.

Chief Petty Officer James Samuel Beadle, O.N. 171735, who remained at his post at the wheel for over an hour after being wounded in the kidneys.

John Galvin, Stoker, Petty Officer, O.N. 279946, who took entire charge, under the engineer officer, of the party who stopped leaks, and accomplished his task although working up to his chest in water.

H.M.S. *Laforey*.

Mr. Ernest Roper, chief gunner, who carried out his duties with exceptional coolness under fire.

I have the honour to be, Sir,
Your obedient Servant,

R. Y. Tyrwhitt,
Commodore (T).

4. Dispatch from Commander Roger J. B. Keyes, commanding the Eighth Submarine Flotilla.

H.M.S. *Maidstone*, 17th October 1914.

Sir, In compliance with Their Lordships' directions, I have the honour to report as follows upon the services performed by Submarines since the commencement of hostilities:—

Three hours after the outbreak of war, Submarines E6 (Lieutenant-Commander Cecil P. Talbot), and E8 (Lieutenant-Commander Francis H. H. Goodhart), proceeded unaccompanied to carry out a reconnaissance in the Heligoland Bight. These two vessels returned with useful information, and had the privilege of being the pioneers on a service which is attended by some risk.

During the transportation of the Expeditionary Force the *Lurcher* and *Firedrake* and all the Submarines of the Eighth Submarine Flotilla occupied positions from which they could have attacked the High Sea Fleet, had it emerged to dispute the passage of our transports. This patrol was maintained day and night without relief, until the personnel of our army had been transported and all chance of effective interference had disappeared.

These submarines have since been incessantly employed on the enemy's coast in the Heligoland Bight and elsewhere, and have obtained much valuable information regarding the composition and movement of his patrols. They have occupied his waters and reconnoitred his anchorages, and, while so engaged, have been subjected to skilful and well executed anti-submarine tactics; hunted for hours at a time by torpedo craft and attacked by gunfire and torpedoes.

At midnight on the 26th August, I embarked in the *Lurcher*, and, in company with *Firedrake* and submarines D2, D8, 4, 5, E6, 7, E8, and E9, of the Eighth Submarine Flotilla, proceeded to take part in the operations in the Heligoland Bight arranged for the 28th August. The destroyers scouted for the submarines until nightfall on the 27th, when the latter proceeded independently to take up various positions from which they could co-operate with the destroyer flotillas on the following morning.

At daylight on the 28th August the *Lurcher* and *Firedrake* searched the area, through which the battle cruisers were to advance, for hostile submarines, and then proceeded towards Heligoland in the wake of Submarines E6, E7, and E8, which were exposing themselves with the object of inducing the enemy to chase them to the westward.

On approaching Heligoland, the visibility, which had been very good to seaward, reduced to 5,000 to 6,000 yards, and this added considerably to the anxieties and responsibilities of the commanding officers of submarines, who handled their vessels with coolness and judgment in an area which was necessarily occupied by friends as well as foes.

Low visibility and calm sea are the most unfavourable conditions under which submarines can operate, and no opportunity occurred of closing with the enemy's cruisers to within torpedo range.

Lieutenant-Commander Ernest W. Leir, commanding Submarine 4, witnessed the sinking of the German Torpedo Boat Destroyer 187 through his periscope, and, observing a cruiser of the *Stettin* class close, and open fire on the British destroyers which had lowered their boats to pick up the survivors, he proceeded to attack the cruiser, but she altered course before he could get within range. After covering the retirement of our destroyers, which had had to abandon their boats, he returned to the latter, and embarked a lieutenant and nine men of *Defender*, who had been left behind.

The boats also contained two officers and eight men of 187, who were unwounded, and eighteen men who were badly wounded. As he could not embark the latter, Lieutenant-Commander Leir left one of the officers and six unwounded men to navigate the British boats to Heligoland. Before leaving he saw that they were provided with water, biscuit, and a compass. One German officer and two men were made prisoners of war.

Lieutenant-Commander Leir's action in remaining on the surface in the vicinity of the enemy and in a visibility which would have placed his vessel within easy gun range of an enemy appearing out of the mist, was altogether admirable.

This enterprising and gallant officer took part in the reconnaissance which supplied the information on which these operations were based, and I beg to submit his name, and that of Lieutenant-Commander Talbot, the commanding officer of E6, who exercised patience, judgment, and skill in a dangerous position, for the favourable consideration of Their Lordships.

On the 13th September, 9 (Lieutenant-Commander Max K. Horton), torpedoed and sank the German light cruiser *Hela* six miles South of Heligoland.

A number of destroyers were evidently called to the scene after 9 had delivered her attack, and these hunted her for several hours.

On the 14th September, in accordance with his orders, Lieutenant-Commander Horton examined the outer anchorage of Heligoland, a service attended by considerable risk.

On the 25th September, Submarine E6 (Lieutenant-Commander C. P. Talbot), while diving, fouled the moorings of a mine laid by the enemy. On rising to the surface she weighed the mine and sinker; the former was securely fixed between the hydroplane and its guard; fortunately, however, the horns of the mine were pointed outboard. The weight of the sinker made it a difficult and dangerous matter to lift the mine clear without exploding it. After half an hour's patient work this was effected by Lieutenant Frederick A. P. Williams-Freeman and Able Seaman Ernest Randall Cremer, Official Number 214235, and the released mine descended to its original depth.

On the 6th October, E9 (Lieutenant-Commander Max K. Horton), when patrolling off the Ems, torpedoed and sank the enemy's destroyer, S126.

The enemy's torpedo craft pursue tactics, which, in connection with their shallow draft, make them exceedingly difficult to attack with torpedo, and Lieutenant-Commander Horton's success was the result of much patient and skilful zeal. He is a most enterprising submarine officer, and I beg to submit his name for favourable consideration.

Lieutenant Charles M. S. Chapman, the second in command of E9, is also deserving of credit.

Against an enemy whose capital vessels have never, and light cruisers have seldom, emerged from their fortified harbours, opportunities of delivering submarine attacks have necessarily been few, and on one occasion only, prior to the 13th September, has one of our Submarines been within torpedo range of a cruiser during daylight hours.

During the exceptionally heavy westerly gales which prevailed between the 14th and 21st September, the position of the submarines on a lee shore, within a few miles of the enemy's coast, was an unpleasant one.

The short steep seas which accompany westerly gales in the Heligoland Bight made it difficult to keep the conning tower hatches open. There was no rest to be obtained, and even when cruising at a depth of 60 feet, the submarines were rolling considerably, and pumping—*i.e.,* vertically moving about twenty feet.

I submit that it was creditable to the commanding officers that they should have maintained their stations under such conditions.

Service in the Heligoland Bight is keenly sought after by the commanding officers of the Eighth Submarine Flotilla, and they have all shown daring and enterprise in the execution of their duties. These officers have unanimously expressed to me their admiration of the cool and gallant behaviour of the officers and men under their command. They are, however, of the opinion that it is impossible to single out individuals when all have performed their duties so admirably, and in this I concur. The following submarines have been in contact with the enemy during these operations:—

D1 (Lieutenant-Commander Archibald D. Cochrane).
D2 (Lieutenant-Commander Arthur G. Jameson).
D3 (Lieutenant-Commander Edward C. Boyle).
D5 (Lieutenant-Commander Godfrey Herbert).
E4 (Lieutenant-Commander Ernest W. Leir).
E5 (Lieutenant-Commander Charles S. Benning).
E6 (Lieutenant-Commander Cecil P. Talbot).
E7 (Lieutenant-Commander Ferdinand E. B. Feilmann).
E9 (Lieutenant-Commander Max K. Horton).

I have the honour to be, Sir,
Your obedient servant,
(Signed)   Roger Keyes,
Commodore (S).

APPENDIX 2

THE BATTLE OF THE FALKLAND ISLANDS

Admiral Sturdee's Dispatch.
Admiralty, 3rd March, 1915.

The following dispatch has been received from Vice-Admiral Sir F. C. Doveton-Sturdee, K.C.B., C.V.O., C.M.G., reporting the action off the Falkland Islands on Tuesday, the 8th of December, 1914:—

Invincible at Sea,
19th December, 1914.

Sir,—I have the honour to forward a report on the action which took place on 8th December, 1914, against a German Squadron off the Falkland Islands.

I have the honour to be, Sir,
Your obedient Servant,
F. C. D. Sturdee,

Vice-Admiral, Commander-in-Chief.

The Secretary, Admiralty.

(A.) Preliminary Movements.

The squadron, consisting of H.M. ships *Invincible*, flying my flag, Flag Captain Percy T. H. Beamish; *Inflexible*, Captain Richard F. Phillimore; *Carnarvon*, flying the flag of Rear-Admiral Archibald P. Stoddart, Flag Captain Harry L. d'E. Skipwith; *Cornwall*, Captain Walter M. Ellerton; *Kent*, Captain John D. Allen; *Glasgow*, Captain John Luce; *Bristol*, Captain Basil H. Fanshawe; and *Macedonia*, Captain Bertram S. Evans, arrived at Port Stanley, Falkland Islands, at 10.30 a.m. on Monday, the 7th December 1914. Coaling was commenced at once, in order that the ships should be ready to resume the search for the enemy's squadron the next evening, the 8th December.

At 8 a.m. on Tuesday, the 8th December, a signal was received from the signal station on shore:—

A four-funnel and two-funnel man-of-war in sight from Sapper Hill, steering northwards.

At this time the positions of the various ships of the squadron were as follows:—

Macedonia: At anchor as look-out ship.
Kent (guard ship): At anchor in Port William.
Invincible and *Inflexible*: In Port William.
Carnarvon: In Port William.
Cornwall: In Port William.
Glasgow: In Port Stanley.
Bristol: In Port Stanley.

The *Kent* was at once ordered to weigh, and a general signal was made to raise steam for full speed.

At 8.20 a.m. the signal station reported another column of smoke in sight to the southward, and at 8.45 a.m. the *Kent* passed down the harbour and took up a station at the entrance.

The *Canopus*, Captain Heathcoat S. Grant, reported at 8.47 a.m. that the first two ships were 8 miles off, and that the smoke reported at 8.20 a.m. appeared to be the smoke of two ships about 20 miles off.

At 8.50 a.m. the signal station reported a further column of smoke in sight to the southward.

The *Macedonia* was ordered to weigh anchor on the inner side of the other ships, and await orders.

At 9.20 a.m. the two leading ships of the enemy (*Gneisenau* and *Nürnberg*), with guns trained on the wireless station, came within range of the *Canopus*, who opened fire at them across the low land at a range of 11,000 yards. The enemy at once hoisted their colours and turned away. At this time the masts and smoke of the enemy were visible from the upper bridge of the *Invincible* at a range of approximately 17,000 yards across the low land to the south of Port William.

A few minutes later the two cruisers altered course to port, as though to close the *Kent* at the entrance to the harbour, but about this time it seems that the *Invincible* and *Inflexible* were seen over the land, as the enemy at once altered course and increased speed to join their consorts.

The *Glasgow* weighed and proceeded at 9.40 a.m. with orders to join the *Kent* and observe the enemy's movements.

At 9.45 a.m. the squadron—less the *Bristol*—weighed, and proceeded out of harbour in the following order:—*Carnarvon*, *Inflexible*, *Invincible*, and *Cornwall*. On passing Cape Pembroke Light, the five ships of the enemy appeared clearly in sight to the south-east, hull down. The visibility was at its maximum, the sea was calm, with a bright sun, a clear sky, and a light breeze from the north-west.

At 10.20 a.m. the signal for a general chase was made. The battle cruisers quickly passed ahead of the *Carnarvon* and overtook the *Kent*. The *Glasgow* was ordered to keep two miles from the *Invincible*, and the *Inflexible* was stationed on the starboard quarter of the flagship. Speed was eased to 20 knots at 11.15 a.m. to enable the other cruisers to get into station.

At this time the enemy's funnels and bridges showed just above the horizon.

Information was received from the *Bristol* at 11.27 am that three enemy ships had appeared off Port Pleasant, probably colliers or transports. The *Bristol* was therefore directed to take the *Macedonia* under his orders and destroy transports.

The enemy were still maintaining their distance, and I decided, at 12.20 p.m., to attack with the two battle cruisers and the *Glasgow*.

At 12.47 p. m. the signal to "Open fire and engage the enemy" was made.

197

The *Inflexible* opened fire at 12.55 pm. from her fore turret at the right-hand ship of the enemy, a light cruiser; a few minutes later the *Invincible* opened fire at the same ship.

The deliberate fire from a range of 16,500 to 15,000 yards at the right-hand light cruiser, who was dropping astern, became too threatening, and when a shell fell close alongside her at 1.20 p.m. she (the *Leipzig*) turned away, with the *Nürnberg* and *Dresden* to the south-west. These light cruisers were at once followed by the *Kent*, *Glasgow*, and *Cornwall*, in accordance with my instructions.

The action finally developed into three separate encounters, besides the subsidiary one dealing with the threatened landing.

(B.) Action with the Armoured Cruisers.

The fire of the battle cruisers was directed on the *Scharnhorst* and *Gneisenau*. The effect of this was quickly seen, when at 1.25 p.m., with the *Scharnhorst* leading, they turned about 7 points to port in succession into line ahead and opened fire at 1.30 p.m. Shortly afterwards speed was eased to 24 knots, and the battle cruisers were ordered to turn together, bringing them into line ahead, with the *Invincible* leading.

The range was about 13,500 yards at the final turn, and increased, until, at 2 p.m., it had reached 16,450 yards.

The enemy then (2.10 p.m.) turned away about 10 points to starboard and a second chase ensued, until, at 2.45 p.m., the battle cruisers again opened fire; this caused the enemy, at 2.53 p.m., to turn into line ahead to port and open fire at 2.55 p.m. The *Scharnhorst* caught fire forward, but not seriously, and her fire slackened perceptibly; the *Gneisenau* was badly hit by the *Inflexible*.

At 3.30 p.m. the *Scharnhorst* led round about 10 points to starboard; just previously her fire had slackened perceptibly, and one shell had shot away her third funnel; some guns were not firing, and it would appear that the turn was dictated by a desire to bring her starboard guns into action. The effect of the fire on the *Scharnhorst* became more and more apparent in consequence of smoke from fires, and also escaping steam; at times a shell would cause a large hole to appear in her side, through which could be seen a dull red glow of flame.

At 4.4 p.m. the *Scharnhorst*, whose flag remained flying to the last, suddenly listed heavily to port, and within a minute it became clear that she was a doomed ship; for the list increased very rapidly until she lay on her beam ends, and at 4.17 p.m. she disappeared.

The *Gneisenau* passed on the far side of her late flagship, and continued a determined but ineffectual effort to fight the two battle cruisers.

At 5.8 p.m. the forward funnel was knocked over and remained resting against the second funnel. She was evidently in serious straits, and her fire slackened very much.

At 5.15 p.m. one of the *Gneisenau's* shells struck the *Invincible*; this was her last effective effort.

At 5.30 p.m. she turned towards the flagship with a heavy list to starboard, and appeared stopped, with steam pouring from her escape pipes and smoke from shell and fires rising everywhere. About this time I ordered the signal "Cease fire," but before it was hoisted the *Gneisenau* opened fire again, and continued to fire from time to time with a single gun.

At 5.40 p.m. the three ships closed in on the *Gneisenau*, and, at this time, the flag flying at her fore truck was apparently hauled down, but the flag at the peak continued flying.

At 5.50 p.m. "Cease fire" was made.

At 6 p.m. the *Gneisenau* heeled over very suddenly, showing the men gathered on her decks and then walking on her side as she lay for a minute on her beam ends before sinking.

The prisoners of war from the *Gneisenau* report that, by the time the ammunition was expended, some 600 men had been killed and wounded. The surviving officers and men were all ordered on deck and told to provide themselves with hammocks and any articles that could support them in the water.

When the ship capsized and sank there were probably some 200 unwounded survivors in the water, but, owing to the shock of the cold water, many were drowned within sight of the boats and ship.

Every effort was made to save life as quickly as possible, both by boats and from the ships; life-buoys were thrown and ropes lowered, but only a proportion could be rescued. The Invincible alone rescued 108 men, 14 of whom were found to be dead after being brought on board; these men were buried at sea the following day with full military honours.

(C.) Action with the Light Cruisers.

At about 1 p.m., when the *Scharnhorst* and *Gneisenau* turned to port to engage the *Invincible* and *Inflexible*, the enemy's light cruisers turned to starboard to escape; the *Dresden* was leading and the *Nürnberg* and *Leipzig* followed on each quarter.

In accordance with my instructions, the *Glasgow, Kent,* and *Cornwall* at once went in chase of these ships; the *Carnarvon,* whose speed was insufficient to overtake them, closed the battle cruisers.

The *Glasgow* drew well ahead of the *Cornwall* and *Kent,* and at 3 p.m. shots were exchanged with the *Leipzig* at 12,000 yards. The *Glasgow's* object was to endeavour to outrange the *Leipzig* with her 6-inch guns and thus cause her to alter course and give the *Cornwall* and *Kent* a chance of coming into action.

At 4.17 p.m. the *Cornwall* opened fire, also on the *Leipzig.*

At 7.17 p.m. the *Leipzig* was on fire fore and aft, and the *Cornwall* and *Glasgow* ceased fire.

The *Leipzig* turned over on her port side and disappeared at 9 p.m. Seven officers and eleven men were saved.

At 3.36 p.m. the *Cornwall* ordered the *Kent* to engage the *Nürnberg,* the nearest cruiser to her.

Owing to the excellent and strenuous efforts of the engine room department, the *Kent* was able to get within range of the *Nürnberg* at 5 p.m. At 6.35 p.m. the *Nürnberg* was on fire forward and ceased firing. The *Kent* also ceased firing and closed to 3,300 yards; as the colours were still observed to be flying in the *Nürnberg,* the *Kent* opened fire again. Fire was finally stopped five minutes later on the colours being hauled down, and every preparation was made to save life. The *Nürnberg* sank at 7.27 p.m., and, as she sank, a group of men were waving a German ensign attached to a staff. Twelve men were rescued, but only seven survived.

The *Kent* had four killed and twelve wounded, mostly caused by one shell.

During the time the three cruisers were engaged with the *Nürnberg* and *Leipzig,* the *Dresden,* who was beyond her consorts, effected her escape owing to her superior speed. The *Glasgow* was the only cruiser with sufficient speed to have had any chance of success. However, she was fully employed in engaging the *Leipzig* for over an hour before either the *Cornwall* or *Kent* could come up and get within range. During this time the *Dresden* was able to increase her distance and get out of sight.

The weather changed after 4 p.m., and the visibility was much reduced; further, the sky was overcast and cloudy thus assisting the *Dresden* to get away unobserved.

(D.) Action with the Enemy's Transports.

A report was received at 11.27 a.m. from H.M.S. *Bristol* that three ships of the enemy, probably transports or colliers, had appeared off Port Pleasant. The *Bristol* was ordered to take the *Macedonia* under his orders and destroy the transports.

H.M.S. *Macedonia* reports that only two ships, steamships *Baden* and *Santa Isabel*, were present; both ships were sunk after the removal of the crew.

I have pleasure in reporting that the officers and men under my orders carried out their duties with admirable efficiency and coolness, and great credit is due to the engineer officers of all the ships, several of which exceeded their normal full speed.

The names of the following are specially mentioned:—

Officers.

Commander Richard Herbert Denny Townsend, H.M.S. *Invincible*.

Commander Arthur Edward Frederick Bedford, H.M.S. *Kent*.

Lieutenant-Commander Wilfred Arthur Thompson, H.M.S. *Glasgow*.

Lieutenant-Commander Hubert Edward Danreuther, First and Gunnery Lieutenant, H.M.S. *Invincible*.

Engineer-Commander George Edward Andrew, H.M.S. *Kent*.

Engineer-Commander Edward John Weeks, H.M.S. *Invincible*.

Paymaster Cyril Sheldon Johnson, H.M.S. *Invincible*.

Carpenter Thomas Andrew Walls, H.M.S. Invincible.

Carpenter William Henry Venning, H.M.S. *Kent*.

Carpenter George Henry Egford, H.M.S. *Cornwall*.

Petty Officers and Men.

Chief P.O. D. Leighton, O.N. 124238, H.M.S. *Kent*.

P.O., 2nd Class, M. J. Walton (R.F.R., A. 1756), O.N. 118358, H.M.S. *Kent*.

Leading Seaman F. S. Martin, O.N. 233301, H.M.S. Invincible, Gunner's Mate, Gunlayer, 1st Class.

Signalman F. Glover, O.N. 225731, H.M.S. *Cornwall*.

Chief E.R. Artificer, 2nd Class, J. G. Hill, O.N. 269646, H.M.S. *Cornwall*.

Acting Chief E.R. Artificer, 2nd Class, R. Snowdon, O.N. 270654, H.M.S. *Inflexible*.

E.R. Artificer, 1st Class, G. H. F. McCarten, O.N. 270023, H.M.S. Invincible.

Stoker P.O. G. S. Brewer, O.N. 150950, H.M.S. *Kent*.

Stoker P.O. W. A. Townsend, O.N. 301650, H.M.S. *Cornwall*.

Stoker, 1st Class, J. Smith, O.N. SS. 111915, H.M.S. *Cornwall*.

Shipwright, 1st Class, A. N. E. England, O.N. 341971, H.M.S. *Glasgow*.

Shipwright, 2nd Class, A. C. H. Dymott, O.N. M. 8047, H.M.S. *Kent*.

Portsmouth R.F.R.B./3307 Sergeant Charles Mayes, H.M.S. Kent.

F. C. D. Sturdee.

APPENDIX 3

THE BATTLE OF THE 24TH OF JANUARY, 1915.

Admiral Beatty's Dispatch.
Admiralty, March 3, 1915.

The following dispatch has been received from Vice-Admiral Sir David Beatty, K.C.B., M.V.O., D.S.O., commanding the First Battle-Cruiser Squadron, reporting the action in the North Sea on Sunday, the 24th of January, 1915:—

H.M.S. *Princess Royal*, February 2, 1915.

Sir,

I have the honour to report that at daybreak on 24th January, 1915, the following vessels were patrolling in company.

The battle cruisers *Lion*, Captain Alfred E. M. Chatfield, C.V.O., flying my flag; *Princess Royal*, Captain Osmond de B. Brock, *Aide-de-Camp*; *Tiger*, Captain Henry B. Pelly, M.V.O.; *New Zealand*, Captain Lionel Halsey, C.M.G., *Aide-de-Camp*, flying the flag of Rear-Admiral Sir Archibald Moore, K.C.B., C.V.O.; and *Indomitable*, Captain Francis W. Kennedy.

The light cruisers *Southampton*, flying the broad pennant of Commodore William E. Goodenough, M.V.O.; *Nottingham*, Captain Charles B. Miller; *Birmingham*, Captain Arthur A. M. Duff; and *Lowestoft*, Captain Theobald W. B. Kennedy, were disposed on my port beam.

Commodore (T) Reginald Y. Tyrwhitt, C.B., in *Arethusa, Aurora*, Captain Wilmot S. Nicholson, *Undaunted*, Captain Francis G. St. John, M.V.O., *Arethusa* and the destroyer flotillas were ahead.

At 7.25 a.m. the flash of guns was observed S.S.E. Shortly afterwards a report reached me from *Aurora* that she was engaged with enemy's ships. I immediately altered course to S.S.E., increased to 22 knots, and ordered the light cruisers and flotillas to chase S.S.E., to get in touch and report movements of enemy.

This order was acted upon with great promptitude; indeed my wishes had already been forestalled by the respective senior officers, and reports almost immediately followed from *Southampton, Arethusa*, and *Aurora* as to the position and composition of the enemy, which consisted of 3 battle cruisers and *Blücher*, 6 light cruisers, and a number of destroyers, steering N.W. The enemy had altered course to S.E. From now onwards the light cruisers maintained touch with the enemy, and kept me fully informed as to their movements.

The battle cruisers worked up to full speed, steering to the southward. The wind at the time was N.E., light, with extreme visibility. At 7.30 a.m. the enemy were sighted on port bow steaming fast, steering approximately S.E., distant 14 miles.

Owing to the prompt reports received we had attained our position on the quarter of the enemy, and so altered course to S.E. parallel to them, and settled down to a long stern chase, gradually increasing our speed until we reached 28.5 knots. Great credit is due to the engineer staffs of *New Zealand* and *Indomitable* these ships greatly exceeded their normal speed.

At 8.52 a.m., as we had closed to within 20,000 yards of the rear ship, the battle cruisers manoeuvred to keep on a line of bearing so that guns would bear, and *Lion* fired a single shot, which fell short. The enemy at this time were in single line ahead, with light cruisers ahead and a large number of destroyers on their starboard beam.

Single shots were fired at intervals to test the range, and at 9.9 a.m. *Lion* made her first hit on the *Blücher*, No. 4 in the line. The *Tiger* opened fire at 9.20 a.m. on the rear ship, the *Lion* shifted to No. 3 in the line, at 18,000 yards, this ship being hit by several salvos. The enemy returned our fire at 9.14 a.m. *Princess*

Royal, on coming into range, opened fire on *Blücher*, the range of the leading ship being 17,500 yards, at 9.35 a.m. *New Zealand* was within range of *Blücher*, which had dropped somewhat astern, and opened fire on her. *Princess Royal* shifted to the third ship in the line, inflicting considerable damage on her.

Our flotilla cruisers and destroyers had gradually dropped from a position broad on our beam to our port quarter, so as not to foul our range with their smoke; but the enemy's destroyers threatening attack, the *Meteor* and M Division passed ahead of us, Captain the Hon. H. Meade, D.S.O., handling this division with conspicuous ability.

About 9.45 a.m. the situation was as follows:—*Blücher*, the fourth in their line, already showed signs of having suffered severely from gunfire; their leading ship and No. 3 were also on fire. *Lion* was engaging No. 1, *Princess Royal* No. 3, *New Zealand* No. 4, while the *Tiger*, who was second in our line, fired first at their No. 1, and when interfered with by smoke, at their No. 4.

The enemy's destroyers emitted vast columns of smoke to screen their battle cruisers, and under cover of this the latter now appeared to have altered course to the northward to increase their distance, and certainly the rear ships hauled out on the port quarter of their leader, thereby increasing their distance from our line. The battle cruisers, therefore, were ordered to form a line of bearing N.N.W., and proceed at their utmost speed.

Their destroyers then showed evident signs of an attempt to attack. *Lion* and *Tiger* opened fire on them, and caused them to retire and resume their original course.

The light cruisers maintained an excellent position on the port quarter of the enemy's line, enabling them to observe and keep touch, or attack any vessel that might fall out of the line.

At 10.48 a.m., the *Blücher*, which had dropped considerably astern of the enemy's line, hauled out to port, steering north with a heavy list, on fire, and apparently in a defeated condition. I consequently ordered *Indomitable* to attack enemy breaking northward.

At 10.54 a.m. submarines were reported on the starboard bow, and I personally observed the wash of a periscope two points on our starboard bow. I immediately turned to port.

At 11.3 a.m. an injury to the *Lion* being reported as incapable of immediate repair, I directed *Lion* to shape course N.W. At

11.20 a.m. I called the *Attack* alongside, shifting my flag to her at about 11.35 a.m. I proceeded at utmost speed to rejoin the squadron, and met them at noon retiring N.N.W.

I boarded and hoisted my flag in *Princess Royal* at about 12. 20 p.m., when Captain Brock acquainted me of what had occurred since the *Lion* fell out of the line namely, that *Blucher* had been sunk and that the enemy battle cruisers had continued their course to the eastward in a considerably damaged condition. He also informed me that a Zeppelin and a seaplane had endeavoured to drop bombs on the vessels which went to the rescue of the survivors of *Blücher*.

The good seamanship of Lieut.-Commander Cyril Callaghan, H.M.S. *Attack*, in placing his vessel alongside the *Lion* and subsequently the *Princess Royal*, enabled the transfer of flag to be made in the shortest possible time.

At 2 p.m. I closed *Lion* and received a report that the starboard engine was giving trouble owing to priming, and at 3.38 p.m. I ordered *Indomitable* to take her in tow, which was accomplished by 5 p.m.

The greatest credit is due to the captains of *Indomitable* and *Lion* for the seamanlike manner in which the *Lion* was taken in tow under difficult circumstances.

The excellent steaming of the ships engaged in the operation was a conspicuous feature.

I attach an appendix giving the names of various officers and men who specially distinguished themselves.

Where all did well it is difficult to single out officers and men for special mention, and as *Lion* and *Tiger* were the only ships hit by the enemy, the majority of those I mention belong to those ships.

> I have the honour to be, Sir,
>> Your Obedient Servant,
> (Signed)

David Beatty,
Vice-Admiral.

Appendix 4

Documents Relating to the Conduct of the War at Sea.

1.

On December 28, 1914, the United States Government addressed a note to Britain on the treatment of American commerce by the

British Fleet. On January 7, 1915, Sir Edward Grey addressed to the American Ambassador in London a provisional reply. The complete British Note was issued on 10th February, and is here reprinted:—

Sir Edward Grey to the Hon. W. Page.

Foreign Office, February 10, 1915.

Sir,

Your Excellency has already received the preliminary answer, which I handed to you on the 7th January, in reply to your note of the 28th December on the subject of the seizures and detentions of American cargoes destined for neutral European ports. Since that date I have had further opportunity of examining into the trade statistics of the United States as embodied in the Customs returns, in order to see whether the belligerent action of Great Britain has been in any way the cause of the trade depression which your Excellency describes as existing in the United States, and also whether the seizures of vessels or cargoes which have been made by the British navy have inflicted any loss on American owners for which our existing machinery provides no means of redress. In setting out the results of my investigation I think it well to take the opportunity of giving a general review of the methods employed by his Majesty's Government to intercept contraband trade with the enemy, of their consistency with the admitted right of a belligerent to intercept such trade, and also of the extent to which they have endeavoured to meet the representations and complaints from time to time addressed to them on behalf of the United States Government.

Towards the close of your note of the 28th December your Excellency described the situation produced by the action of Great Britain as a pitiful one to the commercial interests of the United States, and said that many of the great industries of the country were suffering because their products were denied long-established markets in neutral European countries contiguous to the nations at war.

It is unfortunately true that in these days, when trade and finance are cosmopolitan, any war—particularly a war of any magnitude—must result in a grievous dislocation of commerce, including that of the nations which take no part in the war. Your Excellency will realise that in this tremendous struggle,

for the outbreak of which Great Britain is in no way responsible, it is impossible for the trade of any country to escape all
injury and loss, but for such his Majesty's Government are not
to blame.

INTERFERENCE WITH TRADE.

I do not understand the paragraph which I have quoted from
your Excellency's note as referring to these indirect consequences of the state of war, but to the more proximate and
direct effect of our belligerent action in dealing with neutral
ships and cargoes on the high seas. Such action has been limited
to vessels on their way to enemy ports or ports in neutral countries adjacent to the theatre of war, because it is only through
such ports that the enemy introduces the supplies which he
requires for carrying on the war.

In my earlier note I set out the number of ships which had
sailed from the United States for Holland, Denmark, Norway,
Sweden, and Italy, and I there stated that only eight of the 773
had been placed in the Prize Court, and that only 45 had been
temporarily detained to enable particular consignments of cargo to be discharged for the purpose of Prize Court proceedings. To measure the effect of such naval action it is necessary to
take into consideration the general statistics of the export trade
of the United States during the months preceding the outbreak
of war and those since the outbreak.

Taking the figures in millions of dollars, the exports of merchandise from the United States for the seven months of January to July, 1914, inclusive, were 1,201, as compared with 1,327
in the corresponding months of 1913, a drop of 126 millions
of dollars.

For the months of August, September, October, and November, that is to say, for the four months of the war preceding the
delivery of your Excellency's note, the figures of the exports of
merchandise were (again in millions of dollars) 667, as compared with 923 in the corresponding months of 1913, a drop of
256 millions of dollars.

If, however, the single article of cotton be eliminated from the
comparison, the figures show a very different result. Thus the
exports of all articles of merchandise other than cotton from
the United States during the first seven months of 1914 were
966 millions of dollars, as against 1,127 millions in 1913, a drop

of 161 millions of dollars, or 14½ *per cent.* On the other hand, the exports of the same articles during the months August to November amounted to 608 millions of dollars as compared with 630 millions in 1913, a drop of only 22 millions, or less than 4 *per cent.*

DECREASE IN COTTON EXPORTS.

It is therefore clear that, if cotton be excluded, the effect of the war has been not to increase but practically to arrest the decline of American exports which was in progress earlier in the year. In fact, any decrease in American exports which is attributable to the war is essentially due to cotton. Cotton is an article which cannot possibly have been affected by the exercise of our belligerent rights, for, as your Excellency is aware, it has not been declared by his Majesty's Government to be contraband of war, and the rules under which we are at present conducting our belligerent operations give us no power in the absence of a blockade to seize or interfere with it when on its way to a belligerent country in neutral ships. Consequently no cotton has been touched.

Into the causes of the decrease in the exports of cotton I do not feel that there is any need for me to enter, because, whatever may have been the cause, it is not to be found in the exercise of the belligerent rights of visit, search, and capture, or in our general right when at war to intercept the contraband trade of our enemy. Imports of cotton to the United Kingdom fell as heavily as those to other countries. No place felt the outbreak of war more acutely than the cotton districts of Lancashire, where for a time an immense number of spindles were idle. Though this condition has now to a large extent passed away, the consumption of the raw material in Great Britain was temporarily much diminished. The same is no doubt true of France.

The general result is to show convincingly that the naval operations of Great Britain are not the cause of any diminution in the volume of American exports, and that if the commerce of the United States is in the unfavourable condition which your Excellency describes the cause ought in fairness to be sought elsewhere than in the activities of his Majesty's naval forces.

I may add that the circular issued by the Department of Commerce at Washington on the 23rd January admits a marked improvement in the foreign trade of the United States which we have noted with great satisfaction. The first paragraph of the circular is worth quoting verbatim:—

A marked improvement in our foreign trade is indicated by the latest reports issued by the Department of Commerce through its Bureau of Foreign and Domestic Commerce, sales of food-stuffs and certain lines of manufactures having been unusually large in November, the latest period for which detailed information is at hand. In that month exports aggregated 206,000,000 dollars, or double the total for August last, when, by reason of the outbreak of war, our foreign trade fell to the lowest level reached in many years. In December there was further improvement, the month's exports being valued at 246,000,000 dollars, compared with 233,000,000 in December 1913, and within 4,000,000 of the high record established in December 1912.

A FIVE MONTHS' REVIEW.

A better view of the situation is obtained by looking at the figures month by month. The exports of merchandise for the last five months have been (in millions of dollars):

August	110
September	156
October	194
November	205
December	246

The outbreak of war produced in the United States, as it did in all neutral countries, an acute but temporary disturbance of trade. Since that time there seems to have been a steady recovery, for today the exports from the United States stand at a higher figure than on the same date last year.

Before passing away from the statistics of trade, and in order to demonstrate still more clearly if necessary that the naval operations of Great Britain and her Allies have had no detrimental effect on the volume of trade between the United States and neutral countries, it is worth while to analyse the figures of the exports to Europe since the outbreak of hostilities. For this purpose the European countries ought to be grouped under three heads:—Great Britain and those fighting with her, neutral countries, and enemy countries. It is, however, impossible for me to group the countries in this way satisfactorily, as the figures relating to the export trade of the United States with each country have not yet been published. In the preliminary statement of the export trade of the United States with foreign countries only principal countries are shown, and various countries which are tabulated separately in the more detailed monthly summary of commerce and finance are omitted. Those omitted include not only the Scandinavian countries, the exports to which are of peculiar importance in dealing with this question, but also Austria.

So far as it is possible to distribute the figures under the headings which I have indicated above (all the figures being given in thousands of dollars), the results are as follows:—

Total exports to Europe from the 1st August to the; 30th November, 413,995, as against 597,342 in 1913. Of these, Great Britain and her Allies took 288,312, as against 316,805 in 1913. Germany and Belgium took 1,881, as against 177,136 in 1913; whereas neutral countries (among which Austria-Hungary is unavoidably included) took 123,802, as against 103,401 in 1913.

The general complaint in your Excellency's note was that the action of Great Britain was affecting adversely the trade of the United States with neutral countries. The naval operations of Great Britain certainly do not interfere with commerce from the United States on its way to the United Kingdom and the Allied countries, and yet the exports to Great Britain and her Allies during those four months diminished to the extent of over 28,000,000 dollars, whereas those to neutral countries and Austria increased by over 20,000,000 dollars.

The inference may fairly be drawn from these figures, all of which are taken from the official returns published by the United States Government, that not only has the trade of the United States with the neutral countries in Europe been maintained as compared with previous years, but also that a substantial part of this trade was, in fact, trade intended for the enemy countries going through neutral ports by routes to which it was previously unaccustomed.

One of the many inconveniences to which this great war is exposing the commerce of all neutral countries is undoubtedly the serious shortage in shipping available for ocean transport, and the consequential result of excessive freights.

DETENTION OF NEUTRAL SHIPS.

It cannot fairly be said that this shortage is caused by Great Britain's interference with neutral ships. At the present time there are only seven neutral vessels awaiting adjudication in the Prize Courts in this country, and three in those in the British Dominions. As your Excellency is aware, I have already instructed our Ambassador at Washington to remind the parties who are interested in these vessels that it is open to them to apply to the Court for the release of these ships on bail, and if an application of this sort is made by them it is not likely to be opposed by the Crown. There is therefore no reason why such an application should not be favourably entertained by the Court, and, if acceded to, all these vessels will again be available for the carriage of commerce. Only one neutral vessel is now detained in this country in addition to those awaiting adjudication in the Prize Court.

Every effort has been made in cases in which it has been found necessary to institute proceedings against portions of the cargo to secure the speedy discharge of the cargo and the release of the ship, so as to enable it to resume work. Great Britain is suffering from the shortage of shipping and the rise in freights as acutely as, if not more than, other nations, and his Majesty's Government have taken every step that they could consistently with their belligerent interests to increase the tonnage available for the transport of sea-borne commerce. The enemy ships which have been condemned in the Prize Courts in this country are being sold as rapidly as possible in order that they may become avail able for use; and those which have been condemned in the Prize Courts oversea are being brought to this country in order that they may be disposed of here, and again placed in active employment.

The difficulties have been accentuated by the unforeseen consequences of the convention which was signed at The Hague in 1907 relative to the status of enemy merchant vessels at the outbreak of war. This convention was a well-intentioned effort to diminish the losses which war must impose upon innocent persons, and provided that enemy merchant ships seized by a belligerent in whose ports they lay at the outbreak of war should not be condemned, but should merely be detained for the period of the war, unless they were liberated in the days of grace. We could come to no arrangement with the German Government for the reciprocal grant of days of grace, and the German merchant vessels lying in British ports when the war broke out have therefore been sentenced to detention in lieu of condemnation. The normal result would have been still further to reduce the volume of shipping available for the commerce of the world. To ease the situation, however, his Majesty's Government are resorting to the power of requisitioning which is given by the convention, so that these ships may again be placed in active service.

DESTRUCTION BY MINES.

Your Excellency will see therefore that his Majesty's Government are doing all in their power to increase the volume of shipping available. I hope it will be realised that the detention of neutral ships by his Majesty's Government with a view to the capture of contraband trade on its way to the enemy has not contributed nearly so much to the shortage of shipping as has the destruction of neutral vessels by submarine mines indiscriminately laid by the enemy on the high seas, many miles from the coast, in the track of merchant vessels. Up till now twenty-five neutral vessels have been reported as destroyed by mines on the high seas; quite apart from all questions of the breach of treaties and the destruction of life, there is far more reason for protest on the score of belligerent interference with innocent neutral trade through the mines scattered by the enemy than through the British exercise of the right of seizing contraband.

I trust that what I have said above will be sufficient to convince your Excellency's Government that the complaints that the naval policy of Great Britain has interfered with the shipments of American products to long-established markets in neutral European countries is founded on a misconception.

In justice to the peoples of both countries, I feel that this opportunity should be taken to explain the lines on which his Majesty's Government have been acting hitherto, so as to show that the line they have followed is in no way inconsistent with the general fundamental principle of international law, and to indicate the care with which they have endeavoured to meet the representations which have been made by the United States

Government from time to time during the war on these questions.

No one in these days will dispute the general proposition that a belligerent is entitled to capture contraband goods on their way to the enemy; that right has now become consecrated by long usage and general acquiescence. Though the right is ancient, the means of exercising it alter and develop with the changes in the methods and machinery of commerce. A century ago the difficulties of land transport rendered it impracticable for the belligerent to obtain supplies of seaborne goods through a neighbouring neutral country. Consequently the belligerent actions of his opponents neither required nor justified any interference with shipments on their way to a neutral port. This principle was recognised and acted on in the decisions in which Lord Stowell laid down the lines on which captures of such goods should be dealt with. The advent of steam power has rendered it as easy for a belligerent to supply himself through the ports of a neutral contiguous country as through his own, and has therefore rendered it impossible for his opponent to refrain from interfering with commerce intended for the enemy merely because it is on its way to a neutral port.

AMERICAN USAGE RECALLED.

No better instance of the necessity of countering new devices for dispatching contraband goods to an enemy by new methods of applying the fundamental principle of the right to capture such contraband can be given than the steps which the Government of the United States found it necessary to take during the American Civil War. It was at that time that the doctrine of continuous voyage was first applied to the capture of contraband, that is to say, it was then for the first time that a belligerent found himself obliged to capture contraband goods on their way to the enemy, even though at the time of capture they were *en route* for a neutral port from which they were intended subsequently to continue their journey.

The policy then followed by the United States Government was not inconsistent with the general principles already sanctioned by international law, and met with no protest from his Majesty's Government, though it was upon British cargoes and upon British ships that the losses and the inconvenience due to this new development of the application of the old rule of international law principally fell. The criticisms which have been directed against the steps then taken by the United States came, and come, from those who saw in the methods employed in Napoleonic times for the prevention of contraband a limitation upon the right itself, and failed to see that in Napoleonic times goods on their way to a neutral port were immune from capture, not because the immediate destination conferred a privilege, but because capture under such circumstances was unnecessary.

The facilities which the introduction of steamers and railways have given to a belligerent to introduce contraband goods through neutral ports have imposed upon his opponent the additional difficulty, when endeavouring to intercept such trade, of distinguishing between the goods which are really destined for the commerce of that neutral country and the goods which are on their way to the enemy. It is one of the many difficulties with which the United States Government found themselves confronted in the days of the Civil War, and I cannot do better than quote the words which Mr. Seward, who was then Secretary of State, used in the course of the diplomatic discussion arising out of the capture of some goods on their way to Matamoros which were believed to be for the insurgents:—

> Neutrals engaged in honest trade with Matamoros must expect to experience inconvenience from the existing blockade of Brownsville and the adjacent coast of Texas. While this Government unfeignedly regrets this inconvenience, it cannot relinquish any of its belligerent rights to favour contraband trade with insurgent territory. By insisting upon those rights, however, it is sure that that necessity for their exercise at all, which must be deplored by every friendly commercial Power, will the more speedily be terminated.

BELLIGERENTS' DIFFICULTIES.

The opportunities now enjoyed by a belligerent for obtaining supplies through neutral ports are far greater than they were fifty years ago, and the geographical conditions of the present struggle lend additional assistance to the enemy in carrying out such importation. We are faced with the problem of intercepting such supplies when arranged with all the advantages that flow from elaborate organisation and unstinted expenditure. If our belligerent rights are to be maintained, it is of the first importance for us to distinguish between what is really bona fide trade intended for the neutral country concerned and the trade intended for the enemy country. Every effort is made by organisers of this trade to conceal the true destination, and if the innocent neutral trade is to be distinguished from the enemy trade it is essential that his Majesty's Government should be entitled to make, and should make, careful inquiry with regard to the destination of particular shipments of goods even at the risk of some slight delay to the parties interested.

If such inquiries were not made, either the exercise of our belligerent rights would have to be abandoned, tending to the prolongation of this war and the increase of the loss and suffering which it is entailing upon the whole world, or else it would be necessary to indulge in indiscriminate captures of neutral goods and their detention throughout all the period of the resulting Prize Court proceedings. Under the system now adopted it has been found possible to release without delay, and consequently without appreciable loss to the parties interested, all the goods of which the destination is shown as the result of the inquiries to be innocent.

It may well be that the system of making such inquiries is to a certain extent a new introduction, in that it has been practised to a far greater extent than in previous wars; but if it is correctly described as a new departure, it is a departure which is wholly to the advantage of neutrals, and which has been made for the purpose of relieving them so far as possible from loss and inconvenience.

A CONTESTED PRINCIPLE.

There was a passage in a note which the State Department addressed to the British Ambassador at Washington on 7th November to which I think it may be well to refer:—

> In the opinion of this Government, the belligerent right of visit and search requires that the search should be made on the high seas at the time of the visit, and that the conclusion of the search should rest upon the evidence found on the ship under investigation, and not upon circumstances ascertained from external sources.

The principle here enunciated appears to me to be inconsistent with the practice in these matters of the United States Government, as well as of the British Government. It certainly was not the rule upon which the United States Government acted either during the Civil War or during the Spanish-American War, nor has it ever been the practice of the British Government, nor, so far as I am aware, of any other Government which has had to carry on a great naval war; as a principle I think it is impossible in modern times. The necessity for giving the belligerent captor full liberty to establish by all the evidence at his disposal the enemy destination with which the goods were shipped was recognised in all the leading decisions in the Prize Courts of the United States during the Civil War.

No clearer instance could be given than the reporter's statement of the case of the *Bermuda* (3 Wallace, 514):—

> The final destination of the cargo in this particular voyage was left so skilfully open ... that it was not quite easy to prove, with that certainty which American Courts require, the intention which it seemed plain must have really existed. Thus to prove it required that truth should be collated from a variety of sources, darkened and disguised; from others opened as the cause advanced, and by accident only; from coincidences undesigned, and facts that were circumstantial. Collocations and comparisons, in short, brought largely their collective force in aid of evidence that was more direct.

It is not impossible that the course of the present struggle will show the necessity for belligerent action to be taken in various ways which may at first sight be regarded as a departure from old practice. In my note of the 7th January, I dealt at some length with the question of the necessity of taking vessels into port for the purposes of carrying out an effective search, where search was necessary; to that subject I feel that I need not again recur.

DEFENCE OF BRITISH PRACTICE.

The growth in the size of steamships necessitates in many cases that the vessel should go into calm water, in order that even the right of visit, as apart from the right of search, should be exercised. In modern times a steamer is capable of pursuing her voyage irrespective of the conditions of the weather. Many of the neutral merchantmen which our naval officers are called upon to visit at sea are encountered by our cruisers in places and under conditions which render the launching of a boat impossible. The conditions during winter in the North Atlantic frequently render it impracticable for days together for a naval officer to board a vessel on her way to Scandinavian countries. If a belligerent is to be denied the right of taking a neutral merchantman, met with under such conditions, into calm water in order that the visiting officer may go aboard, the right of visit and of search would become a nullity.

The present conflict is not the first in which the necessity has arisen; as long ago as the Civil War the United States found it necessary to take vessels to United States ports in order to determine whether the circumstances justified their detention.

The same need arose during the Russo-Japanese War, and also during the second Balkan War, when it sometimes happened that British vessels were made to deviate from their course and follow the cruisers to some spot where the right of visit and of search could be more conveniently carried out. In both cases this exercise of belligerent rights, although questioned at first by his Majesty's Government, was ultimately acquiesced in.

No Power in these days can afford during a great war to forgo the exercise of the right of visit and search. Vessels which are apparently harmless merchantmen can be used for carrying and laying mines, and even fitted to discharge torpedoes. Supplies for submarines can without difficulty be concealed under other cargo. The only protection against these risks is to visit and search thoroughly every vessel appearing in the zone of operations, and if the circumstances are such as to render it impossible to carry it out at the spot where the vessel was met with, the only practicable course is to take the ship to some more convenient locality for the purpose.

To do so is not to be looked upon as a new belligerent right, but as an adaptation of the existing right to the modern conditions of commerce. Like all belligerent rights it must be exercised with due regard for neutral interests, and it would be unreasonable to expect a neutral vessel to make long deviations from her course for this purpose. It is for this reason that we have done all we can to encourage neutral merchantmen, on their way to ports contiguous to the enemy country, to visit some British port lying on their line of route in order that the necessary examination of the ship's papers, and, if required, of the cargo, can be made under conditions of convenience to the ship herself. The alternative would be to keep a vessel which the naval officers desired to board waiting, it might be for days together, until the weather conditions enabled the visit to be carried out at sea.

REDRESS OF NEUTRALS' GRIEVANCES.

No war has yet been waged in which neutral individuals have not occasionally suffered from unjustified belligerent action; no neutral nation has experienced this fact more frequently in the past than Great Britain. The only method by which it is possible to harmonise belligerent action with the rights of neutrals is for the belligerent nation to provide some adequate machinery by which in any such case the facts can be investigated and appropriate redress can be obtained by the neutral individual. In this country such machinery is provided by the powers which are given to the Prize Court to deal not only with captures, but also with claims for compensation.

Order V., Rule 2, of the British Prize Court Rules provides that where a ship has been captured as prize, but has been subsequently released by the captors, or has by loss, destruction, or otherwise ceased to be detained by them, without proceedings for condemnation having been taken, any person interested in the ship (which by Order I., Rule 2, includes goods) wishing to make a claim for costs and damages in respect thereof shall issue a writ as provided by Order II. A writ so issued will initiate a proceeding, which will follow its ordinary course in the Prize Court.

This rule gives the Prize Court ample jurisdiction to deal with any claim for compensation by a neutral arising from the interference with a ship or goods by our naval forces. The best evidence that can be given of the discrimination and the moderation with which our naval officers have carried out their duties is to be found in the fact that up to this time no proceedings for the recovery of compensation have been initiated under the rule which I have quoted.

RECOURSE TO DIPLOMACY DEPRECATED.

It is the common experience of every war that neutrals whose attempts to engage in suspicious trading are frustrated by a belligerent are wont to have recourse to their Government to urge that diplomatic remonstrances should be made on their behalf, and that redress should be obtained for them in this way. When an effective mode of redress is open to them in the Courts of a civilized country by which they can obtain adequate satisfaction for any invasion of their rights which is contrary to the law of nations, the only course which is consistent with sound principle is that they should be referred to that mode of redress, and that no diplomatic action should be taken until their legal remedies have been exhausted, and they are in a position to show *prima facie* denial of justice.

The course adopted by his Majesty's Government during the American Civil War was in strict accordance with this principle. In spite of remonstrances from many quarters, they placed full reliance on the American Prize Courts to grant redress to the parties interested in cases of alleged wrongful capture by American ships of war, and put forward no claims until the opportunities for redress in those Courts had been exhausted. The same course was adopted in the Spanish-American War, when all British subjects who complained of captures or detentions of their ships were referred to the Prize Courts for relief.

Before leaving this subject may I remind your Excellency of the fact that at your request you are now supplied immediately by this Department with particulars of every ship under American colours which is detained, and of every shipment of cargo in which an American citizen appears to be the party interested? Not only is the fact of detention notified to your Excellency, but so far as is practicable the grounds upon which the vessel or cargo has been detained are also communicated to you; a concession which enables any United States citizen to take steps at once to protect his interests.

His Majesty's Government have also done all that lies in their power to ensure rapid action when ships are reported in British ports. They realise that the ship and cargo owners may reasonably expect an immediate decision to be taken as to whether the ship may be allowed to proceed, and whether her cargo or any part of it must be discharged and put into the Prize Court. Realising that the ordinary methods of inter-departmental correspondence might cause delays which could be obviated by another method of procedure, they established several months ago a special Committee, on which all the departments concerned are represented. This Committee sits daily, and is provided with a special clerical staff. As soon as a ship reaches port full particulars are telegraphed to London, and the case is dealt with at the next meeting of the Committee, immediate steps being taken to carry out the action decided upon. By the adoption of this procedure it has been found possible to reduce to a minimum the delays to which neutral shipping is exposed by the exercise of belligerent rights, and by the necessity, imposed by modern conditions, of examining with care the destination of contraband articles.

CONDITIONAL CONTRABAND.

Particular attention is directed in your Excellency's Note to the policy we are pursuing with regard to conditional contraband, especially foodstuffs, and it is there stated that a number of American cargoes have been seized without, so far as your Excellency's Government are informed, our being in possession of facts which warranted a reasonable belief that the shipments had in reality a belligerent destination, and in spite of the presumption of innocent use due to their being destined to neutral territory. The Note does not specify any particular seizures as those which formed the basis of this complaint, and I am therefore not aware whether the passage refers to cargoes which were detained before or since the Order in Council of the 29th October was issued.

Your Excellency will, no doubt, remember that soon after the outbreak of war an Order of his Majesty in Council was issued under which no distinction was drawn in the application of the doctrine of continuous voyage between absolute contraband and conditional contraband, and which also imposed upon the neutral owner of contraband somewhat drastic conditions as to the burden of proof of the guilt or innocence of the shipment. The principle that the burden of proof should always be imposed upon the captor has usually been admitted as a theory. In practice, however, it has almost always been otherwise, and any student of the Prize Court decisions of the past or even of modern wars will find that goods seldom escape condemnation unless their owner was in a position to prove that their destination was innocent. An attempt was made some few years ago, in the unratified Declaration of London, to formulate some definite rules upon this subject, but time alone can show whether the rules there laid down will stand the test of modern warfare.

RELAXED RULES.

The rules which his Majesty's Government published in the Order in Council of the 20th August, 1914, were criticized by the United States Government as contrary to the generally recognised principles of international law, and as inflicting unnecessary hardship upon neutral commerce, and your Excellency will remember the prolonged discussions which took place between us throughout the month of October with a view to finding some new formulae which should enable us to restrict supplies to the enemy forces, and to prevent the supply to the enemy of materials essential for the making of munitions of war, while inflicting the minimum of injury and interference with neutral commerce. It was with this object that the Order in Council of the 29th October was issued, under the provisions of which a far greater measure of immunity is conferred upon neutral commerce. In that Order the principle of non-interference with conditional contraband on its way to a neutral port is in large measure admitted; only in three cases is the right to seize maintained, and in all those cases the opportunity is given to the claimant of the goods to establish their innocence.

Two of those cases are where the ship's papers afford no information as to the person for whom the goods are intended. It is only reasonable that a belligerent should be entitled to regard as suspicious cases where the shippers of the goods do not choose to disclose the name of the individual who is to receive them. The third case is that of goods addressed to a person in the enemy territory. In the peculiar circumstances of the present struggle, where the forces of the enemy comprise so large a proportion of the population, and where there is so little evidence of shipments on private as distinguished from Government account, it is most reasonable that the burden of proof should rest upon the claimant.

QUESTION OF FOODSTUFFS.

The most difficult questions in connexion with conditional contraband arise with reference to the shipment of foodstuffs.

No country has maintained more stoutly than Great Britain in modern times the principle that a belligerent should abstain from interference with the foodstuffs intended for the civil population. The circumstances of the present struggle are causing his Majesty's Government some anxiety as to whether the existing rules with regard to conditional contraband, framed as they were with the object of protecting so far as possible the supplies which were intended for the civil population, are effective for the purpose, or suitable to the conditions present. The principle which I have indicated above is one which his Majesty's Government have constantly had to uphold against the opposition of continental Powers. In the absence of some certainty that the rule would be respected by both parties to this conflict, we feel great doubt whether it should be regarded as an established principle of international law.

Your Excellency will, no doubt, remember that in 1885, at the time when his Majesty's Government were discussing with the French Government this question of the right to declare foodstuffs not intended for the military forces to be contraband, and when public attention had been drawn to the matter, the Kiel Chamber of Commerce applied to the German Government for a statement of the latter's views on the subject. Prince Bismarck's answer was as follows:—

> In answer to their representation of the 1st instant, I reply to the Chamber of Commerce that any disadvantage our commercial and carrying interests may suffer by the treatment of rice as contraband of war does not justify our opposing a measure which it has been thought fit to take in carrying on a foreign war. Every war is a calamity which entails evil consequences not only on the combatants, but also on neutrals. These evils may easily be increased by the interference of a neutral Power with the way in which a third carries on the war, to the disadvantage of the subjects of the interfering Power, and by this means German commerce might be weighted with far heavier losses than a transitory prohibition of the rice trade in Chinese waters. *The measure in question has for its object the shortening of the war by increasing the difficulties of the enemy, and is a justifiable step in war if impartially enforced against all neutral ships.*

His Majesty's Government are disposed to think that the same view is still maintained by the German Government.

GERMAN CONTROL OF FOOD.

Another circumstance which is now coming to light is that an elaborate machinery has been organised by the enemy for the supply of foodstuffs for the use of the German Army from overseas. Under these circumstances it would be absurd to give any definite pledge that in cases where the supplies can be proved to be for the use of the enemy forces they should be given complete immunity by the simple expedient of dispatching them to an agent in a neutral port.

The reason for drawing a distinction between foodstuffs intended for the civil population and those for the armed forces or enemy government disappears when the distinction between the civil population and the armed forces itself disappears. In any country in which there exists such a tremendous organisation for war as now obtains in Germany there is no clear division between those whom the government is responsible for feeding and those whom it is not. Experience shows that the power to requisition will be used to the fullest extent in order to make sure that the wants of the military are supplied, and however much goods may be imported for civil use it is by the military that they will be consumed if military exigencies require it, especially now that the German Government have taken control of all the foodstuffs in the country.

EXPORTS TO NEUTRALS.

I do not wish to overburden this note with statistics, but in proof of my statement as to the unprecedented extent to which supplies are reaching neutral ports, I should like to instance the figures of the exports of certain meat products to Denmark during the months of September and October. Denmark is a country which in normal times imports a certain quantity of such products, but exports still more. In 1913, during the above two months, the United States exports of lard to Denmark were *nil*, as compared with 22,652,598 lb. in the same two months of 1914. The corresponding figures with regard to bacon were: 1913, *nil*, 1914, 1,022,195 lb,; canned beef, 1913, *nil*; 1914, 151,200 lb.; pickled and cured beef, 1913, 42,901 lb.; 1914, 156,143 lb.; pickled pork, 1913, *nil*; 1914, 812,872 lb.

In the same two months the United States exported to Denmark 280,176 gallons of mineral lubricating oil in 1914, as compared with 179,252 in 1913; to Norway, 335,468 gallons in 1914, as against 151,179 gallons in 1913; to Sweden, 896,193 gallons in 1914, as against 385,476 gallons in 1913.

I have already mentioned the framing of the Order in Council of the 29th October, and the transmission to your Excellency of particulars of ships and cargoes seized as instances of the efforts which we have made throughout the course of this war to meet all reasonable complaints made on behalf of American citizens, and in my note of the 7th January I alluded to the decision of our Prize Court in the case of the *Miramichi*, as evidencing the liberal principles adopted towards neutral commerce.

RELEASE OF CARGOES.

I should also like to refer to the steps which we took at the beginning of the war to ensure the speedy release of cargo claimed by neutrals on board enemy ships which were captured or detained at the outbreak of war. Under our Prize Court rules release of such goods can be obtained without the necessity of entering a claim in the Prize Court if the documents of title are produced to the officer representing his Majesty's Government, and the title to the goods is established to his satisfaction. It was shortly found, however, that this procedure did not provide for the case where the available evidence was so scanty that the officer representing the Crown was not justified in consenting to a release. In order, therefore, to ameliorate the situation we established a special Committee, with full powers to authorize the release of goods without insisting on full evidence of title being produced.

This Committee dealt with the utmost expedition with a large number of claims. In the great majority of cases the goods claimed were released at once. In addition to the cases dealt with by this Committee a very large amount of cargo was released at once by the Procurator-General on production of documents. Claimants therefore obtained their goods without the necessity of applying to the Prize Court and of incurring the expense involved in retaining lawyers, and without the risk, which was in some cases a considerable one, of the goods being eventually held to be enemy property and condemned. We have reason to know that our action in this matter was highly appreciated by many American citizens.

Transfer to Neutral Flag.

Another instance of the efforts which his Majesty's Government have made to deal as leniently as possible with neutral interests may be found in the policy which we have followed with regard to the transfer to a neutral flag of enemy ships belonging to companies which were incorporated in the enemy country, but all of whose shareholders were neutral. The rules applied by the British and by the American Prize Courts have always treated the flag as conclusive in favour of the captors in spite of neutral proprietary interests (see the case of the *Pedro*, 175 U.S. 354). In several cases, however, we have consented to waive our belligerent right to treat as enemy vessels ships belonging to companies incorporated in Germany which were subsidiary to and owned by American corporations. The only condition which we have imposed is that these vessels should take no further part in trade with the enemy country.

Consideration of Neutrals.

I have given these indications of the policy which we have followed, because I cannot help feeling that if the facts were more fully known as to the efforts which we have made to avoid inflicting any avoidable injury on neutral interests, many of the complaints which have been received by the Administration in Washington, and which led to the protest which your Excellency handed to me on the 29th December, would never have been made. My hope is that when the facts which I have set out above are realised, and when it is seen that our naval operations have not diminished trade with neutral countries, and that the lines on which we have acted are consistent with the fundamental principles of international law, it will be apparent to the Government and people of the United States that his Majesty's Government have hitherto endeavoured to exercise their belligerent rights with every possible consideration for the interests of neutrals.

It will still be our endeavour to avoid injury and loss to neutrals, but the announcement by the German Government of their intention to sink merchant vessels and their cargoes without verification of their nationality or character, and without making any provision for the safety of non-combatant crews or giving them a chance of saving their lives, has made it necessary for his Majesty's Government to consider what measures they should adopt to protect their interests. It is impossible for one belligerent to depart from rules and precedents and for the other to remain bound by them.   I have, etc.,

E. Grey.

2.

On 9th March the American Ambassador raised various questions concerning this declaration by the British Government, which Sir Edward Grey adumbrated in the above dispatch,.

Mr. Page to Sir Edward Grey.
Received March 9.

With regard to the recent communications received by my government from His Britannic Majesty's Government and that of France concerning restraints upon commerce with Germany, I have received instructions to address to you certain inquiries with a view to a more complete elucidation of the situation which has arisen from the action contemplated by the governments of the two allied countries.

My government finds itself in some difficulty in determining its attitude towards the British and French declarations of intended retaliation upon commerce with Germany by reason of the nature of the proposed measures in their relation to the commerce of neutral countries.

While it appears that the intention is to interfere with and take into custody all ships, both outgoing and incoming, engaged in trade with Germany, which, in effect, seems to constitute a blockade of German ports, there is no assertion of the rule of blockade permitting the condemnation, regardless of the character of its cargo, of any ship which attempts to enter or leave a German port. In the language of the declaration:—

> The British and French Governments will therefore hold themselves free to detain and take into port ships carrying goods of presumed enemy destination, ownership, or origin. It is not intended to confiscate such vessels or cargoes unless they would otherwise be liable to condemnation.

The former sentence above quoted claims a right pertaining only to a state of blockade, while the latter sentence proposes a treatment of ships and cargoes as if no blockade existed. The two together present a proposed course of action previously unknown to international law, and neutrals have in consequence no standard by which to measure their rights or to avoid danger to their ships and cargoes. It seems to the Government of the United States that the paradoxical situation thus created should be altered, and that the declaring Powers ought to make a definite assertion as to whether they rely upon the rules governing a blockade, or the rules applicable when no blockade exists.

The declaration presents other perplexities. The latter of the two sentences above quoted indicates that the rules of contraband are to be applied to cargoes detained. The existing rule covering non-contraband articles carried in neutral bottoms is that the cargoes be released and the ships allowed to proceed. This rule cannot, under the other sentence quoted, be applied as to destination, and the question then arises as to what is to be done with a cargo of non-contraband goods which might be detained under the declaration. The same question may be asked as to cargoes of conditional contraband.

The foregoing comments apply to cargoes destined for German ports. Cargoes issuing from them present another problem under the terms of the declaration.

Pursuant to the rules governing enemy exports, the only goods subject to seizure and condemnation are those owned by enemy subjects, carried in enemy bottoms, and yet under the declaration it is proposed to seize and take into port all goods of enemy "ownership and origin." A particular significance attaches to the word "origin." The origin of goods in neutral ships destined to neutral territory is not and never has been a ground for forfeiture except in cases where a blockade is declared and not maintained. To what then would the seizure under the present declaration amount except to delay the delivery of the goods? The declaration does not indicate what disposition would be made of such cargoes owned by a neutral; and another question arises in the case of enemy ownership as to what rule should then come into play. If another rule is to be applied, upon what principle of international law would it rest, and upon what rules, if no blockade is declared and maintained, could the cargo of a neutral ship issuing from a German port be condemned? If it is not to be condemned, what legal course exists but to release it?

My government is fully alive to the possibility that the methods of modern naval warfare, particularly in the use of the submarine for both defensive and offensive operations, may make the former means of maintaining a blockade a physical impossibility; but it nevertheless feels that the point of the desirability of limiting " the radius of activity " can be urged with great force, especially so if this action by the belligerents can be construed to be a blockade. A very complicated situation would undoubtedly be created if, for example, an American vessel laden with cargo of German origin should escape the British patrol in European waters only to be held up by a cruiser off New York and taken into Halifax.

I have the honour to add, for your information, that a communication similar to the above has been addressed to the Government of the French Republic.

On 15th March Sir Edward Grey replied:—

Foreign Office, March 15, 1915.

1. His Majesty's Government have had under careful consideration the inquiries which, under instructions from your government, your Excellency addressed to me on the 8th instant regarding the scope and mode of application of the measures, foreshadowed in the British and French declarations of the 1st March, for restricting the trade of Germany. Your Excellency explained, and illustrated by reference to certain contingencies, the difficulty of the United States Government in adopting a definite attitude towards these measures, by reason of uncertainty regarding their bearing upon the commerce of neutral countries.

2. I can at once assure your Excellency that, subject to the paramount necessity of restricting German trade, His Majesty's Government have made it their first aim to minimize inconvenience to neutral commerce. From the accompanying copy of the Order in Council, which is to be published today, you will observe that a wide discretion is afforded to the Prize Court in dealing with the trade of neutrals in such manner as may in the circumstances be deemed just, and that full provision is made to facilitate claims by persons interested in any goods placed in the custody of the marshal of the Prize Court, under the Order. I apprehend that the perplexities to which your Excellency refers will for the most part be dissipated by the perusal of this document, and that it is only necessary for me to add certain explanatory observations.

3. The effect of the Order in Council is to confer certain powers upon the executive officers of His Majesty's Government. The extent to which those powers will be actually exercised, and the degree of severity with which the measures of blockade authorized will be put

into operation, are matters which will depend on the administrative orders issued by the government and the decisions of the authorities specially charged with the duty of dealing with individual ships and cargoes, according to the merits of each case. The United States Government may rest assured that the instructions to be issued by His Majesty's Government to the fleet, and to the customs officials and executive committees concerned, will impress upon them the duty of acting with the utmost dispatch consistent with the object in view, and of showing in every case such consideration for neutrals as may be compatible with that object, which is, succinctly stated, to establish a blockade to prevent vessels from carrying goods for, or coming from, Germany.

4. His Majesty's Government have felt most reluctant at the moment of initiating a policy of blockade to exact from neutral ships all the penalties attaching to a breach of blockade. In their desire to alleviate the burden which the existence of a state of war at sea must inevitably impose on neutral sea-borne commerce, they declare their intention to refrain altogether from the exercise of the right to confiscate ships or cargoes which belligerents have always claimed in respect of breaches of blockade. They restrict their claim to the stopping of cargoes destined for or coming from the enemy's territory.

5. As regards cotton, full particulars of the arrangements contemplated have already been explained. It will be admitted that every possible regard has been had to the legitimate interests of the American cotton trade.

6. Finally, in reply to the penultimate paragraph of your Excellency's note, I have the honour to state that it is not intended to interfere with neutral vessels carrying enemy cargo of non-contraband nature outside European waters, including the Mediterranean.

3

On 22nd February the United States Government addressed an Identic Note to Britain and Germany, suggesting a compromise:—

Mr. Page to Sir Edward Grey.
Received February 22.

Pursuant to instructions from my government, I have the honour to submit for your consideration the following communication which I have just received by telegraph from the Secretary of State, dated at Washington on the 20th instant, with the information that it forms the text of an identic note to the Government of His Britannic Majesty and that of Germany. I have been in some uncertainty as to the reading of some of its passages on account of omissions in the enciphering of the telegram or mistakes in its transmission; but in view of the desirability of laying the matter before you immediately, and since these passages do not appear to affect the general sense of the note, I have not waited to obtain an authoritative correction. I shall not fail, however, to furnish you with a corrected copy with the least possible delay.

In view of the correspondence which has passed between this Government and Great Britain and Germany respectively relative to the declaration of a war zone by the German Admiralty, and the use of neutral flags by British merchant vessels, this Government ventures to express the hope that the two belligerent Governments may, through reciprocal concessions, find a basis for agreement which will relieve neutral vessels engaged in peaceful commerce from the great dangers which they will incur on the high seas adjacent to the coasts of the belligerents.

The Government of the United States respectfully suggests that an agreement in terms like the following might be entered into. This suggestion is not to be regarded as in any sense a proposal made by this Government, for it of course fully recognises that it is not its privilege to propose terms of agreement between Great Britain and Germany, even though the matter be one in which it and the people of the United States are directly and deeply interested. It is merely venturing to take the liberty which may be accorded a sincere friend desirous of embarrassing neither nation involved, and of serving, if it may, the common interests of humanity.

The course outlined is offered in the hope that it may draw forth the views and elicit the suggestions of the British Government on a matter of capital interest to the whole world.

Germany and Great Britain to agree:—

First. That neither will sow any floating mines, whether upon the high seas or in territorial waters; that neither will plant in the high seas anchored mines except within cannon range of harbours for defensive purposes only; and that all mines shall bear the stamp of the government planting them, and be so constructed as to become harmless if separated from their moorings.

Second. That neither will use submarines to attack merchant vessels of any nationality except to enforce the right of visit and search.

Third. That each will require their respective merchant vessels not to use neutral flags for the purpose of disguise or *ruse de guerre*.

Germany to agree that all importations of food or foodstuffs from the United States (and from such other neutral countries as may ask it) into Germany shall be consigned to agencies to be designated by the United States Government; that these American agencies shall have entire charge and control, without interference on the part of the German Government, of the receipt and distribution of such importations, and shall distribute these solely to retail dealers bearing licences from the German Government entitling them to receive and furnish such food and foodstuffs to non-combatants only; that any violation of the terms of the retailers' licences shall work a forfeiture of their rights to receive such food and food supplies for this purpose; and that such food and food supplies will not be requisitioned by the German Government for any purpose whatsoever or be diverted to the use of the embarcation [*sic*] forces of Germany. Great Britain to agree that food and food supplies will not be placed upon absolute contraband list, and that shipments of such commodities will not be interfered with or detained by British authorities if consigned to agencies designated by the United States Government in Germany for the receipt and distribution of such cargoes to licensed German retailers for distribution solely to the non-combatant population.

In submitting this proposed basis of agreement this Government does not wish to be understood as admitting or denying any belligerent or neutral right established by principles of international law, but would consider the agreement, if acceptable to the interested Powers, a *modus vivendi*, based upon expediency rather than legal right, and as not binding upon the United States either in its present form or in a modified form until accepted by this government."

On 15th March Sir Edward Grey issued the following Memorandum in reply to the American Note:—

On the 22nd February last I received a communication from your Excellency of the identic note addressed to His Majesty's Government and to Germany respecting an agreement on certain points as to the conduct of the war at sea.

The reply of the German Government to this note has been published, and it is not understood from the reply that the German Government are prepared to abandon the practice of sinking British merchant vessels by submarines; and it is evident from their reply that they will not abandon the use of mines for offensive purposes on the high seas, as contrasted with the use of mines for defensive purposes only within cannon range of their own harbours, as suggested by the Government of the United States.

This being so, it might appear unnecessary for the British Government to make any further reply than to take note of the German answer. We desire, however, to take the opportunity of making a fuller statement of the whole position, and of our feeling with regard to it.

We recognise with sympathy the desire of the Government of the United States to see the European War conducted in accordance with the previously recognised rules of international law and the dictates of humanity. It is thus that the British forces have conducted the war, and we are not aware that these forces, either naval or military, can have laid to their charge any improper proceedings, either in the conduct of hostilities or in the treatment of prisoners or wounded.

On the German side it has been very different:—

1. The treatment of civilian inhabitants in Belgium and the north of France has been made public by the Belgian and French Governments, and by those who have had experience of it at first hand. Modern history affords no precedent for the sufferings that have been inflicted on the defenceless and noncombatant population in the territory that has been in German military occupation. Even the food of the population was confiscated, until, in Belgium, an International Commission, largely influenced by American generosity, and conducted un-

der American auspices, came to the relief of the population, and secured from the German Government a promise to spare what food was still left in the country, though the Germans still continue to make levies in money upon the defenceless population for the support of the German army.

2. We have from time to time received most terrible accounts of the barbarous treatment to which British officers and soldiers have been exposed after they have been taken prisoner, while being conveyed to German prison camps. One or two instances have already been given to the United States Government, founded upon authentic and first-hand evidence which is beyond doubt. Some evidence has been received of the hardships to which British prisoners of war are subjected in the prison camps, contrasting, we believe, most unfavourably with the treatment of German prisoners in this country. We have proposed, with the consent of the United States Government, that a commission of United States officers should be permitted in each country to inspect the treatment of prisoners of war. The United States Government have been unable to obtain any reply from the German Government to this proposal, and we remain in continuing anxiety and apprehension as to the treatment of British prisoners of war in Germany.

3. At the very outset of war a German minelayer was discovered laying a minefield on the high seas. Further minefields have been laid from time to time without warning, and, so far as we know, are still being laid on the high seas, and many neutral as well as British vessels have been sunk by them.

4. At various times during the war German submarines have stopped and sunk British merchant vessels, thus making the sinking of merchant vessels a general practice, though it was admitted previously, if at all, only as an exception; the general rule, to which the British Government have adhered, being that merchant vessels, if captured, must be taken before a Prize Court. In one case, already quoted in a note to the United States Government, a neutral vessel carrying foodstuffs to an unfortified town in Great Britain has been sunk. Another case is now reported, in which a German armed cruiser has sunk an American vessel, the *William P. Frye,* carrying a cargo of wheat from Seattle to Queenstown. In both cases the cargoes were

presumably destined for the civil population. Even the cargoes, in such circumstances, should not have been condemned without the decision of a Prize Court, much less should the vessels have been sunk. It is to be noted that both these cases occurred before the detention by the British authorities of the *Wilhelmina* and her cargo of foodstuffs, which the German Government allege is the justification for their own action.

The Germans have announced their intention of sinking British merchant vessels by torpedo without notice and without any provision for the safety of the crew. They have already carried out this intention in the case of neutral as well as of British vessels, and a number of non-combatant and innocent lives on British vessels, unarmed and defenceless, have been destroyed in this way.

5. Unfortified, open, and defenceless towns, such as Scarborough, Yarmouth, and Whitby, have been deliberately and wantonly bombarded by German ships of war, causing in some cases considerable loss of civilian life, including women and children.

6. German aircraft have dropped bombs on the East Coast of England, where there were no military or strategic points to be attacked.

On the other hand, I am aware of but two criticisms that have been made on British action in all these respects:—

1. It is said that the British naval authorities also have laid some anchored mines on the high seas. They have done so; but the mines were anchored and so constructed that they would be harmless if they went adrift, and no mines whatever were laid by the British naval authorities till many weeks after the Germans had made a regular practice of laying mines on the high seas.

2. It is said that the British Government have departed from the view of international law, which they had previously maintained, that foodstuffs destined for the civil population should never be interfered with; this charge being founded on the submission to a Prize Court of the cargo of the *Wilhelmina*. The special considerations affecting this cargo have already been presented in a Memorandum to the United States Government, and I need not repeat them here. Inasmuch as the stoppage of

all foodstuffs is an admitted consequence of blockade, it is obvious that there can be no universal rule, based on considerations of morality and humanity, which is contrary to this practice. The right to stop foodstuffs destined for the civil population must, therefore, in any case be admitted if an effective "cordon" controlling intercourse with the enemy is drawn, announced, and maintained.

Moreover, independently of rights, arising from belligerent action in the nature of blockade, some other nations, differing from the opinion of the Government of the United States and Great Britain, have held that to stop the food of the civil population is a natural and legitimate method of bringing pressure to bear on an enemy country, as it is upon the defence of a besieged town. It is also upheld on the authority of both Prince Bismarck and Count Caprivi, and therefore presumably is not repugnant to German morality. The following are the quotations from Prince Bismarck and Count Caprivi on this point:—

Prince Bismarck, in answering in 1885 an application from the Kiel Chamber of Commerce for a statement of the view of the German Government on the question of the right to declare as contraband foodstuffs that were not intended for military forces, said:—

> I reply to the Chamber of Commerce that any disadvantage our commercial and carrying interests may suffer by the treatment of rice as contraband of war does not justify our opposing a measure which it has been thought fit to take in carrying on a foreign war. Every war is a calamity which entails evil consequences not only on the combatants but also on neutrals. These evils may easily be increased by the interference of a neutral Power with the way in which a third carries on the war, to the disadvantage of the subjects of the interfering Power, and by this means German commerce might be weighted with far heavier losses than a transitory prohibition of the rice trade in Chinese waters. The measure in question has for its object the shortening of the war by increasing the difficulties of the enemy, and is a justifiable step in war if impartially enforced against all neutral ships.

Count Caprivi, during a discussion in the German Reichstag on the 4th March, 1892, on the subject of the importance of international protection for private property at sea, made the following statements:—

> A country may be dependent for her food or for her raw produce upon her trade, in fact, it may be absolutely necessary to destroy the enemy's trade."

> The private introduction of provisions into Paris was prohibited during the siege, and in the same way a nation would be justified in preventing the import of food and raw produce.

The Government of Great Britain have now frankly declared, in concert with the Government of France, their intention to meet the German attempt to stop all supplies of every kind from leaving or entering British or French ports by themselves stopping supplies going to or from Germany. For this end, the British fleet has instituted a blockade, effectively controlling by cruiser "cordon" all passage to and from Germany by sea. The difference between the two policies is, however, that, while our object is the same as that of Germany, we propose to attain it without sacrificing neutral ships or non-combatant lives, or inflicting upon neutrals the damage that must be entailed when a vessel and its cargo are sunk without notice, examination, or trial.

I must emphasise again that this measure is a natural and necessary consequence of the unprecedented methods, repugnant to all law and morality, which have been described above, which Germany began to adopt at the very outset of the war, and the effects of which have been constantly accumulating.

LEONAUR

ALSO FROM LEONAUR
AVAILABLE IN SOFTCOVER OR HARDCOVER WITH DUST JACKET

OFFICERS & GENTLEMEN *by Peter Hawker & William Graham*—Two Accounts of British Officers During the Peninsula War: Officer of Light Dragoons by Peter Hawker & Campaign in Portugal and Spain by William Graham .

THE WALCHEREN EXPEDITION *by Anonymous*—The Experiences of a British Officer of the 81st Regt. During the Campaign in the Low Countries of 1809.

LADIES OF WATERLOO *by Charlotte A. Eaton, Magdalene de Lancey & Juana Smith*—The Experiences of Three Women During the Campaign of 1815: Waterloo Days by Charlotte A. Eaton, A Week at Waterloo by Magdalene de Lancey & Juana's Story by Juana Smith.

JOURNAL OF AN OFFICER IN THE KING'S GERMAN LEGION *by John Frederick Hering*—Recollections of Campaigning During the Napoleonic Wars.

JOURNAL OF AN ARMY SURGEON IN THE PENINSULAR WAR *by Charles Boutflower*—The Recollections of a British Army Medical Man on Campaign During the Napoleonic Wars.

ON CAMPAIGN WITH MOORE AND WELLINGTON *by Anthony Hamilton*—The Experiences of a Soldier of the 43rd Regiment During the Peninsular War.

THE ROAD TO AUSTERLITZ *by R. G. Burton*—Napoleon's Campaign of 1805.

SOLDIERS OF NAPOLEON *by A. J. Doisy De Villargennes & Arthur Chuquet*—The Experiences of the Men of the French First Empire: Under the Eagles by A. J. Doisy De Villargennes & Voices of 1812 by Arthur Chuquet .

INVASION OF FRANCE, 1814 *by F. W. O. Maycock*—The Final Battles of the Napoleonic First Empire.

LEIPZIG—A CONFLICT OF TITANS *by Frederic Shoberl*—A Personal Experience of the 'Battle of the Nations' During the Napoleonic Wars, October 14th-19th, 1813.

SLASHERS *by Charles Cadell*—The Campaigns of the 28th Regiment of Foot During the Napoleonic Wars by a Serving Officer.

BATTLE IMPERIAL *by Charles William Vane*—The Campaigns in Germany & France for the Defeat of Napoleon 1813-1814.

SWIFT & BOLD *by Gibbes Rigaud*—The 60th Rifles During the Peninsula War.

www.ingramcontent.com/pod-product-compliance
Lightning Source LLC
Chambersburg PA
CBHW032048080426
42733CB00006B/195